REGNUM EDINBURGH 2010 SERIES

The Church Going Glocal

Mission and Globalisation

REGNUM EDINBURGH 2010 SERIES

The Centenary of the World Missionary Conference of 1910, held in Edinburgh, was a suggestive moment for many people seeking direction for Christian mission in the twenty-first century. Several different constituencies within world Christianity held significant events around 2010. From 2005, an international group worked collaboratively to develop an intercontinental and multi-denominational project, known as Edinburgh 2010, and based at New College, University of Edinburgh. This initiative brought together representatives of twenty different global Christian bodies, representing all major Christian denominations and confessions, and many different strands of mission and church life, to mark the Centenary.

Essential to the work of the Edinburgh 1910 Conference, and of abiding value, were the findings of the eight think-tanks or 'commissions'. These inspired the idea of a new round of collaborative reflection on Christian mission – but now focused on nine themes identified as being key to mission in the twenty-first century. The study process was polycentric, open-ended, and as inclusive as possible of the different genders, regions of the world, and theological and confessional perspectives in today's church. It was overseen by the Study Process Monitoring Group: Miss Maria Aranzazu Aguado (Spain, The Vatican), Dr Daryl Balia (South Africa, Edinburgh 2010), Mrs Rosemary Dowsett (UK, World Evangelical Alliance), Dr Knud Jørgensen (Norway, Areopagos), Rev. John Kafwanka (Zambia, Anglican Communion), Rev. Dr Jooseop Keum (Korea, World Council of Churches), Dr Wonsuk Ma (Korea, Oxford Centre for Mission Studies), Rev. Dr Kenneth R. Ross (UK, Church of Scotland), Dr Petros Vassiliadis (Greece, Aristotle University of Thessalonikki), and coordinated by Dr Kirsteen Kim (UK, Edinburgh 2010).

These publications reflect the ethos of Edinburgh 2010 and will make a significant contribution to ongoing studies in mission. It should be clear that material published in this series will inevitably reflect a diverse range of views and positions. These will not necessarily represent those of the series' editors or of the Edinburgh 2010 General Council, but in publishing them the leadership of Edinburgh 2010 hopes to encourage conversation between Christians and collaboration in mission. All the series' volumes are commended for study and reflection in both church and academy.

Series Editors

REGNUM EDINBURGH 2010 SERIES

The Church Going Glocal

Mission and Globalisation

Edited by Tormod Engelsviken, Erling Lundeby and Dagfinn Solheim

Proceedings of the Fjellhaug Symposium 2010

Sponsored by Fjellhaug International University College and The Egede Institute

Fjellhaug internasjonale Høgskole

Egede Instituttet

First published 2011 by Regnum Books International

Regnum is an imprint of the Oxford Centre for Mission Studies
St. Philip and St. James Church
Woodstock Road
Oxford OX2 6HR, UK
www.ocms.ac.uk/regnum

09 08 07 06 05 04 03 7 6 5 4 3 2 1

British Library Cataloguing in Publication Data
A catalogue record for this book is available from the British Library

ISBN: 978-1-506476-06-3

Typeset by Words by Design

Proceedings of the Fjellhaug Symposium, April 14th-15th 2010, arranged at Fjellhaug International University College, Oslo, Norway

Distributed by 1517 Media in the US and Canada

Contents

FOREWORD

Witnessing to Christ Today was the overall topic when June 2010 saw the centenary celebration of the well-known Edinburgh 1910 World Missionary Conference. Like Edinburgh 1910 its centenary triggered a lot of meaningful preparations. Edinburgh 1910 had its documents neatly organized in nine big volumes; Edinburgh 2010 will see a series of varied contributions from a decentralised study process in different parts of the world under its umbrella. The present book – coming out of the Fjellhaug Symposium, Oslo, 2010 – is part of this. It represents a Norwegian attempt to deal adequately with the challenge of witnessing to Christ in a globalized world.

The year 2010 does not only mark the centenary of the 1910 World Missionary Conference. A century has also passed since the death of Gustav Warneck, the famous German pioneer missiologist and 'pathfinder of world mission'. In the wake of the two events in 1910 not only did the world mission of the church expand, but the study of Christian world mission as an academic discipline expanded as well. The new and somewhat controversial theological discipline influenced theology as a whole in the course of the twentieth century, not least in the understanding of ecclesiology. New terminology was born and new catchwords were eventually coined to carry the content of new insights in the nature of the church. On the threshold of the next century – the twenty-first – it had become quite common to talk of the church as being missional.

The interesting terminological process continues and may well be taken as an encouraging sign of life in the church. A new catchword seemingly in the coming is the designation of the church as glocal – i.e. the church being global and local at the same time. Time will show whether the term will establish itself as more than a clever play of words. The following pages indicate however that it may well deserve to be adopted as a meaningful ecclesiological concept. In fact, it might have been coined already on the basis of New Testament ecclesiology itself without the midwifery of today's globalisation. It is elementary biblical insight that the New Testament portrays the church in a dual way, sometimes as the universal body of Christ, sometimes as a certain gathering of believers in Corinth, Ephesus, Philippi or Jerusalem. The New Testament church is not the one or the other of the two, not universal or local. She is universal and local at the same time. The universal, one and holy apostolic church appears in local manifestations.

It is not far-fetched then to talk of the church of Christ as glocal. Missiologically speaking it is to say that the church can take courage as she faces the increasing impact of globalisation on local communities today. Being from her very birth both universal and concrete the church is geared for the challenging simultaneity of the global and the local. Our question to ask is how her dual nature may best be expressed to enhance her continuous witness to Christ – locally and globally. To ponder the question I highly recommend the book in your hand, written as it is by people of great competence and experience with mission in our globalized world.

Jan-Martin Berentsen
Oslo, September 2010

Introduction

Tormod Engelsviken, Erling Lundeby and Dagfinn Solheim

The centenary of the mission conference in Edinburgh 1910 is celebrated in 2010 through a number of conferences and publications. The present volume is one of several contributions to the necessary reflection on mission today in the context of this celebration.

One of the most significant features of contemporary society is what is commonly called globalisation. This phenomenon, which, as this book will show, is not unique for our time, is nevertheless more widespread, more pervasive and more rapidly changing the world in which we live than ever before. Just as globalisation has become a reality in areas such as communication, culture, economics and politics, the two largest religions in the world, i.e. Christianity and Islam, have also become global in an unprecedented way. One hundred years after Edinburgh 1910 the global vision of that conference has been fulfilled in ways and places that nobody at that time could imagine. The global reality of the church and the globalisation of the world happen at the same time – and in our time. Is this coincidence accidental? What is the relationship between globalisation and the global church? What precisely is the global vision of the church as a missional church? What is the impact of globalisation on the church and the cultures in which the church finds itself? What is the role of religion, and more specifically Christianity, in the globalized world today? These are some of the questions that the authors of this book want to explore.

The background of the volume is an international symposium on the theme "Mission and Globalisation" that was held at Fjellhaug International University College in Oslo, Norway, April 14-15, 2010. Fjellhaug International University College is owned by the Norwegian Lutheran Mission, the largest mission organization in Northern Europe, founded in 1891. Norwegian Lutheran Mission has from its inception had a particular vision for China, but is today engaged in mission work in Asia, Africa and Latin America. It is known as a theologically conservative, evangelical, Lutheran organization. The symposium was ecumenical – as is appropriate in memory of the Edinburgh 1910 conference – with representation from various churches in and outside of Norway. While most of the contributors and participants at the symposium were Norwegians, there was also a strong international representation, first and foremost by two of the main speakers, Dr. Eckhard Schnabel from Germany/USA and Dr. Chawkat Moucarry from Syria/United Kingdom. In addition there were a significant number of representatives from churches in Asia, Africa and Latin-America, in particular churches that are cooperating with Norwegian Lutheran Mission.

The Egede Institute, an independent ecumenical institute for mission research and information, located at the MF Norwegian School of Theology in Oslo, was delegated the task of coordinating the theological preparations for the celebration of Edinburgh 2010 in the Nordic countries with a special responsibility for the commission on 'Mission and Postmodernities'. The Egede Institute was also a co-sponsor of the symposium on 'Mission and Globalisation' at Fjellhaug International University College and this book.

The book is divided into two major parts. The first part consists of what we have called the 'main papers', while the second is made up of various 'case studies'. The 'main papers' have two major foci; first, those that deal with different aspects of mission and globalisation, and second, those that deal with the relationship between the two global religions Christianity and Islam. Two of the four case studies also deal with Christianity and Islam while the last two deal with the global youth culture and the question of a global truth in a pluralistic age. All the papers, both the main papers and the case studies, are followed by a 'response'.

In the final section of the book the General Secretaries of the three largest Lutheran mission organizations in Norway discuss the priorities for global mission in the decade ahead. The president of Fjellhaug International University College sums up the conference with some closing remarks.

In the first of the main papers Dr. Knud Jørgensen raises some of the main issues of the celebration of the centenary of Edinburgh 1910 in a chapter titled 'Edinburgh 2010 in Global Perspective'. Jørgensen has been actively involved in the preparation of the centenary celebrations. In this chapter he reflects on his own participation in the study process leading up to Edinburgh 2010. The chapter is mainly historical and the author deals with some of the major changes that have taken place between 1910 and 2010. He then proceeds to reflect on the challenges for the global church in mission today.

The second of the main papers is the annual Brandtzæg Memorial Lecture. Johannes Brandtzæg was one of the founders of the Norwegian Lutheran Mission and its general secretary for many years (1892-1931). In this paper Dr. Eckhard J. Schnabel presents a foundational biblical study on the theme 'Global Strategies and Local Methods of Missionary Work in the Early Church: Jesus, Peter, and Paul'. Dr. Schnabel draws on his vast knowledge of mission in the Bible to present a theological synthesis. He argues that in the Bible mission has a global dimension, most specifically expressed in Acts 1:8. However, although the apostle Paul had a global missionary strategy, he and other missionaries used flexible local methods. They served in weakness so that the power of the risen Lord, that is the power of the Holy Spirit, could work in and through them.

The respondent, professor Hans Kvalbein, emphasizes the particularity of Jesus Christ in agreement with Dr. Schnabel. Further he praises him for his combination of biblical scholarship and personal commitment to mission, which is rather unusual among professors of biblical studies.

The third of the main papers, 'The Church as Both Local and Global – A Missiological Perspective' deals especially with aspects of a missional ecclesiology. It emphasizes that the church is both local and global, and that it is therefore charged with the task of combining the two in what can be termed a 'glocal' perspective. The chapter, written by professor Tormod Engelsviken, argues for the contextualization of a normative, universal, biblical message in a time when some understandings of contextualization may lead to relativizing the gospel and challenge the uniqueness of Christ. He also presents a missiological understanding of the marks of the church.

The respondent to this paper, Assistant Professor Egil Grandhagen, unfortunately did not receive Engelsviken's manuscript before the symposium. Nevertheless, he shows in a short but instructive paper how mission work in Asia by Asians brought about early globalisation of the church during the first centuries of Christian history, prior to the Muslim conquest in the seventh and eighth centuries.

The fourth of the main papers initially carried the intriguing title, 'When the Gods Do Not Respond as Expected: An Anthropological Perspective on Religion and Globalisation". It is written by anthropologist Dr. Asle Jøssang who draws on his extensive research experience from Bolivia. He also uses the term glocalization in an anthropological context but argues that the resurgence of popular religion and especially the growth of Protestantism may be termed 'disharmonious glocalization'. He holds a rather negative view of globalisation especially with regard to the disadvantaged, and challenges mission agencies to increased sensitivity.

The respondent to Jøssang's paper is Professor Emeritus Øyvind Dahl, an anthropologist and communication specialist. He makes a significant contribution relating the subject to recent critiques of the traditional concept of culture.

The two last 'main papers' deal with another global religion, i.e. Islam and its relationship to Christianity. The first is written by Dr. Chawkat Moucarry, originally from Syria. He describes how the two missionary religions with exclusive, universal and conflicting claims have a history of polarisation and enmity. He is critical of Christian Zionism and concerned with the plight of Christian minorities in Muslim-majority countries. He calls the Open Letter written by Muslim scholars and leaders in 2007 a 'Landmark Islamic Initiative' with its insistence on love for God and the neighbor. He further suggests several points that could help the church in its future relationship with Islam.

The respondent Dr. Terje Østebø emphasizes the need for and possibility of cooperation between Muslims and Christians without either party giving up their essential tenets. He also points out that there is empirical evidence that conflicts have been caused by the two traditions' emphasis of universal mission and *dawa*.

In the last 'main paper' a historian of religion, Professor Jan Opsal, depicts the history of Christian mission to Muslim in a paper called, 'Mission to

Muslims – What Lessons Has the Missional Church Learned?' He identifies ten lessons (all beginning with a c!) and explores them in a historical perspective. Among these a number could be mentioned: competition which led to a certain mission strategy in Africa, colonialism and the image of Islam in the West, conversion for different reasons, and contextualization. This wide-ranging paper gives a short, but comprehensive overview of Christian-Muslim relations especially when it comes to mission.

In his response Dr. Moucarry would wish for Opsal to engage more critically with the issues raised by Christian mission in Islamic contexts. He concludes that the one lesson we as Christians must learn from history is that confrontation is not the way to do mission. Compassion – God's and ours – should be our main motive.

The four case studies are rather different as far as style is concerned. The first one, written by Nasser Fard, Iranian immigrant to Norway and founder of ethnic Iranian churches in Norway, is a very personal account. After presenting some statistics and discussing the role of religion for Iranians in Norway, he gives an account of the history of the work among Iranians including his own conversion and the founding of several churches. He points out the challenges and dangers that faces Christian Iranians both in Iran and in Norway. "As pastor I have baptized 70 Iranians, and since 2008 I have received three anonymous death threats."

In her response Assistant Professor Solveig Omland expands on the topic of immigrant Christians, and takes a look at the challenges of communication that both immigrant and ethnically Norwegian Christians are faced with. She also favours integration of immigrant Christians from non-Western cultures into Norwegian churches. To her Iranian and other Christian immigrants should be seen as a resource in a Norwegian Christian context.

The second case study by F.O. Thoresen, who has experience as a missionary on the Horn of Africa, raises important questions about how Somalis may use chat rooms on the internet for Christian witness and fellowship. After a discussion of Somali culture with emphasis on holism and individualism, Thoresen relates how two Christian Somalis living in Norway use the internet. He concludes that the social media may be of particular relevance for communication in a context where people live more individualized but remain within culturally defined religious limitations. He shows that through the process of globalisation and with increased mobility the traditional understanding of religious space has become more complex. The internet provides a new territory for developing religious and ethnic identities.

In his response Assistant Professor Thomas Sundnes Drønen, a former missionary in Cameroon, points out how globalisation, which he sees as something qualitatively new and characterized by "transplanetary relations and supraterritoriality" (Scholte), and not least migration, has an impact on global mission. He brings in examples from Nigeria and Cameroon demonstrating the active use of social media creating a cyber church, and then discusses how this kind of church or mission may affect Christian commitment and identity.

The third case study is written by Bård Eirik Hallesby Norheim. He is a Ph.D. candidate at MF Norwegian School of Theology and a former missionary to Estonia. His theme is 'The Global Youth Culture – Targeting and Involving Youth in Global Mission'. He describes the global youth culture and focuses particularly on the gap between the developing and developed world. He then discusses two types of addressing the global youth culture: culture-pessimistic and culture-optimistic church responses. In the end he advocates discipleship and involvement as part of *Missio Dei.*

In his response the director of the Bible School at Fjellhaug International University College, and general secretary elect of IFES in Norway, Tor Erling Fagermoen, focuses on the term 'targeting'. He notes that the young generation is not only the future but the present generation and in many ways leading the world. To be an authentic Christian is a key to winning young people.

The fourth case study is written by Stefan Gustavsson who is the director of CredoAkademin, an apologetic study centre in Stockholm, Sweden. He is also the general secretary of the Swedish Evangelical Alliance. His theme is 'Can we – and dare we – present a global truth in a pluralistic age?' Gustavsson argues that Christians should not only witness for the truth but argue for the Christian faith and present it as global truth in the midst of modern and post-modern thinking. He shows that the concept of global truth is still with us in scientific, ethical and religious discussions, and there is no reason for the Christian church to downplay the absolute and universal claim of the gospel. He therefore wants to see a recovery of Christian apologetics.

The response from Ingrid Eskilt, Assistant Professor of Missiology at Ansgar School of Theology and Mission, emphasizes the pluralistic character of post-modern Western society, yet argues that although a presentation of a global truth may easily be rejected as arrogant and as an out-dated legacy from the time of Western imperialism, the proclamation of one global truth is ethically legitimate if it is done in humility and with respect towards people with other faiths.

The final essays of the General Secretaries of the three largest Lutheran mission organizations in Norway express a vision for future mission, a mission in which European Christians work in partnership with people from other continents: "Elisha asked for a double portion of Elijah's Spirit. European Christians seem to be in need of the same prayer – and for the deep and long lasting partnership with the churches of Asia, Africa and Latin-America" (Kjøde).

In the closing comments Dr. Hans A. Gravaas, the President of Fjellhaug International University College, summarizes some of the highlights of the conference and closes with the following statement: "Mission is a joint endeavour of the global church, based on God's message, commandment, support and blessing."

Hopefully this volume will explore important aspects of God's message and convey His blessing.

PART A

MAIN PAPERS

EDINBURGH 2010 IN GLOBAL PERSPECTIVE

Knud Jørgensen

For the last four years I have had the privilege of being involved in the process towards Edinburgh 2010. It has been challenging, time-consuming, and inspiring. Sometimes it has felt like a roller coaster, at other times it has opened new vistas when I worked together with people from traditions and outlooks different from mine. In that sense I have in very practical and concrete ways tasted the global perspectives of Edinburgh 2010. Some of these perspectives have changed my own views and transformed my traditional thinking of mission.

My primary involvement has been in the study processes (see www.edinburgh2010.org). The programme of the 1910 World Missionary Conference was built on the reports from eight commissions. The agenda for each day was to debate one such report. The impact of Edinburgh 1910 was due to these eight reports, in the form of eight books – books that one will also find today in most theological and missiological libraries worldwide. As occurred in the preparation for 1910, studies for Edinburgh 2010 have been commissioned on nine of the most relevant and challenging topics facing mission and church in a new century. The result of the work on these nine study themes is now available in the form of a major volume entitled *Edinburgh 2010 Witnessing to Christ Today* (edited by Daryl Balia and Kirsteen Kim).[1] In addition six of the study groups/commissions will in the course of 2011 publish volumes on their findings and collected position papers and case studies.

The material in the volume on *Witnessing to Christ Today* will then feed into a centenary conference in Edinburgh in June 2010 where a cross-section of world Christianity will gather and spend most of the time on these nine reports, just as the conference did with the eight reports in 1910.

I have been chairing the Study Process Monitoring Group and have therefore followed closely the work on the nine themes. In addition I have been directly involved in the study themes on *Forms of Missionary Engagement* and *Christian Mission among Other Faiths*. In the following this involvement is clearly reflected; I sometimes draw directly or indirectly on what I personally have contributed towards these two study themes.

Why have we set in motion this comprehensive process and carried out the cumbersome work on the nine study themes? The answer is simple: we dream

---

[1] Daryl Balia and Kirsteen Kim (eds), *Edinburgh 2010 Witnessing to Christ Today* (Oxford: Regnum, 2010).

of having the same impact on mission in the twenty-first century as Edinburgh 1910 has had on the twentieth century. It is this same dream that lies behind the following pages.

Where is the Non-Christian World?

As a young student I remember people quoting the so-called Edinburgh 1910 by-line *The Evangelization of the World in This Generation.* In my mind that became the watchword of what happened in Edinburgh. Only recently did I discover that this motto, coined by John R. Mott, was never adopted as the Edinburgh 1910 watchword, maybe because the German missiology pioneer Gustav Warneck did not like it. Instead the rallying call was the title of the first of the eight commissions *Carrying the Gospel to the Non-Christian World.*[2] I mention this because it calls attention to the basic working assumption of Edinburgh that Christian mission was a movement from the Christian world of the West and the North to the non-Christian world of the East and the South.

Today we react to this crude division of the world between Christendom and the non-Christian world. Such a territorial understanding of Christendom has been out-dated for a long time, at least in theory. Already four years later "some gigantic prehistoric catastrophe"[3] occurred, opening up "a huge fault" in the unity of the Christian West and in the superiority of Christendom. Edinburgh 1910 was mistaken in its foundational assumption that Christian mission should be viewed as a movement from the Christian nations of the West to the non-Christian nations of the East. Viewing the world in the rear-mirror of two world wars, one may wonder how it has been possible for us to uphold the notion of 'Christian nations' almost until the end of the twentieth century, if not longer? Any delineation made on the basis of geography is today completely out of the question. Or does it still linger on in western minds and in the minds of western mission when we talk about our 'missionary calling' or about 'reaching the unreached peoples'?

In the course of the last 20-30 years western mission societies have increasingly realized the need for, and aimed at joining hands with, local churches and congregations in outreach to new people groups. Even so the partnership has been quite uneven in terms of leadership, initiative and resources. Edinburgh 1910 implied a relegation of the South to a secondary place on the agenda of mission, especially as regards Africa and Oceania. Today we know that such relegation was mistaken, but it is still openly or covertly influencing our western mindset, in terms of power, funds, resources and our own needs.

---

[2] David Kerr, 'Missiological Developments from Edinburgh 1910 to Today', *Swedish Missiological Themes,* 96, 1 (2008), 9-26.

[3] Quoted from Brian Stanley, *The World Missionary Conference, Edinburgh 1910* (Grand Rapids/Cambridge: Eerdmans, 2009), 304.

If we were to envisage God's people from the many nations bringing their gifts to the big basket of Christ, many of these peoples would bring their prayers, songs, testimonies, sorrows and joys; we westerners would bring our resources and strategies and education to this basket. All the gifts would belong to Christ and be his gifts. But when the Lord then would invite us to come and take from the basket what we need, one may wonder whether we in the West would take anything?

Why Celebrate?

Does this mean there is little to celebrate as we mark the centenary for 1910? We may ridicule Edinburgh for its mistake in expecting the church to grow particularly in Asia. They did not foresee the extraordinary growth of the church in Africa. Nor did they anticipate how Latin America would become the scene of a powerful renewal of the faith.[4] But there is no denying that the century has shown that the gospel can take root in every culture across the world and result in fruit in church and society everywhere.

Andrew Walls calls this 'a huge reversal' of the Christian geography: "The map of the Christian Church, its demographic and cultural make-up, changed more dramatically during the twentieth century than (probably) in any other since the first."[5] One may even wonder whether we today could have talked about Christianity as a world religion without an event like Edinburgh 1910. The seeds of the Good News that had been sown by the missionary movement in the nineteenth century were here spread further, and Edinburgh 1910 became the occasion for lifting up the vision of this missionary movement in a concentrated and focused manner.

At one and the same time Edinburgh marked the climax and end of an era: the climax of the Enlightenment model of mission and the western missionary movement. In that sense we may view it as the close of one chapter and the beginning of another, a chapter about how Edinburgh became the birthplace of the modern ecumenical movement.[6] Walls has called it, "the high point of the modern Western missionary movement and the point from which it declined," but at the same time it became "the launch-pad of the modern ecumenical movement; the point at which Christians first began to glimpse something of what a world church would be like."[7] *Ecumenical movement* should in my view

---

[4] Kenneth Ross, 'The Centenary of Edinburgh 1910: Its Possibilities', *International Bulletin of Missionary Research,* Vol. 30, No.4 (2006), 177-179.

[5] Andrew Walls, 'Commission One and the Church's Transforming Century', in David Kerr & and Kenneth Ross (eds), *Edinburgh 2010. Mission then and now* (Oxford: Regnum 2010).

[6] Kenneth Scott Latourette, 'Ecumenical Bearings of the Missionary Movement and the International Missionary Council', in Ruth Rouse and Stephen C. Neill (eds), *A History of the Ecumenical Movement, 1517-1948* (Geneva: World Council of Churches, 1993), 362.

[7] Andrew Walls, *The Cross-Cultural Process in Christian History: Studies in the*

here be understood in a broad sense to ensure that both the conciliar and the evangelical movements are included. One of the things we should celebrate in this connection is the achievement of the agencies represented to commit themselves to work in cooperation with one another. At the same time it should be remembered that the push towards such cooperation in mission, and even more towards unity, came primarily from the non-Western delegates.

Mapping Mission

One of the publications marking the centenary is the *Atlas of Global Christianity* from 1910 to 2010.[8] The salient trend documented in this atlas is that Christianity moves South and East. The Christian faith is no longer a European or American phenomenon. In a series of maps the 1910 situation is compared to the situation today. To this end the atlas also uses 'towers' to contrast the growth in percentage: in 1910 the number of Christians in Africa was 9.4% of the population (just under 12 million Christians). By 2010 the total has risen to 47.9% or almost 500 million.

But the maps also indicate the extent of the growth of Christianity in Asia. In 1910 the number of Christians in Asia was just over 25 million (2.4% of the population) while in 2010 it is just over 350 million (8.5% of the population). Edinburgh 1910 made a mistake in not expecting the phenomenal growth in Africa, but their expectations about growth in Asia have not been put entirely to shame. In this connection it is also of interest to mention that the statistical 'centre of gravity' of the Christian faith in Asia (the geographical point at which an equal number of believers in a given religion lives to the north, south, east and west of that point) has moved from Bengal in north-east India to a point in southern China just north of Vietnam: Christianity has grown significantly in eastern Asia since 1910.

Worldwide the centre of gravity has since 1910 moved from southwest Spain to Timbuktu in Mali.

Why this Growth?

Christianity has undergone several 'transformations' in the course of the century – from living with Enlightenment to living with modernity and today with post-modernity, the collapse of the Constantine model of church-state relations, the defeat of 'the crusading mind' to 'the crucified mind' (the expression used by the Japanese Kosuke Koyama) – but the greatest transformation is this enormous growth of Christianity in the Global South where more than 60% of the Christians now live. How could this happen?

Transmission and Appropriation of Faith (Maryknoll and Edinburgh: Orbis Books and T. & T. Clark, 2002), 53.

[8] Todd M. Johnson and Kenneth R. Ross (eds), *Atlas of Global Christianity 1910-2010* (Edinburgh: Edinburgh University Press, 2009).

Surely there is more to this than the transmission of the missionary message, even though we know from Scripture about the power of God's word in creation and redemption.

I shall return several times to this question. Let me here mention that in the attempt to find answers to the growth, the science of mission has enlisted insights of ethnography, anthropology and sociology.[9] Examples of this are the church growth studies at Fuller Theological Seminary, the work on enculturation within Roman Catholic mission and the focus on contextualization.[10] These studies on culture, society and receptivity have helped us understand some of the ways in which the gospel is received, interpreted and applied by churches and communities in the Global South. This endeavour should not be sharply separated from God acting in history and culture; rather we have learnt to broaden our view of how the Spirit works and paves the way for the gospel.

Contextualization as a Key Concern

In this way *contextualization* has become a key concern in contemporary missiology, and the inspiration towards this concern has largely come from scholars in the Global South (e.g. John Mbiti, Kwame Bediako, Hwa Yung, Kosuke Koyama, etc). One of several reasons for this concern among scholars in the Global South has been the fact that numerical growth has not always been matched by a concurrent discipleship. Church leaders have described the growth of Christianity as being 'a mile broad, but only an inch deep'. In addition the emphasis on Christian values in society, culture and politics has often been lagging behind the growth in numbers. Sometimes churches have been compromised when they have taken part in corrupt politics and supported military coups which promoted ethnic separation (e.g. Rwanda, Burundi, and DR Congo).[11] This has challenged the credibility of the witness of the churches and encouraged them to uphold basic Christian values in their struggle for justice and peace.[12]

Contextualization and its focus on context and society have taken us a major step further than indigenization and enculturation. Contextualization is not just a question of relevance in terms of culture, but also of being salt and light in a broken world.

David Bosch calls contextual theology "a theology 'from below', from the underside of history; its main source (apart from Scripture and tradition) is the *social sciences,* and its main interlocutor the *poor* or the *culturally*

---

[9] Kerr, 'Missiological Developments', 16.

[10] Stephen Bevans, *Models of Contextual Theology* (Maryknoll, N.Y.: Orbis, 2003).

[11] Featuna'I Ben Liua'na, 'Christianity in Melanesia, Micronesia and Polynesia, 1910-2010', in Johnson and Ross, *Atlas of Global Christianity,* 201.

[12] Fohle Lygunda, 'Christianity in Middle Africa, 1910-2010', in Johnson and Ross, *Atlas of Global Christianity,* 119.

marginalized."[13] The strong focus on contextual theology marks a decisive difference between 1910 and 2010. In the course of the century mission has increasingly struggled with how, on the one hand, to be relevant to and involved in the world and, on the other hand, how to maintain its identity in Christ. The most essential part of this has involved the construction of a variety of 'local theologies'. 1910 still believed that Western theology vas universally valid and based on the ecclesiastical confessions. Contextualization implies an experimental nature of all theology and an on-going dialogue between text and context, and therefore a theology which always will be provisional, at the same time as it is part of a universal dimension of theology.[14]

This calls, as an illustration, for theological institutions in the West to offer courses on theological developments in the Global South and not just the other way round.

But at the same time as we have come to understand the crucial role of the context, it is also important not to make the context the sole and basic authority for theological reflection. Related to this, David Kerr would seem to support a change with regard to the ordering of truth and action. Edinburgh 1910 clearly believed that truth prevails through right action or praxis.[15] Theologies in the Global South have, according to Kerr, reversed the order and argued that Scripture should not be read as the revelation of transcendent truths (that are then applied in action), but as the story of Israel's struggle for justice and truth. This implies that mission no longer begins with a transcendent truth (that demands action) but with action, modelled on Scripture (e.g. the Exodus event), which then discovers the truth of the gospel in the actual context. Along this way *praxis* may gain absolute priority, unless we affirm the need for a critical theology of mission that relates to the context, but keeps the context in a dialectical tension with biblical theology and the Christian tradition. The missionary message is not contextual because it grows out of the context, but when it lives in a hermeneutical dialogue between text and context.

Dark Sides of 1910

One dark side of Edinburgh 1910 that relates to the question of a universally valid theology has to do with the concepts of racial distinctiveness that we find expressed in the language of the reports.[16] Here are expressions about the influence of the white man among "the primitive races" and warnings against importing ideas and practices derived from heathenism into native evangelism. The reports talk about the "vigorous and progressive" races of the west and the "contemplative and mystical" spirituality of the oriental races.[17] Especially with

[13] David Bosch, *Transforming Mission. Paradigm Shifts in Theology of Mission* (Maryknoll, N.Y.: Orbis Books, 1991), 423.
[14] Bosch, *Transforming Mission,* 427.
[15] David Kerr, 'Missiological Developments', 17.
[16] Stanley, *The World Missionary Conference,* 307.
[17] Stanley, *The World Missionary Conference,* 308-309.

regard to Africa there is a widespread uncertainty over whether Africans had anything that westerners could recognize as 'religion'. Today we shudder when hearing such expressions. But they are there.

In the same way we need to pay heed to the militaristic language used when talking about relations to non-Christian religions. John R. Mott would call the church to go into and take possession of the world for Christ, and the report on *The Missionary Message in Relation to Non-Christian Religions* concludes by celebrating, "the spectacle of the advance of the Christian Church along many lines of action to the conquest of the five great religions of the modern world."[18] The reports talked about "mission fields", about missionaries as "soldiers" and "Christian forces". Mission was associated with "army", "crusade", "council of war", "conquest" and "marching orders".[19] This sort of language should have been shattered by two world wars, but as a matter of fact even towards the turn of the twentieth century remnants of such language prevailed. I am sure that many illustrations could be cited from mission magazines and mission strategies. There is still room for repentance and redirection.

Powerlessness and Vulnerability of Mission

An essential dimension of such a redirection is to discover the powerlessness of the gospel and of mission. Edinburgh 1910 marked the climax of the western belief in its own power to civilize and open up the rest of the world. Edinburgh looked at this as something God had prepared, making the whole world accessible to this generation. In the view of John R. Mott all this was, "to further some mighty and beneficent purpose. Every one of these wonderful facilities has been intended primarily to serve as a handmaiden to the sublime enterprise of extending and building up the kingdom of Jesus Christ in all the world."[20] There was a strong optimism around the power of improved communication (railways, steamships, cable and telegraph systems, news agencies, and the printing press), and an equally strong belief in the money power of western mission; this was the time when giving to foreign mission was rapidly increasing. The power of steam and electricity had brought the world together.

Certainly, there will always in mission be a need for a spirit of optimism and confidence, but such confidence can be a real hindrance for grasping the vulnerability of mission.[21] 'Vulnerable Mission' refers both to mission in contexts of poverty and mission by the powerless. Could it be that in 2010 vulnerability contains the potential, the capacity and power so much needed for a renewal of mission and church? Is vulnerability to be considered "an enabling

---

[18] Quoted from Ross, 'The Centenary of Edinburgh 1910', 177.
[19] Bosch, *Transforming Mission,* 338.
[20] Quoted from Bosch, *Transforming Mission,* 338.
[21] Balia and Kim, *Edinburgh 2010 Witnessing to Christ Today,* 121-124.

condition for mission"?[22] In the Bible's image of a God among us we meet his vulnerability, and in Christ God makes God himself vulnerable, to the extent that Jesus Christ is God's 'wound in the world'. The vulnerable God calls the church in mission to liberate the vulnerable in service and diakonia. Here is one of the signs of the church, a sign which also encompasses liberating action in solidarity with the oppressed.

At the same time there is power in powerlessness. It makes us gain new insights into the gospel and opens up for a new understanding of how God's power is hidden under its contradiction (*sub contrarie specie*, Luther said). Vulnerable mission begins from below. Samuel Escobar calls it the heart-beat and the thrust of mission today: "There is an element of mystery when the dynamism of mission does not come from the people of position of power and privilege... but from below, from the little ones, those who have few material financial or technical resources."[23] Do we here find an essential reason for the growth of the Christian faith among the poor and the persecuted?

The theology of Vinay Samuel (for many years the director of the Oxford Center for Mission Studies) is in a similar manner a reflection on mission among the poor in the Indian context. In this context he has realized that the meaning of the good news for the poor defines the meaning of the good news for all. As the poor are called, the real nature of the gospel becomes evident to others. The gospel therefore has to be mediated through what it means to be poor and vulnerable.[24] Unless we hear and receive the gospel from the poor and the vulnerable, from below, there is a genuine risk of a shift of emphasis from the grace of God to the works of humans.

A Shift in Missionaries: The Importance of Migration

The focus on vulnerability and the poor today also finds expression in the global shift in missionaries. The typical missionary in 2010 is no longer the white foreigner. Instead the sending of missionaries is from many different countries. There is little doubt that a missionary from the Global South is more easily accepted as one of their own and that she/he understands better the ways of thinking and communicating. Lalsangkima Pachuau says it in this way: "If the 1910 World Missionary Conference in Edinburgh represents the high point of the modern missionary movement from the West to Asia, Edinburgh 2010 marks another high point, namely Christian missions from Asia, by Asians, in Asia and around the world.'"[25] It is this new missionary movement that will set the stage for mission in the next one hundred years.

---

[22] Balia and Kim, *Edinburgh 2010 Witnessing to Christ Today,* 123-124.

[23] Samuel Escobar, *A Time for Mission* (Leicester: Intervarsity Press, 1995), 17.

[24] See Hwa Yung, *Mangoes or Bananas? The Quest for an Authentic Asian Christian Theology* (Oxford: Regnum, 1997).

[25] Lalsingkima Pachuau, 'Missionaries Sent and Received, Asia, 1910-2010' in Johnson and Ross *Atlas of Global Christianity,* 268.

This new missionary movement finds new expressions and new patterns. Today's *migration* is one such expression. Migration and mission were very much part of mission in the nineteenth and the twentieth centuries, but most often in such a way that migration and mission moved from the powerful to the poor and powerless. Today it is the migrants and refugees themselves rather than the missionaries who bring the faith from one place to another. This migration in reverse, from the Global South to the North and the West, represents a new dynamic witness in the midst of a faltering Christianity. The routes of migration are also the pathways of mission.

A majority of the migrants are profoundly Christian and explicitly evangelistic.[26] Some would see this mobilization of the masses in the South as the driving force in Christian mission. Jehu Hanciles from Sierra Leone has helped us see the link between migration and the transformation of the West.[27] He paints a broad picture of the consequences for the West of the European migration and mission activity (the encounter with other religious worldviews, emerging new disciplines like anthropology, comparative religion and linguistics), and he helps us understand that migration always has been the most important factor in religious expansion and in the spread of the Christian faith (the Jewish Diaspora, the migration of Christians in the Roman Empire after the fall of Jerusalem, the great movements of peoples within and out of Europe from the sixth century, the network of trade routes over land and sea bringing the gospel to India, Afghanistan, India and Arabia, the migration of 60 million Europeans from 1800 till 1914 to the Americas, Oceania and Africa).

Also today, Hanciles says, every Christian migrant is a potential missionary. Why are these Christian migrants from the South so important? Because they have a larger experience in witnessing to Christ and in winning converts among other migrants; because they are in a better position to comprehend religious pluralism; because they, in a society where the Christian faith is faltering, understand better than we that the countries in the West are 'mission fields'. "Hence many migrants come from the new heartlands of Christianity and bring the flame of faith to the old centres in the North where the fire is burning low."[28] Hanciles claims that this non-Western missionary movement represents mission beyond Christendom:

> …mission de-linked from structures of power and domination; mission undertaken from positions of vulnerability and need; mission freed from the bane of territoriality and one-directional expansion from a fixed centre; mission involving agents who reflect the New Testament reference to the 'weak things of the world' (1 Cor 1:27).[29]

---

26 Jonathan Bonk, 'Finance', in Johnson and Ross, *Atlas of Global Christianity*, 295.
27 Jehu J. Hanciles, *Beyond Christendom: Globalisation, African Migration and the Transformation of the West* (Maryknoll, Maryknoll: Orbis Books, 2008).
28 Kenneth R. Ross, 'From Edinburgh 1910 to Edinburgh 2010', in Mogens Mogensen (ed), *Edinburgh 1910 – 100 år efter* (København: Dansk Missionsråd, 2009), 30.
29 Hanciles, *Beyond Christendom,* 369.

The structures for this new migratory mission movement differ from the mission societies of 1910. There is no head office, no organizing committee, no command structure, no centralized fund, and no comprehensive strategic direction.[30] Rather than structures, people in the new movement talk about networking, requiring lesser resources. The emphasis is on relations and less on strategies. Our western models will not prove useful, and our models cannot be used for understanding and analyzing this movement. The movement will represent a great variety in experience and forms of expression, and it will largely be post-confessional. Among its members there will be a strong understanding of spiritual powers and spiritual conflicts and a long experience with religious pluralism. In that way it will represent a *mission in reverse* which may embrace our spiritual poverty and meet our cry for renewal.

Forms of Missionary Engagement: The Local Church

Another global perspective of Edinburgh 2010 has to do with the *change in forms of missionary engagement and with the missional identity of the church.*[31] Edinburgh 1910 was a missionary conference with a focus on traditional mission, mission societies, missionaries, and the missionary encounter in foreign lands. The past century has radically changed our way of thinking. We have come to see the church as essentially missionary, it exists in being sent. Missionary activity is not the work of the church but the church at work.[32] God is a missionary God (*missio Dei*) wherefore God's people are a missionary people. Edinburgh 1910 talked about church *and* mission; today we must talk about the mission *of* the church. In the words of David Bosch, "It is not the church which 'undertakes' mission; it is *the missio Dei* which constitutes the church."[33]

The church-in-mission is today primarily the local church everywhere in the world. This local church is part of the church universal (hence, the church is *glocal*). From the very beginning the local churches were *complete* churches. Roland Allen suggested that their success was due to the fact that they trusted both the Lord and the people to whom they had gone.[34] It took decades before foreign mission took the views and advice of Roland Allen to heart. Slowly the Edinburgh 1910 concept of 'older' and 'younger' churches was replaced, and the church-*for*-others was turned into the church-*with*-others[35].

---

[30] Ross, 'From Edinburgh 1910 to Edinburgh 2010', 31.

[31] Daryl Balia and Kirsteen Kim (eds), *Edinburgh 2010 Witnessing to Christ Today*, 117-121. The material I am referring to in this section was written by me for this study theme.

[32] Bosch, *Transforming Mission,* 372.

[33] Bosch, *Transforming Mission,* 519.

[34] Allen, Roland, *Missionary Methods: St. Paul's or Ours?* (London: World Dominion Press, 1956 (1912)), 183-190.

[35] Bosch, *Transforming Mission,* 379.

In the past the parish structure prevailed. In some places this may also today be an appropriate structure. The parish structure grew up together with the notion of *Corpus Christianum* where the church was married to the holders of power. This turned the church into a pastoral institution where the church adopted the shape of society's structure with parochial churches and a division between *clerici* (priests) and *idiotes* (lay people). However, even with the parish structure as the dominant scheme, there have always been alternate models with more focus on the small community (*ecclesiola* within the *ecclesia*), e.g. the monastic community, the fellowship of believers, and the *missionary bands*.

Today we see experiments with new forms and structures. One such model is the *house church* which e.g. in the Chinese context exemplifies the characteristics of the Early Church: no church building, often no professional form of leadership, and sometimes considered an illegal religion. Using the images of *clan, synagogue* and *temple*,[36] the house church is the clan living together in a small 'hamlet'; the synagogue is a community where the smaller groups gather regularly; and the temple is the place for the bigger celebration where the many come together.

Other models are called *emerging churches*[37] – new forms that try to bind together the original apostolic core with new imaginative, relatively disorganized forms, and gathering in cafés, dance clubs, on riverbanks, in theatres etc. These emerging churches live as communities that transform secular space and live in a spirituality similar to the Desert Fathers.

Or we may go to what has been called *independent* churches (or African indigenous or initiated churches) which encompass a total of 400 million people worldwide – churches that reject historical denominationalism and seek a more effective missionary lifestyle.

All these new forms signal more *fluid* communities, providing multiple options depending on context and target group. At the same time there is a growing dissatisfaction with traditional forms of church, and more and more Christians, primarily in the West, live without a local church, alienated from current expressions of church.

Missionary and Missional

Edinburgh 1910 often used the word *missionary* to refer to specific mission activities of the church. That word and concept will remain on the mission agenda of the twenty-first century. But increasingly the word *missional* will be employed when we want to talk about *the nature of the church* as sent by God to the world. The primary form of missionary engagement in the new century

---

[36] Lausanne Committee for World Evangelization, *The Local Church in Mission: Becoming a Missional Congregation in the Twenty-First Century Global Context* (Lausanne Committee for World Evangelization, 2004).

[37] Gibbs, Eddie and Ryan K. Bolger, *Emerging Churches. Creating Christian Community in Postmodern Culture* (Grand Rapids: Baker Academic, 2006).

will most likely be such missional congregations and churches in both the West and the Global South, using missional structures that go beyond the hierarchies of the past and providing a balance between worship, community and mission.

In such churches a primary missional vocation will be *witness*. Mission has always been and will always remain *witness*. *Martyria* is the sum of *kerygma*, *koinonia* and *diakonia* – all three of which constitute important dimensions of the witness of the church in mission.[38] Also here is an area where churches in the North could learn from churches in the South. One of the explanations of their growth – and of the growth of churches at any time in history – is that they are witnessing churches, in practise. So how may we in the North re-learn to do and practice what we are ecclesiologically, i.e. God's witnessing people in mission?

Come- and Go-Structures

If the primary form of missionary engagement is the local church, which implications will that have for the voluntary structure of the mission society? This question relates to what Ralph Winter at the Lausanne Congress on World Evangelization in 1974 termed 'modalities' and 'sodalities', i.e. the two structures of the church (*come* and *go*). Already in Antioch we find the two structures (Acts 13:1-3) – when the local church wanted to move beyond its own borders, the Holy Spirit told them to send out a missionary team of Paul and Barnabas. So both structures are needed, *and together they constitute the church*.

The history of the church lists a number of examples of this twofold structure – itinerant evangelists from Ireland and Scotland (*perigrini*), the monastic movements, monks from the Nestorian and Syrian churches, the Jesuits in India, Japan and China, the Moravian brethren, and the model that Edinburgh 1910 and we know best in the form of 'mission societies'.

Also today we need, in one form or another, the go- and the come-structures. And we should not forget the reasons why many mission societies came into being:

- a state-church with no structure for going beyond Christendom;
- a church that did not take up the call to go;
- Christians on fire from revivals and searching for new, effective ways of crossing the borders.

1910 represented the division between 'foreign' and 'home' mission and a separation between church and mission. This separation creates so-called 'para-church' organisations, separated from the come-structure of the parish church. In 2010 the two structures are in both the South and the North searching for ways of joining hands. Within the 'free' or independent churches in the North that problem has never existed because mission from the outset was an integral

[38] Darrell L. Guder, *The Continuing Conversion of the Church* (Grand Rapids: Eerdmans, 2000), 53-55.

part of the church; the same applies to most churches in the Global South. But in the so-called established churches this has been a sore and complex point for more than a century. As established churches today realise that they are churches in *a mission situation*, they will increasingly come to view themselves as both 'missional' and 'missionary'. Mission societies in the West are increasingly linking up with local congregations in new and imaginative ways.

Also in a new century we shall need the missionary band, but probably taking new forms in new contexts – missionary movements in and from the South, Christian migratory movements and congregations, short-term mission, tentmakers, etc.

Christian Mission Among Other Faiths

One of the most crucial missiological questions facing Christians in both 1910 and 2010 is how we should relate with and witness to people of other faiths.[39] This question may be expressed in various ways:

- How do we understand mission in the religiously pluralistic context of today, and how has the concept of mission been shaped by our understanding of other religious faiths and our relationship with people of other faiths?
- How can an inter-faith dialogue enhance our common Christian witness without relativizing our Christian faith?
- How may churches in the West gain new insights from churches in the Global South about witness and dialogue in a pluralistic setting?
- What could churches in the Global South gain from discussions on pluralism in the North?

Such questions were in Edinburgh 1910 primarily dealt with in the report of Commission IV: *The Missionary Message in Relation to Non-Christian Religions*.[40] The theology of religions in this report is 'fulfillment theology', and the task was therefore to a large extent to identify 'points of contact' in non-Christian religions, with the aim of drawing people of other faiths toward the full revelation found in Christ. The use of fulfillment theology as a lens implied a focus on the 'high religions' while other more 'animistic' traditions did not fit; the commission was not even sure that such traditions would qualify as 'religion'.

The fulfillment theology was seriously challenged by Hendrik Kraemer in 1938.[41] Rather than fulfillment, Kraemer, influenced by Karl Barth, advocated

---

[39] Daryl Balia and Kirsteen Kim (eds), *Edinburgh 2010 Witnessing to Christ Today*, 34-60. Part of the material I am using in this section was written by me for this study theme.

[40] World Missionary Conference, 1910, *Report of Commission IV: The Missionary Message in Relation to Non-Christian Religions* (Edinburgh and London: Oliphant, Anderson & Ferrier; New York, Chicago and Toronto: Fleming H. Revell Company, n.d.).

[41] Hendrik Kraemer, *The Christian Message in a Non-Christian World* (London: International Missionary Council, 1938).

'discontinuity'. Also Kraemer had great respect for non-Christian religions, but he viewed the search for contacts as misguided. God's revelation in Jesus Christ is *sui generis* and can therefore not be related in that way to other religions. This revelation contradicts human wisdom and religion, and there can therefore not be continuity from non-Christian religions to Christianity. Kraemer's thinking has influenced Protestant theologies of religions and has met with positive as well as negative response.

One of the more critical responses came from the debates on dialogue in a pluralistic context following World War II. Within both WCC and Roman Catholic circles interreligious dialogue posited an affirmative posture to non-Christian religions. The church cannot be opposed to anything 'true and holy' in other religions. And so Karl Rahner talked about 'anonymous Christians' and Raymond Pannikar about 'the unknown Christ of Hinduism'. Here was no room for Christian superiority. The focus was rather on respect and openness, an openness that among several of the proponents ended up in a pluralistic theology affirming the salvific validity of different religions. Such views had little or no room for mission in any traditional sense. The same critical view applies to 'conversion', which remains a key concern among evangelicals, together with the focus on *the uniqueness of Christ*.

However, evangelicals have also learned to talk about dialogue as a mode of mission.[42] In a similar manner people like Timothy Tennent[43] and Veli-Matti Kärkkäinen[44] have dealt extensively with issues of dialogue and theology of religions.

Today we affirm the plurality of religions as a fact of life. This calls for a dialogical way of living and witnessing. Mission is not only what the church is sent to be and do, but also what the church is sent to *say* – proclamation of the Gospel, dialogue and apologetics. In this perspective dialogue means witnessing to our deepest convictions, while listening to those of our neighbors. 'Neighbor' means that we cannot dialogue with or witness to people if we from the outset resent their views. Christian theology must today everywhere be a theology of dialogue, in the same way as it is a theology of contextualization. Both contextualization and dialogue are specific ways of being in mission, and not alternatives to mission. And so we need to affirm dialogue as a basic way of life because Christians share life and contexts with neighbors of other faiths. In this way dialogue has to do with family, working place and neighborhood; it calls for creating meeting places and using opportunities. When dialoguing in such meeting places we can be committed to dialogue and to Christian witness at the same time: "We affirm that witness does not preclude dialogue but

---

[42] John R. W. Stott, *Christian Mission in the Modern World* (Downers Grove: InterVarsity Press, 1975), 58-81.

[43] Timothy C. Tennent, *Christianity at the Religious Roundtable: Evangelicalism in Conversation with Hinduism, Buddhism, and Islam* (Grand Rapids: Baker Academic, 2002).

[44] Veli-Matti Kärkkäinen, *An Introduction to the Theology of Religions* (Downers Grove: Intervarsity Press, 2003).

invites it, and that dialogue does not preclude witness but extends and deepens it."[45]

Committed Pluralism

In contemporary theology of religions there is a broad spectrum of ways to understand other faiths. One such way that I have found valuable is what Lesslie Newbigin calls *committed pluralism* in contrast to agnostic pluralism.[46] Committed pluralism takes other worldviews seriously, but dares to raise questions about the other's faith. Truth is to be found in a life of discipleship to Jesus Christ as he is known through a life lived in the community of disciples, in faithfulness to the tradition about him (Scripture), and in openness to all truth which may be discovered in history. I am therefore not afraid of what I may learn in the encounter with other living faiths because my ultimate commitment is to the Christ of Scripture and history.

In the encounter with other living faiths we should, however, be aware that religions are worlds in themselves, with their own structures and worldviews. As Bosch says, they face in different directions and ask different questions. The gospel relates differently to Islam than it does to Hinduism or Buddhism. These differences are for real. Other living faiths are not a sort of reduced copy of Christianity or simply echoes of Christianity's own voice.[47]

Revelation in Other Religions?

Every religion has a dark side, also Christianity, but in terms of creation we may still recognize 'revelation' in all of them. We may listen to Paul's claim, in his speech on Areopagos, that every part of the created world and every human being are already related to Jesus. And so the light of God may be seen in the lives of women and men even though they do not know him as Lord. But the Areopagos speech also challenges the listeners with a call for confrontation with the idols and a call to repentance, conversion to and faith in him who is no longer an unknown God, but has revealed his face in the crucified and risen Christ. It is his cross that in a sense becomes *the master clue* for Christians in the search for salvation and the encounter with other faiths.

This does not solve the difficult question of salvation for those who have not had and will not have the opportunity to respond to the Gospel. Some will look for an answer in the World Council of Churches' statement at San Antonio in 1989: "We cannot point to any other way of salvation than Jesus Christ. At the

---

[45] World Council of Churches, *The San Antonio Report,* ed F. R. Wilson (Geneva: World Council of Churches, 1990), quoted in Bosch, *Transforming Mission,* 487.
[46] Lesslie Newbigin, *The Gospel in a Pluralist Society* (Grand Rapids: Eerdmans, 1989).
[47] Bosch, *Transforming Mission,* 485.

same time we cannot set limits to God's saving power.... We appreciate this tension, and do not attempt to solve it."[48]

Others, also evangelicals, will cling to God's 'amazing grace' and the confidence that this grace is sufficient for all. Alister McGrath, a well-known evangelical Anglican, says:

> We cannot draw the conclusion... that only those who respond will be saved. God's revelation is not limited to the explicit human preaching of the good news, but extends beyond it. We must be prepared to be surprised at those whom we will meet in the kingdom of God.[49]

Also I hope and pray that God will work in the hearts and lives of people in order to open them to his grace. At the same time I affirm what Scripture says about salvation and perdition. In a number of places the New Testament refers to both (e.g. Jn 3:16 and Eph 2:1-3). Scripture makes it quite clear that it is faith in Jesus that saves. Perdition or being lost is therefore a result of the disobedience that says no to the word of the Gospel about salvation. I dare believe that all of us in one way or another shall have an opportunity to choose between faith and unbelief. Along these lines I read Jn 3:16 to say that those who deliberately say no to faith in Christ are lost. The verses in Eph 2 emphasize that all of us as humans (by nature) are under the wrath of God, in the same way as Paul argues in Rom 1-2, but this does not *eo ipso* imply that those who have not heard the Gospel, are lost. Based on a biblical theology of religion, I will claim that anyone who ever has been, is now or ever will be saved is accepted by God on the grounds of the sacrifice of Christ and our union with him. There is no other ground. The rest I leave to the hidden God (*Deus absconditus*).

This discussion on theology of religion shows that also with regard to this question, and more so than in the other questions, we have since Edinburgh 1910 experienced a major transformation in thinking about gospel, other faiths and dialogue. The questions still remain, in my view, on the very top of any agenda for mission in the twenty-first century.

Conclusion

I recall having heard or read that John R. Mott concluded the 1910 conference with the following: "The end of the conference is the beginning of the Conquest. The end of the Planning is the beginning of the Doing." Edinburgh 2010 will hardly talk about 'conquest', but it will talk about 'doing' if it aspires to impact mission in a new century. It will celebrate what God has done in the growth of the church worldwide. It will commit to God the witness of the churches in the twenty-first century. Even more so, one would hope that it will

---

[48] *The San Antonio Report,* quoted in Bosch, *Transforming Mission*, 489.

[49] Alister E. McGrath, 'A Particularist View: A Post-Enlightenment Approach', in Dennis L. Okholm and Timothy R. Philips (eds), *More than One Way? Four Views on Salvation in a Pluralistic World* (Grand Rapids: Zondervan, 1995), 177-178.

affirm the biblical call to mission with particular focus on witnessing to Christ today. This affirmation should, in my view, grow out of a conversation among mission leaders from the older mission movements of the North and the new mission movements from the South and the East. Representatives from all Christian traditions will be part of this conversation.

This is the global perspective of Edinburgh 2010. May a new vision of God's purpose for creation in Christ and a renewed spirituality grow out of this and impact the life of churches worldwide.

Global Strategies and Local Methods of Missionary Work in the Early Church: Jesus, Peter and Paul (Brandtzæg Memorial Lecture)

Eckhard J. Schnabel

Introduction

In the beginning, "when God created the heavens and the earth" (Gen 1:1), after he had created *Adam* in his image, both male and female, commanding them to be fruitful and multiply and "fill the earth" (Gen 1:27-28), "God saw everything that he had made, and indeed, it was very good" (Gen 1:31). After the eyes of Adam and Eve were opened to see not only the good that God had created but also the evil that had intruded (Gen 3:5, 7), they were banished to live outside of God's perfect world, among the pain, the toil, the sweat, and the thorns and thistles of a ground that had now been cursed (Gen 3:16-24). When Jesus called disciples to follow him and to be trained to "fish for people" (Mk 1:17), he called them to join his mission, which is "to seek out and to save the lost" (Luke 19:10). The 'lost' include not only the notorious sinners who despise and flout the will of God, but also the 'righteous' according to the Law who have not insulted God the Father by demanding what is their due, but who stand outside the house of the Father having to decide whether they welcome the lost son who has been found and rejoice in the Father's love and grace (Luke 15:11-32). The goal of God's mission now is not to bring about perfection in this present world. Perfection is re-established only when the first heaven and the first earth have passed away, when God creates a new heaven and a new earth, when God's holy city will come down, uniting heaven and earth, when God will dwell among mortals whose tears have been wiped away when death, mourning, crying, and pain will have been eliminated (Rev 21:1-4). The goal of God's mission now, for the people living in a seriously damaged world, is to seek out the lost, to find them, and to integrate them into the life in the Father's house.

As we think about global strategies and local methods of missionary work, we think about God's mission as the mission that Jesus fulfilled when he was walking on this earth, a mission that he continues to lead and empower as the risen and exalted Lord on the throne at God's right hand (Acts 1:6-11; 2:32-35), a mission that has been entrusted to the Twelve (Mt 28:18-20; Acts 1:8) and to other missionaries in the first century (Rom 10:14-15) and in the centuries since these beginnings. The global dimension involves the globe, i.e. all the people who live in the world. The local dimension involves localities, i.e. all the individual people who live in specific cities, towns, and villages. The missionary dimension involves the sending and going of followers of Jesus to people who are lost and need to be saved, to people who do not know the one true God and need to worship him, to people who do not submit to the one true God and need forgiveness of sins, to people who do not belong to God's people and need to receive God's love and grace through faith in Jesus Christ. The term 'work' in 'missionary work' is understood as an act or action involving effort or exertion directed to a definite end, a deed, a proceeding, often difficult to do[1] rather than being merely a thought, or a principle, or a discussion. Missionary work is what Christians do; it involves going to people who have not heard the gospel or who do not live according to the gospel, it involves proclaiming and explaining the gospel, it involves helping people come to faith in Jesus, it involves helping people become members of congregations of followers of Jesus. When we speak of 'method' we speak about the work of missionaries, about their 'tactics', i.e. the way of doing evangelistic outreach, the implementation of a defined and regular plan, the produces that we adopt in a particular region or city or situation. When we speak of strategies, we refer to the goals of missionary work, to the overall plan for reaching people with the gospel.

Reaching the World

The promises and prophecies of the Old Testament Scriptures

The world is affected by sin, thus missionary work, as God's mission, targets the world. In the Old Testament, the logic of this connection can be seen in the covenant that God granted Abraham which combines the particularistic promise of descendants and land with the universalistic promise, "in you all the families of the earth shall be blessed" (Gen 12:3).

The global dimension of God's mission is expressed most explicit in the prophets, particularly in Isaiah.[2] Isaiah prophecies that the Davidic king who is

---

[1] Cf. *Oxford English Dictionary* s.v. 'Work'.

[2] See Friedrich Huber, *Jahwe, Juda und die anderen Völker beim Propheten Jesaja* (BZAW, 137: Berlin: De Gruyter, 1976); Graham Davies, 'The Destiny of the Nations in the Book of Isaiah', in J. Vermeylen (ed), *The Book of Isaiah/Le Livre d'Isaïe: Les Oracles et Leurs Reflectures Unitè Complexitè de L'ouvrage* (BETL, 81: Leuven: Leuven University Press, 1989), 93-120; John N. Oswalt, 'The Mission of Israel to the Nations', in W. V. Crockett and J. G. Sigountos (eds), *Through No Fault of Their Own? The Fate of Those Who Have Never Heard* (Grand Rapids: Baker, 1991), 85-95; Walter Groß, 'Israel und die Völker: Die Krise des YHWH-Volk-Konzepts im Jesajabuch', in

expected to come will judge the godless and re-establish righteousness (Isa 11:3-5) and create peace not only in Israel, but in all of creation, as he will fill the world with the knowledge of the Lord, drawing the Gentile nations to himself (Isa 11:6-10). The servant of the Lord whose ministry Isaiah prophecies brings about the restoration of God's people (Isa 49:6) by replacing the original "servant Israel" (Isa 49:3) who is deaf and blind (Isa 42:18-20). And he takes God's justice (or righteousness) to the nations so that his salvation reaches "to the end of the earth" (Isa 49:6). The suffering of the Servant affects many nations (Isa 52:15) as he atones for sins (Isa 53:5). The Servant is thus "a covenant to the people" and a "light to the nations" opening the eyes of people who are blind and sit in darkness (42:6, 7). A day will come when pagan nations will come to Mt. Zion and inquire after the instructions of the Lord.[3] The Gentiles come to Zion drawn by God's redemptive acts (Isa 55:3-5; 56:6-8). At this time, when the nations will bring burnt offerings and other sacrifices to the altar in the Temple, the Temple will be a "house of prayer for all peoples" (Isa 56:6). This vision promises the Gentiles' "participation, on equal terms with Israel, in eschatological salvation in the sanctuary on Zion."[4]

While the emphasis in most of Isaiah's prophecies is on the movement of the nations from the periphery to the center, to Mt. Zion and to the Temple in Jerusalem, there is a twofold 'centrifugal' movement from Israel to the nations. The first movement is connected with the Servant of the Lord who, as light of the nations, carries the will of the Lord to the nations (Isa 42:1, 6-7; 49:6). The second movement from the center to the periphery is connected with the "survivors of Israel" whom Jahwe sends to the nations so that foreigners may become priests and Levites (Isa 66:19-21). In the context of Isa 66, these 'survivors' (*pĕlēṭîm*) are either Jews who have survived God's judgment, or they are converted Gentiles from the neighboring nations who are sent to the more remote nations as God's envoys.

Jesus' ministry, call, and commission

In Jesus' ministry, the global dimension is seen not so much in his actual work, which was mostly limited to Galilee, but rather in the call and commission with which he charged the Twelve.[5] Jesus called the Twelve with the words, "Follow

---

E. Zenger (ed), *Der Neue Bund im Alten. Studien zur Bundestheologie der beiden Testamente* (QD, 146: Freiburg: Herder, 1993), 149-67; John N. Oswalt, 'The Nations in Isaiah: Friend or Foe; Servant or Partner', *BBR* 16 (2006), 41-51.

[3] On the 'pilgrimage' of the nations to Zion cf. Isa 2:1-4 (Mic 4:1-4); 25:6-9; 56:6-7; 60:1-5; Jer 3:17; Zeph 3:8-9; Hag 2:6-9; Zech 8:20-23.

[4] Jostein Ådna, *Jesu Stellung zum Tempel. Die Tempelaktion und das Tempelwort als Ausdruck seiner messianischen Sendung* (WUNT, 2/119: Tübingen: Mohr Siebeck, 2000), 282.

[5] On Jesus and the disciples' mission to the Gentiles see Eckhard J. Schnabel, *Early Christian Mission* (Downers Grove: InterVarsity Press, 2004), 327-82; Michael F. Bird, *Jesus and the Origins of the Gentile Mission* (Library of New Testament Studies:

me and I will make you fish for people" (Mk 1:17; cf. Mt 4:19). While the use of the term ἄνθρωπος should not be over-interpreted in terms of referring to both Jews and Gentiles – given Jesus' ministry in Galilee, these first disciples would surely have understood the term as referring to Jews[6] – Jesus describes the target of the disciples' future preaching and teaching activity in the most general terms.

Jesus' encounters with Gentiles foreshadowed the inclusion of non-Jews in the people of God.[7] And Jesus' prophetic action in the Temple announces the inauguration of the era in which the nations would come to Mt. Zion to worship Jahweh.[8] The quotation of Isa 56:7 in Mk 11:17 ("My house shall be called a house of prayer for all the nations") uses the general reference πᾶσιν τοῖς ἔθνεσιν. Jesus' commission to the Twelve, after his crucifixion and resurrection, also refers to 'all nations' (πάντα τὰ ἔθνη) to whom the Twelve are sent (Mt 28:19).

The global dimension of the mission of the Twelve is most dramatically formulated when Jesus says, "All authority in heaven and on earth has been given to me" (Mt 28:18). The risen and exalted Jesus, who is the Son of Man of Dan 7:14, is Lord over all people and over all things, over heaven and earth and therefore over all nations. The universal dimension of this statement informs the word of commission that follows: as Jesus has been given 'all authority' in all realms of God's creation, the Twelve are directed to make disciples of 'all nations' and to teach all people everywhere, "all things that I have commanded you" as Jesus' authority empowers them 'all days' until the end of the age (Mt 28:20).[9] Since Jesus has 'all authority' there is no human or demonic authority that the disciples have to fear; since Jesus sends them to 'all nations' there are no people, no matter where they live or what their ethnicity or social status

---

London / New York: T& T Clark, 2006).

[6] The term Ἰουδαίος occurs in Mark only in 7:3; 15:2, 9, 12, 18, 26, and in Matthew in 2:2; 27:11, 29, 37; 28:15, i.e. nearly exclusively in the passion narrative. William D. Davies and Dale C. Allison, *The Gospel According to Saint Matthew* (ICC: Edinburgh: T & T Clark, 1988-97), vol. 1, 398-99, suggest that "perhaps Matthew thought of the Gentiles as included in the ἀνθρώπων (cf. 5:16; 10:22; 12:41)." For a discussion of the passage see Ernest Best, *Following Jesus: Discipleship in the Gospel of Mark* (JSNTSup, 4: Sheffield: JSOT Press, 1981), 166-74; John P. Meier, *A Marginal Jew: Rethinking the Historical Jesus* (New York: Doubleday, 1991-2009), vol. 3, 159-61.

[7] The centurion in Capernaum (Mt 8:5-13 / Lk 7:1-10; cf. Jn 4:46-54); the demon-possessed man in Gadara (Mt 8:28-34 / Mk 5:1-20 / Lk 8:26-39); the woman in Syro-Phoenicia (Mt 15:21-28 / Mk 7:24-31); the mute-deaf man in the Decapolis (Mk 7:32-37); the 4,000 people east of the Sea of Galilee (Mk 8:1-10 / Mt 15:32-39). On Jesus and the Gentiles in the view of the authors of the synoptic gospels see Florian Wilk, *Jesus und die Völker in der Sicht der Synoptiker* (BZNW, 109: Berlin: De Gruyter, 2001).

[8] Cf. Mt 21:12-13 / Mk 11:15-17 / Lk 19:45-46. Cf. Rudolf Pesch, *Das Markus-evangelium* (HThK, 2: Freiburg: Herder, 1976-77), vol. 2, 199.

[9] Cf. Christof Landmesser, *Jüngerberufung und Zuwendung zu Gott. Ein Exegetischer Beitrag zum Konzept der Matthäischen Soteriologie im Anschluß an Mt 9,9-13* (WUNT, 133: Tübingen: Mohr Siebeck, 2001), 15-16.

happens to be, who do not need to hear about Jesus; since the risen and exalted Jesus is with the disciples 'all days' there is no time in which Jesus is not present and in which the disciples have to remain quiet about the gospel.[10] The famous phrase 'all nations' (πάντα τὰ ἔθνη) refers to all peoples, including both the Jews and the Gentile nations.[11]

The global perspective of the missionary commission of the Twelve and thus of the community of Jesus' followers is expressed in geographical terms most specifically in Acts 1:8. Before his ascension to the throne at God's right hand, Jesus asserts, "you will receive power when the Holy Spirit has come upon you; and you will be my witnesses in Jerusalem, in all Judea and Samaria, and to the ends of the earth." The expression 'ends of the earth' can be understood in the context of Greek-Roman geography quite literally as referring to the farthest reaches of the inhabited world known at the time, i.e. to Iberia (Spain) in the west, to Ethiopia (Sudan) in the south, to India in the east, and to Scythia (Ukraine, Belarus, Russia) in the north.[12] The mission of the disciples is world mission. Jesus directs the Twelve, and with the Twelve the entire messianic people of God, to embark on an international initiative telling people about Jesus and the forgiveness of sins that God offers through faith in Jesus, an initiative that begins in Jerusalem, that reaches the surrounding regions of Judea and Samaria, and then moves out to all other places as far as the border regions of the earth.

The early church evidently took Jesus' commission to reach people with the gospel in all regions between Jerusalem, Judea, and Samaria and the end of the earth literally.[13] Luke reports that Philip leads a royal official from Ethiopia to faith in Jesus (Acts 8:26-39). Paul wants to go to Spain (Rom 15:24, 28). In his letter to the Colossian believers he refers to a Scythian (Col 3:11), and he twice mentions barbarians (Rom 1:14; Col 3:11). As far as India is concerned, the 'end of the earth' in the east, there is good evidence which suggests that the apostle Thomas explained the gospel at the court of Gondophernes, the Indo-Parthian ruler in Taxila between AD 20–46.[14] When Luke lists the regions from

[10] Cf. Theo K. Heckel, *Vom Evangelium des Markus zum viergestaltigen Evangelium* (WUNT, 120: Tübingen: Mohr-Siebeck, 1999), 71, who limits the universal statement to the view of the author of the Gospel of Matthew.

[11] Cf. Schnabel, *Early Christian Mission*, 361-65.

[12] For Spain cf. Strabo 1.2.31; 2.5.14; 3.1.4; 3.1.8; Lucanus, *Pharsalia* 3.454; Diodoros Siculus 25.10.1; Juvenal, *Sat.* 10.1-2; Silius, *Punica* 17.637; on Ethiopia cf. Homer, *Od.* 1.23; Herodotus 3.25; for India cf. Procopius, *De bellis* 2.3.52; 6.30.9; for Scythia cf. Propertius 2.7.18. See also Philostratus, *Vit. Apoll.* 5.4; 4.47; 6.1.1; Philo, *Cher.* 99; *Somn.* 1.134; *Migr.* 181; Josephus, *C. Ap.* 1.67; Tacitus, *Hist.* 4.3; Pliny, *Nat.* 3.1.3-7; Livy 21.43.13; 23.5.11. See Earle E. Ellis, '"The End of the Earth" (Acts 1:8),' *BBR* 1 (1991), 123-32; James S. Romm, *The Edges of the Earth in Ancient Thought. Geography, Exploration, and Fiction* (Princeton: Princeton University Press, 1992); Schnabel, *Early Christian Mission*, 373-75.

[13] Cf. Schnabel, *Early Christian Mission*, 469-99; for the mission to India see ibid. 880-95.

[14] *Gospel of Thomas* 1-2, 17-61; missionary work in the land of Mizdaios is described

which the diaspora Jews came who attended the Feast of Pentecost in Jerusalem in AD 30, he possibly describes the regions that the disciples would later reach as missionaries (Acts 2:9-11). The list reflects a geographical perspective that goes beyond the confines of the Roman Empire: neither Parthia, nor Media, Elam, Mesopotamia, or Arabia were Roman provinces in the first century. Christian sources of the second and third centuries illustrate and confirm the wide range of contacts that Christians maintained, and the cultural curiosity that informed their activities. It was precisely as a result of their missionary activity, based on the conviction that all people and nations were created by Israel's God and that all people need salvation, and also on account of the fact that they were not tied to Greek-Roman literary and philosophical traditions, that they were open for and eager to obtain ethnographic information.[15]

The Letter to Diognetus, written around AD 150, reflects the cultural openness and the willingness to adapt to local, foreign cultures, which finds its most plausible explanation in the missionary work of Christians in the second century, which continued to the missionary work of the apostles of the first century. The (unknown) author writes, "For Christians are no different from other people in terms of their country, language, or customs. Nowhere do they inhabit cities of their own, use a strange dialect, or live life out of the ordinary.... They inhabit both Greek and barbarian cities, according the lot assigned to each. And they show forth the character of their own citizenship in a marvelous and admittedly paradoxical way by following local customs in what they wear and what they eat and in the rest of their lives. They live in their respective countries, but only as resident aliens; they participate in all things as citizens, and they endure all things as foreigners. Every foreign territory (πᾶσα ξένη) is a homeland (πατρίς) for them, every homeland foreign territory" (*Diogn.* 5:1-5). It is thus not surprising that Clement of Alexandria provides a description of India in general and of the Brahmans in particular, with the first explicit reference in the ancient sources to Buddhism, that is independent of the descriptions in Greek and Roman sources (*Stromata* 1.15.71).

---

ibid. 66-68, 82-158. For the oral Travancore tradition see the south Indian work *Thoma Parvam*. Eusebius knows that when the Alexandrian teacher Pantaenus traveled to India in the late second century, he encountered Christians who had a copy of the Gospel of Matthew written in Hebrew, given to them by the apostle Bartholomew (Eusebius, *Hist. eccl.* 5.10). Cf. Benedict Vadakkekara, *Origin of India's St Thomas Christians: A Historiographical Critique* (Delhi: Media House, 1995).

[15] Guy G. Stroumsa, 'Philosophy of the Barbarians: On Early Christian Ethnological Representations,' in H. Cancik (ed), *Geschichte, Tradition, Reflexion. Band II: Griechische und Römische Religion* (FS Martin Hengel: Tübingen: Mohr Siebeck, 1996), 339-68, here 357; cf. ibid. 356-58 on Clement of Alexandria. On the latter see also Albrecht Dihle, 'Indische Philosophen bei Clemens Alexandrinus [1964],' in V.Pöschl and H. Petersmann (eds), *Antike und Orient. Gesammelte Aufsätze* (Heidelberg: Winter, 1984), 78-88.

Peter's global missionary vision

After he explained the coming of the Holy Spirit as the gift granted by the risen and exalted Jesus, who is the Lord and Messiah through whom God fulfills his promises (Acts 2:14-36), and when his listeners – Jews from all over the world – ask him what they should do, Peter's answer includes a description the scope of the reality of God's promise of new life through his Spirit. Peter asserts, "Repent, and be immersed, every one of you, in the name of Jesus the Messiah, for the forgiveness of sins, and you will receive the gift of the Holy Spirit. For the promise is for you and for your children and for all those who are far away, whom the Lord our God will call to himself" (Acts 2:38-39). In Acts 2:39, the phrase "for your children" indicates distance in time: God's promise of his Spirit, of forgiveness and of new life, remains valid for future generations of Jews. And the phrase "for all those who are far away" (πᾶσιν τοῖς εἰς μακράν) marks distance in space: the promise of God's Spirit and of his salvation will reach Gentiles. The phrase echoes Isa 57:19.[16] Interpretations which limit the announcement of future conversions to Jews from the diaspora[17] are not plausible.[18] First, God's covenant promises (since the Abrahamic covenant) include blessing for pagans,[19] promises that were reiterated in the prophéts' vision of the nations coming to Jerusalem to worship Israel's God.[20] Since Peter connects the arrival of the Holy Spirit, granted by the risen Jesus who is Israel's promised Messiah, with the 'last days' (Acts 2:17), he anticipates here in 2:39 the conversion of Gentiles. Second, in Eph 2:13, 17 the expression 'far away' clearly refers to Gentiles who once were 'far off' but now have come 'near'[21] since there is now only one single people of God in which

---

[16] Isa 57:19: "Peace, peace, to the far and the near, says the Lord, and I will heal them" (εἰρήνην ἐπ' εἰρήνην τοῖς μακρὰν καὶ τοῖς ἐγγὺς οὖσιν, καὶ εἶπεν κύριος Ἰάσομαι αὐτούς).

[17] Cf. Jürgen Roloff, *Die Apostelgeschichte* (NTD, 5: Göttingen: Vandenhoeck & Ruprecht, 1988), 63; Rebecca I. Denova, *The Things Accomplished Among Us: Prophetic Tradition in the Structural Pattern of Luke-Acts* (JSNTSup, 141: Sheffield: Sheffield Academic Press, 1997), 169-75. Jacob Jervell, *Die Apostelgeschichte* (KEK, 3: Göttingen: Vandenhoeck & Ruprecht, 1998), 150-51, interprets the phrase as a reference to the Godfearers in the diaspora synagogues, which is not indicated by the context.

[18] Cf. David W. Pao, *Acts and the Isaianic New Exodus* (WUNT, 2/130: Tübingen: Mohr Siebeck, 2000), 230-31; I. Howard Marshall, 'Acts,' in G. K. Beale and D. A. Carson (eds), *Commentary on the New Testament Use of the Old Testament* (Grand Rapids: Baker, 2007), 534.

[19] Gen 12:3: "in you all the families of the earth shall be blessed." Cf. Gen 15:3; Gen 22:16-18. Cf. Paul R. Williamson, *Abraham, Israel and the Nations: The Patriarchal Promise and its Covenantal Development in Genesis* (JSOTSup, 315: Sheffield: Sheffield Academic Press, 2000).

[20] Cf. Isa 2:2-5 / Mic 4;1-4; Isa 14:2; Is 45:14; 49:22-23; 55:5; 66:20; Jer 16:19-21; Zeph 3:9-10; Zech 8:20-23; 14:16-19; cf. Tob 13:13.

[21] Eph 2:13: "But now in Christ Jesus you who once were far off have been brought near (οἵ ποτε ὄντες μακρὰν ἐγενήθητε ἐγγύς) by the blood of Christ.... So he came and proclaimed peace to you who were far off (ὑμῖν τοῖς μακράν) and peace to those who

ethnic origins no longer play a role. Third, later rabbis interpreted Isa 57:19 in terms of proselytes, i.e. Gentiles who had converted to Judaism (*Num. Rab.* 8:4). Thus, Peter expresses a universal vision of salvation in which he and the Twelve would play a major role as Jesus' witnesses (1:8, 22).

While Peter's ministry among the Jews of Jerusalem (Acts 2–6) and in the Jewish cities of the coastal plain (Acts 9:32-43) is to be expected, his pastoral and missionary work in Samaritan cities, towns, and villages (Acts 8:14-25) signals that he takes the commission of Jesus seriously, and literally, who had directed the Twelve to be his witnesses not only in Jerusalem and in Judea (which, for Luke at the time of writing, included Galilee) but also in Samaria.

The trajectory from Jerusalem, the holy city, to Judea and to Samaria and then to the end of the earth includes Gentiles living in Judea. Peter probably would not have had problems having some contact with Gentiles, given Jesus' encounters with Gentiles and given Jesus' commission. However, contacts with Gentiles were always a potential source of moral defilement for Jews. A Jewish text exhorts its readers, "Keep yourself separate from the nations, and do not eat with them; and do not imitate their rites, nor associate yourself with them" (*Jub.* 22:16). The Essenes bathed after contact with foreigners (Josephus, *B.J.* 2.150). A devout Jew had the following options when they were invited by a Gentile:[22] he could refuse to enter the house of a Gentile and refuse to have table fellowship with Gentiles; he could accept the invitation and bring his own food; he could eat at the table of Gentiles with the explicit or implicit understanding that the food served was not prohibited in the Torah and was not tainted by idolatry, or he could eat only certain foods from the menu provided by the Gentile host.[23] Peter's assertion that since he is a practicing Jew he

---

were near."

[22] Cf. Markus Bockmuehl, *Jewish Law in Gentile Churches: Halakhah and the Beginning of Christian Public Ethics* (Grand Rapids: Baker, 2003), 58; he considers Peter's attitude expressed in v. 28 as belonging to the "clearly hard-line views about Gentile intentions that would most obviously include conservative Palestinian Jews to enter a Gentile's house 'unlawful'" (ibid. 59).

[23] Some argue that a strict position was the norm among Palestinian Jews, but also among diaspora Jews; cf. Gedalyahu Alon, *Jews, Judaism and the Classical World: Studies in Jewish History in the Times of the Second Temple and Talmud* (Jerusalem: Magnes, 1977), 146-89; Philip F. Esler, *Community and Gospel in Luke-Acts: The Social and Political Motivations of Lucan Theology* (SNTSMS, 57: Cambridge: Cambridge University Press, 1987), 71-86 (note the critique of Esler in Bockmuehl, *Jewish Law in Gentile Churches*, 57-59). Others regard the situation as more fluid, allowing for the possibility that Jews could eat with Gentiles without transgressing the Jewish law; cf. John M. G. Barclay, *Jews in the Mediterranean Diaspora: From Alexander to Trajan (323 BCE – 117 CE)* (Edinburgh: T & T Clark, 1996), 434-37; Martin Goodman, *Rome and Jerusalem: The Clash of Ancient Civilizations* (New York: Vintage, 2007), 111-12, who suggests that Tacitus' statement that Jews stay "separate in their meals and apart in their beds" was a caricature "that was largely, but not totally, true" (ibid. 111).

should not really be associating with a Gentile (Acts 10:28)[24] is probably a polite way of saying that he should not be consorting with an officer of the Roman army and his friends, who would likely be defiled by idolatry, despite the fact that Cornelius is a Godfearer who has a good reputation among some local Jews.[25] The three-times repeated vision of the big sheet with clean and unclean animals and with the heavenly voice commanding him to slaughter and eat (Acts 10:9-16; cf. 11:5-10) prepared Peter for accepting Cornelius' invitation and for eventually accepting Gentiles who believe in Jesus and who receive the Holy Spirit into God's people. When Peter defends his actions in Caesarea before the congregation of Jewish believers in Jerusalem, he asserts that when he saw that the Holy Spirit fell upon the Gentile believers in Jesus in Caesarea just as he had fallen on the Jewish believers in Jerusalem on the day of Pentecost, he remembered Jesus' word who had said, "John immersed in water, but you will be immersed in the Holy Spirit" (Acts 11:16). Peter learnt from his vision that God was impartial (Acts 10:15, 28) and that he had to be willing to accept both Jews and Gentiles, without distinction, into the messianic congregation of 'the Israel of fulfillment" since the Gentiles become 'clean" through their faith in Jesus.[26] Peter remembers John's promise (Luke 3:16), which Jesus had reiterated (Acts 1:5), because it spoke of the work of the Messiah who cleanses and restores Israel through the power of the Spirit of God which he pours out as the crucified, risen, and exalted Lord who sits at God's right hand. Jesus' promise of 'immersion in the Holy Spirit' implies that the Gentiles who had come to faith in Jesus and who had incontrovertibly received the Holy Spirit should be considered 'clean' because God's Spirit who cleanses and restores 'Israel' and calls Gentiles in the last days, as God had promised through the prophets. The vision that God used to teach Peter announced the removal of defilement from Gentiles who come to faith in Jesus and who receive the Spirit who cleanses them. Thus Peter was justified to associate with Gentiles, and thus he was justified to incorporate them into the congregation of God's messianic people by immersion in water and to eat with them. With this divine intervention, which changed central commandments of the Law about the distinction between holy and profane and between clean and unclean, the path to the ends of the earth was fully opened up.

Paul's global missionary strategy

When Paul describes the scope of his missionary work, he repeatedly comments on the ethnic dimension of his global strategy. He asserts that he

---

[24] The term translated as 'Gentile' (ἀλλόφυλος) describes foreigners (lit. people 'from another tribe'); from a Jewish perspective 'foreigners' are Gentiles (BDAG).

[25] Cf. Richard J. Bauckham, 'James, Peter, and the Gentiles', in B.D. Chilton and C.A. Evans (eds), *The Missions of James, Peter, and Paul: Tensions in Early Christianity* (NTSup, 115: Leiden: Brill, 2005), 107-14.

[26] Max M. B. Turner, *Power from on High: The Spirit in Israel's Restoration and Witness in Luke-Acts* (JPTSup, 9: Sheffield: Sheffield Academic Press, 1996), 385.

preaches the saving news of Jesus the messianic Savior and Lord before Jewish and Gentile audiences (1 Cor 9:19-23).[27] For Paul, 'global' (a term that he of course does not use) refers specifically to the Jewish people as well. While the need for Gentiles to receive forgiveness from God was accepted by all Jews, and while Paul certainly argues at some length that Gentiles are under God's wrath (Rom 1:18-32), he takes greater pains to argue that Jews are under God's wrath and in need of forgiveness, justification, and salvation just as the Gentiles (Rom 2:1–3:20). The reason for this ethnic dimension of Paul's global missionary strategy is consistently theological: there is no distinction between Jews and Gentiles with regard to their status before God as far as their sins are concerned, both are helplessly exposed to God's wrath who condemns sinners, both are justified on Judgment Day only by faith in Jesus Christ. It is this conviction which is downplayed in those new perspectives on Paul which reject the view that Paul was in conflict with Judaism.[28] Since "all have sinned and fall short of the glory of God" (Rom 3:23), all people, without exception, need to hear, understand, and accept the good news of Jesus Christ.

The cultural and social dimension of Paul's global mission strategy is formulated in the statement that he is, "a debtor both to Greeks and to barbarians, both to the wise and to the foolish" (Rom 1:14); that "there is no longer Jew or Greek, there is no longer slave or free, there is no longer male and female" (Gal 3:28); that he seeks to reach those who are "wise by human standards" and those with little or no education, those who belong to the powerful elite in the cities which he visits and those who have no political or economic influence, those who are of noble birth and those who are ordinary or who belong to the despised people (1 Cor 1:26-29). While Paul is fully aware of these social and cultural distinctions, and while he can differentiate among his audience who belongs to which group and social class, he sees himself under the obligation to "become all things to all people" so that some people might come to saving faith in Jesus Christ (1 Cor 9:22). Not surprisingly, here again the reason for this comprehensive or 'global' approach to missionary work is theological, expressed in the next sentence where he asserts, "I do it all for the sake of the gospel" (1 Cor 9:23). The saving news of Jesus Christ does not allow Paul to omit any ethnic, social, religious, or cultural group from the preaching of the gospel. Everybody needs to hear the gospel, because there is no salvation apart from faith in the crucified and risen Jesus, Israel's Messiah and Lord.

Thus we find Paul in contact with Jews, proselytes, Godfearers, and pagans (cf. Acts 13:13-48; 14:8-18), with slaves such as the woman who was a medium in Philippi (Acts 16:15-18) and the jailer in Philippi (Acts 16:23-34), with simple people such as the lame beggar in Lystra (Acts 14:8-10), with city magistrates (Acts 13:50), with philosophers (Acts 17:18), with members of the

---

[27] On 1 Cor 9:19-23 cf. Eckhard J. Schnabel, *Paul the Missionary: Realities, Strategies, and Methods* (Downers Grove: InterVarsity Press, 2008), 135-37.

[28] See most recently Magnus Zetterholm, *Approaches to Paul: A Student's Guide to Recent Scholarship* (Minneapolis: Fortress, 2009).

venerable Areopagus Council in Athens (Acts 17:19-34), one of whom, a certain Dionysios, was converted, with the Asiarchs in Ephesus (Acts 19:31), with Roman governors in Paphos and in Caesarea (Acts 13:6-12; 24:1–26:32), and with men such as the synagogue officials in Pisidian Antioch and in Corinth (Acts 13:15; 18:8), with women such as Lydia in Philippi (Acts 17:14-15) and with Damaris in Athens (Acts 17:34).

The geographical dimension of Paul's global mission strategy is expressed in his assertion that he proclaimed the good news of Jesus Christ "from Jerusalem and as far around as Illyricum" (Rom 15:19).[29] Paul preached the gospel in Arabia and in Judea, then in Syria and Cilicia, then on Cyprus and in the provinces of Galatia and Pamphylia in central and southern Asia Minor, then in the provinces of Macedonia and Achaia, then in the province of Asia, then evidently briefly in Illyricum, then during his imprisonment in Caesarea and in Rome, then evidently in Spain. While Paul moved from city to city, and from province to province, he was obviously less interested in a grand geographical strategy than in reaching as many people as possible: Jews and Greeks, men and women, the educated and the simple, the powerful and the slaves, in synagogues and in lecture halls, in marketplaces and in private homes.

Reaching People

Without a local focus, global strategies remain mere talk. When Jesus called the Twelve to fish for people, and when he commissioned them to go to all nations that exist between Jerusalem and the end of the earth, he sent them to real people living in real cities. He did not set up a think-tank in Jerusalem with his followers talking among themselves, but he send them out to other cities, towns, and villages where his envoys were to visit and live among the people, to preach and teach sympathizers and skeptics, and to establish local congregations in which the new converts worship God and learn about Jesus and witness to their friends and neighbors. People do not 'live globally': they live locally. This is why the exploration of global strategies in missionary outreach must be firmly anchored in a consistent and realistic focus on local realities and local methods, if it wants to avoid the risk of degenerating into the arrogant imposition of one's own views on others, and the imperialistic export of methods from one part of the world to another. We see such a consistent local focus in the work of Jesus, Peter, and Paul.

Jesus and the people of Galilee

A brief look at the evidence in the Gospels regarding the beginning of Jesus' ministry is revealing. In Matthew 4, after relating Jesus' testing in the

[29] On the likelihood that Paul preached in Illyricum, the province west of Macedonia, before his winter sojourn in Corinth cf. Robert Jewett, *Romans* (Hermeneia: Minneapolis: Fortress, 2007), 913-14.

wilderness, the evangelist reports that Jesus “left” Nazareth and “went and lived” in Capernaum (4:12), that he was “walking” by the Sea of Galilee and that he “saw” two brothers who were fishing (4:18), whom he then called to follow him, and that he “went” on and “saw” two other brothers who were in a fishing boat (4:21). The following summary statement reports that Jesus “went” throughout Galilee, that he “taught” in synagogues, that he “proclaimed” the good news of the kingdom, and that he “healed” the sick, with the result that large crowds followed him (4:23-25). The next chapter begins with the statement that Jesus “saw” the crowds, that he “went” up on a mountainside, that he “sat down” and that he “began to teach” (5:1-2). When the narrative is resumed after the Sermon on the Mount, Matthew relates that Jesus “came down” from the mountainside, that he “reached out his hand” and “touched” the man with leprosy who knelt before him (8:1, 3). In Mk 1, several of the incidents after Jesus’ testing in the wilderness are identical to Matthew’s; he also relates that Jesus “went” with his disciples to Capernaum, that he “went into” the synagogue on the Sabbath and “began to teach”, that Jesus rebuked and drove out a an evil spirit (1:21, 25), that one day Jesus “got up” very early in the morning while it was still dark, that he “left” the house in which he and his disciples were staying, and that the “went off” to a solitary place where he prayed (1:35). Luke reports after the incident of Jesus’ testing in the wilderness that Jesus “returned” to Galilee, that he was “teaching” in the synagogues, that he “went” to Nazareth, that he “went into” the synagogue on the Sabbath, that he “stood up” to read the Scripture text, that he “unrolled” the scroll, that he “found” the place of the Isaiah text, that he “rolled up” the scroll, that he “gave it back” to the attendant, that he “sat down” and that he explained the text (1:14-17, 20-21).

Jesus’ activities are described with verbs of geographical movement, verbs of seeing, verbs describing body movements, and verbs of speaking. Jesus walks along the lake and he enters synagogues. Jesus sees people in boats and the crowds who follow him. Jesus takes a scroll with the text of Isaiah and he touches a man who is suffering from leprosy. Jesus’ activities are local activities: they take place in Galilee, a small region only about 40 kilometers from east to west; they take place in the towns and villages of Galilee;[30] they take place in synagogues, which were rather small affairs in Galilee in the first century.[31] The references to Jesus’ geographical movement in Mk 6:6 (“Then Jesus went around [περιῆγεν... κύκλῳ] teaching from village to village”,

---

[30] Towns and villages as the place of Jesus’ activities are specifically mentioned in Mt 9:35; Mk 6:6, 56; 8:23, 27; Lk 8:1; 9:6; 10:38; 13:22; 17:12. In Mk 5:56 farms are mentioned besides villages and towns.

[31] Cf. Lee I. Levine, *The Ancient Synagogue: The First Thousand Years* (New Haven: Yale University Press, 2nd edition, 2005), 45-55. The synagogue of Modi’in (Khirbet Umm el-’Umdan), excavated in 2000/2001 by A. Onn and others, is a good example of a village synagogue; the hall of the second and main phase of the building which dates from the Herodian period, measured 10 by 12 meters (ibid. 70; cf. Alexander Onn, ‘Khirbet Umm el-’Umdan’, *Ḥadashot Arkheologiyot* 114 [2002], 64-68).

NRSV) and in Lk 4:43 ("I must proclaim the good news of the kingdom of God to the other towns also, because that is why I was sent", NRSV) might be taken to indicate that Jesus planned his travels in some organized manner.

Jesus addresses people sitting in fishing boats, he explains the Scriptures to local people sitting in their synagogue, he proclaims his message of the dawn of God's kingdom to crowds of people sitting on a mountainside, and he speaks with individuals who kneel before him and ask to be healed. Jesus does not wait for people to come to him, he goes to people wherever they live and work, in the towns and villages of Galilee, at the Sea of Galilee, in the synagogues. When they come to him, whether individuals or crowds of people, he interacts with them individually when they ask for healing, and he uses these opportunities to proclaim and explain his message about God's new initiative of salvation.

The later chapters in the Gospels confirm this picture, providing more details about Jesus encounters with individuals, among them scribes and Pharisees (Mk 2:16, 24; 7:1; 8:11, etc.), Sadducees (Mk 12:18, 27), synagogue presidents (Mk 5:21-24, 35-43), with sympathizers (Mk 10:17-31) and sceptics (Mk 8:11-12; 10:2, 13-17), with devout Jews who tithe even spices (Mt 23:23) and with sinners such as tax collectors and prostitutes (Mt 21:31), with more people who seek healing (Mk 3:1-6; 8:22-26; etc.), with men and women (Mk 5:25-34; Lk 13:10-17; etc.) and children (Mk 10:13-16), as well as encounter with more crowds (Mk 3:20, 32; 4:1; 5:21, 24; 6:34; etc.). Jesus speaks with anyone who is willing to listen. He explained his message to the simple and the sophisticated, to powerless Galileans and to influential leaders of the Jerusalem establishment, to people with bad reputations and to the pious. Jesus models what he teaches his disciples in the parable in which he compares the arriving kingdom of God with a drag-net that is tied to two boats and is let down into the lake and which then catches of "all kinds" (ἐκ παντὸς γένους; Mt 13:47).

Jesus' instructions to the Twelve whom he sends on a preaching tour into the towns and villages of Galilee (Mt 10:5-16 par Lk 9:1-6) reflects the model of Jesus' own activity and constitutes basic training for their later, ethnically and geographically wider missionary ministry.[32] The target audience is specified in ethnic-cultural terms: the Twelve are told to visit with "the lost sheep of the house of Israel", i.e. with Jews and, specifically, not with Gentiles or Samaritans (10:5-6). The basic task involves going (πορεύομαι), proclaiming (κηρύσσειν) the good news of the dawn of God's kingdom, curing (θεραπεύειν) the sick and casting out (ἐκβάλλειν) demons (10:7-8). The prohibition of provisions (10:9-10) presupposes the hospitality that the local Jews, many of whom would be sympathizers of Jesus, would extend to the Twelve. The stipulations concerning room and board – when they enter a village, and when they are invited to stay in a house, they should greet the family and stay there until they leave (10:11-12) – highlight the local nature of the ministry of Jesus

---

[32] For a fuller exposition, with a discussion of questions of authenticity, cf. Schnabel, *Early Christian Mission*, 1:290-311.

and of his disciples: they are based not simply in Galilee, or in a town or village, but in a house in which a family lives willing to take them in.[33] Jesus speaks of people who will welcome them and of people who will reject them (10:13-15). Jesus statement, "See, I am sending you out like sheep into the midst of wolves; so be wise as serpents and innocent as doves" (10:16) implies local personal encounters: sheep are 'local' animals as are serpents, encounters between sheep and wolves take place on local pastures. The wisdom and the innocence that Jesus advises his disciples to display, as they rely on the promised divine protection, is related to their preaching and healing activity in the towns and villages of Galilee which will not be appreciated by everybody. Neither global strategies nor local methods can avoid conflicts. These conflicts can be fierce, even deadly. While the disciples are advised to seek to avoid conflicts if possible (as serpents move away from danger), they are at the same time instructed not be play tactical games but to be open and consistent in their preaching and healing activity (as innocent doves).

Peter and the people in Jerusalem, Samaria, and Judea

Peter has been commissioned, as the 'rock' on whom Jesus will build his church (Mt 16:18),[34] to lead the way in the mission from Jerusalem, Judea, and Samaria to all nations and to the end of the earth (Mt 28:19; Acts 1:8). He begins, however, with a 'local' mission in Jerusalem, in Samaria, and in Judea. Looking at Peter's mission from a geographical and topographical perspective,[35] we encounter Peter on the Mount of Olives (1:12), in an upstairs room in Jerusalem (1:13), sitting in a house in Jerusalem (2:1), standing before a large crowd of people in Jerusalem (2:14), going to the Temple (3:1), in Solomon's Portico on the east side of the Temple Mount (3:11; 5:12, 20, 25, 42),[36] in the prison of the Sanhedrin (4:3), in the Sanhedrin hall (4:7; 5:27),[37] in

[33] The typical Israelite house, measuring ca. 8 by 10 meters, had four rooms. The 'house of the vintner' in Bethsaida measured 16 by 18 meters, with a large room measuring 4.5 by 5.4 meters; cf. Rami Arav and Richard A. Freund, eds, *Bethsaida: A City by the North Shore of the Sea of Galilee* (4 vols.; Bethsaida Excavations Project: Kirksville: Thomas Jefferson University Press/Truman State University Press, 1995-2009), vol. 2, 97-98.

[34] Cf. Chrys C. Caragounis, *Peter and the Rock* (BZNW, 58: Berlin: De Gruyter, 1990); Benedict T. Viviano, 'Peter as Jesus' Mouth: Matthew 16:13-20 in the Light of Exodus 4:10-17 and other Models', in C. A. Evans (ed), *The Interpretation of Scripture in Early Judaism and Christianity: Studies in Language and Tradition* (JSPSup, 33: Sheffield: Sheffield Academic Press, 2000), 312-41.

[35] On geography in Acts, with an emphasis on the 'third space' geography of the risen and exalted Jesus who intervenes from the throne at God's right hand, cf. Matthew Sleeman, *Geography and the Ascension Narrative in Acts* (SNTSMS, 146: Cambridge: Cambridge University Press, 2009).

[36] Josephus describes Solomon's Portico as being 400 cubits (ca. 200 meters) long, with a single nave of 15 meters width, with two rows of columns which were 12.5 meters high. The portico was constructed "of square stones, completely white", each stone

the public jail (5:18), in Samaria in the city in which Philip had been active (8:14-15), in Samaritan villages (8:25), in Lydda in the Plain of Sharon (9:32), in an upstairs room in Joppe (9:36), in the house of a tanner named Simon in Joppe (9:43), on the roof of that house (10:9), on the road from Joppe to Caesarea (10:23), in the house of Cornelius in Caesarea (10:24), on the road from Caesarea to Jerusalem (11:2), in the prison in Herod's palace in Jerusalem (12:3), in the house of Mary in Jerusalem (12:12).

Unfortunately for us, the "other place" (ἕτερος τόπος) for which he left Jerusalem (12:17) is not specified, reflecting perhaps the necessity of keeping Peter's whereabouts secret.[38] Read against the background of Gal 2:11-15 and 1 Cor 9:5, Luke's comment should be interpreted in terms of intensive and extensive missionary work undertaken by Peter after his departure from Jerusalem. Peter had several options. (1) He could travel to remote regions with Jewish diaspora communities where he could continue to preach the gospel; early traditions point to the northern regions of Asia Minor (cf. 1 Pet 1:1).[39] (2) He could travel to larger centers of Jewish life outside of Palestine, notably the diaspora communities in Mesopotamia, Alexandria in Egypt, Antioch in Syria,[40] Ephesus in the province of Asia, or Rome, the capital of the empire. Rome is a possible destination[41] since early church tradition places Peter in

being ca. 10 meters long and 3 meters high (Josephus, *A.J.* 20.221; *B.J.* 5.185). On the Herodian Temple and the Temple Mount see Ehud Netzer, *The Architecture of Herod, the Great Builder* (Grand Rapids: Baker, 2008), 137-78, 273-75. Note that the 'local' Temple Mount, as built by Herod I, had 'global' implications. Byron R. McCane, 'Simply Irresistible: Augustus, Herod, and the Empire', *JBL* 127 (2008), 725-35, concludes from a comparison with Augustus' reconfiguration of the Forum Romanum in the center of the city of Rome that "the Court of the Gentiles altered Jews' image of the empire, for in its wide and sunny plaza the Jewish temple was symbolically opened up to the empire. Whenever a Gentile entered that generous space, and whenever a Jew crossed it on the way to offer sacrifice, empire and temple came together" (ibid. 732). Whether this is what the Jews actually thought when they visited the Temple, must remain open to question, however.

[37] The council of the Sanhedrin may have met in the magnificent hall dating to the Second Temple period, remains of which have been discovered near Wilson's Arch, which is part of this bridge over the Tyropoean Valley which led to the Kipunus Gate, called the Hasmonean Hall; cf. H. Geva, 'Jerusalem. The Temple Mount and its Environs', in Ephraim Stern (ed), *The New Encyclopedia of Archaeological Excavations in the Holy Land* (Jerusalem/New York: Israel Exploration Society/Carta, 1993), vol. 2, 742; with reference to Josephus, *B.J.* 5.144.

[38] James D. G. Dunn, *Beginning from Jerusalem* (Christianity in the Making II: Grand Rapids: Eerdmans, 2009), 410.

[39] Cf. Stephen Mitchell, *Anatolia: Land, Men, and Gods in Asia Minor* (Oxford: Oxford University Press, 1995), vol. 2, 3.

[40] Assumed by many, cf. Ernst Haenchen, *The Acts of the Apostles* (Philadelphia: Westminster, 1971), 386 n. 1.

[41] Cf. Eusebius, *Hist. eccl.* 2.14.5; see John W. Wenham, 'Did Peter go to Rome in AD 42?' *TynBul* 23 (1972), 94-102; Marta Sordi, *The Christians and the Roman Empire* (Norman: University of Oklahoma Press, 1986), 29.

Rome, at least by the time of Nero during whose reign he is said to have died as martyr (*Acts Pet.* 38), although that would have taken place over twenty years later in the Neronian persecution in AD 64. It has been suggested that the major disturbances in Rome, linked with the proclamation of Jesus as Messiah which prompted the emperor Claudius to issue a second edict against the Jews (after the first edict in AD 41) evicting the Jews from Rome in AD 49,[42] can best be explained with the presence and activity of a major Christian figure such as Peter.[43] What we know is that Peter was active as a missionary, traveling with his wife (1 Cor 9:5), surfacing in Antioch probably in AD 48 (Gal 2:11-14), and in Jerusalem in AD 48 (Acts 15:7). What is certainly true is the fact that there is no place that Peter is not willing to go to.

In terms of actions of Peter that can be integrated into a survey of his 'methods' of missionary ministry, we find Peter explaining Scripture (1:16, 20-20; 2:16-21, 25-36; 3:24-25), leading the followers of Jesus in replacing Judas as a member of the Twelve (1:15-26), explaining the visible manifestations connected with the Spirit being poured out by Jesus on his followers (2:1-36), explaining the significance of Jesus as Israel's crucified and risen Messiah before crowds of people (2:22-36; 3:13-26) and before the Sanhedrin (4:10-12; 5:30-32), pleading with the Jews of Jerusalem to confess their sins and find forgiveness in pledging allegiance to Jesus (2:38-40), presumably assisting people to be immersed in one of the large immersion pools in Jerusalem (2:41), praying in the Temple (3:1), praying with believers (4:24-30), praying alone and/or with the other members of the Twelve (6:4), healing the sick (3:1-10; 5:12, 15; 9:32-35, 36-42), explaining miracles (3:11-26), confronting followers of Jesus who want to deceive the church (5:1-10), teaching daily in the Temple court (5:42), teaching daily in private homes (5:42), suffering repeated arrest (4:1-3; 5:18; 12:3-4), suffering the punishment of flogging (5:40), reporting to the congregation about his arrest and interrogation by the Sanhedrin (4:23), supervising the distribution of funds among the needy members of the congregation (4:35, 37; 6:1-2), reorganizing the structure of the church for improved efficiency of the distribution of funds and food to the needy followers of Jesus (6:1-6), installing and praying for new ministry leaders (6:6), going to Samaria in order to consolidate the missionary expansion of the church that had happened through the work of Philip (8:14-25), helping new converts to receive the Holy Spirit (8:15-17), confronting and correcting new converts who have a defective understanding of faith in Jesus (8:18-23), preaching about Jesus in Samaria (8:25), traveling about Judea (9:32), visiting believers in Judean towns (9:32), receiving and responding to a divine audio-vision (10:9-29), explaining

---

[42] Cf. Suetonius, *Claud.* 25.3-4: Claudius initiated measures against 'men of foreign birth' (*peregrinae condicionis*), and 'since the Jews constantly made disturbances at the instigation of Chrestus, he expelled them from Rome' (*Judaeos impulsore Chresto assidue tumultuantes Roma expulit*). See Acts 18:2.

[43] Helga Botermann, *Das Judenedikt des Kaisers Claudius. Römischer Staat und Christiani im 1. Jahrhundert* (Hermes Einzelschriften, 71: Stuttgart: Steiner, 1996), 136-40.

the good news about Jesus to Gentiles (10:34-43), accepting the hospitality of new converts (10:48), defending his actions that other believers find problematic (11:11-18), leaving Jerusalem when his life is in danger (12:1-17). Most of the verbs are verbs of speaking, which confirms Peter's stated priority of engaging in the 'ministry of the word' (6:2, 4) and agrees with his call to be a witness for Jesus (1:8; cf. 1:23). There is nothing that Peter is not willing to do.[44]

In terms of the people that Peter is in contact with, we note the following. Peter speaks with the 120 followers of Jesus in Jerusalem (1:15-22), he preaches before thousands of Jews from Jerusalem and from the Jewish diaspora (2:14-39), he teaches the thousands of believers in Jerusalem (2:42; cf. 4:23), he addresses a beggar (3:1-8), he preaches before Jews visiting the Temple (3:12-26; 5:42), he speaks to groups of people meeting in private homes (5:42), he speaks to the members of the Sanhedrin (4:8-12; 5:29-32), he confronts Ananias and Sapphira, rich members of the church (5:1-10), he consults with the Greek speaking Jewish Christians who complain about their widows being overlooked (as a member of the Twelve, 6:2-4), he presumably speaks with the priests who are converted in Jerusalem (6:7), he is in contact with new converts in Samaria (8:15-17), he speaks with a converted Jewish magician (8:18-24), he speaks with the paralyzed Aeneas (9:32-34), he encounters the deceased Christian woman Dorcas/Tabitha who comes back to life and speaks with the believers in Joppe (9:36-41), he speaks with Cornelius, a Roman centurion, and his family and friends (10:24-48), he interacts with critics in the church in Jerusalem (11:1-18). Peter is in contact with followers of Jesus, with critics in the church, with sinners in the church, with new converts, with sympathizers who are willing to listen to his explanations of the significance of Jesus, and with the people who arrested him and who interrogate him, opponents who helped execute Jesus and who are eager to eliminate him and the other Christian leaders as well. There is nobody that Peter is not willing to speak to.

Paul and the people living in cities in the eastern Mediterranean

The geographical scope of Paul's missionary work was not controlled by a grand global strategy (such as focusing on big cities,[45] or on Roman colonies,

---

[44] On Peter's missionary work see William Thomas Kessler, *Peter as the First Witness of the Risen Lord: An Historical and Theological Investigation* (Tesi Gregoriana, Serie Teologia, 37: Rom: Gregorian University Press, 1998). More generally see Peter Dschulnigg, *Petrus im Neuen Testament* (Stuttgart: Katholisches Bibelwerk, 1996). An older study on Peter still worthwhile reading is Oscar Cullmann, *Peter: Disciple – Apostle – Martyr* (Second Edition: London: SCM, 1962 [1953]).

[45] Cf. Roland Allen, *Missionary Methods: St. Paul's or Ours?* (Grand Rapids: Eerdmans, 2001 [1912]), 12. See Conrad Gempf, 'Mission and Misunderstanding: Paul and Barnabas in Lystra (Acts 14:8-20)', in A. Billington (ed), *Mission and Meaning* (FS P. Cotterell: Carlisle: Paternoster, 1995), 58-59, for Paul's mission after the experience

or on the regions in which the descendants of Japhet settled,[46] or because he wanted to fulfill the 'program' of Isa 66:19[47]) which he used to decide in which cities he should start a new missionary initiative. The evidence indicates that Paul moved to geographically adjacent areas which were open for missionary work, which means that it was 'local methods" that drove his movements.[48]

Paul began his missionary work in Damascus (Acts 9:19-21, 23-25; Gal 1:17) because this is where he happened to be when he was converted, because there was a congregation which could be the basis for his work, and because it was a city in which he could reach Jews in the local synagogues and Gentiles in the city at large. The next phase of his missionary work was Arabia/Nabatea (Gal 1:17; cf. 2 Cor 11:32; Acts 9:23-25), presumably because this was a region close-by, immediately to the south of Damascus, and perhaps due to the fact that Jews regarded the Nabateans as descendants of Ishmael the son of Abraham, i.e. as kindred tribes.[49] Paul then was active in the synagogues of Jerusalem (Acts 9:26-29; Rom 15:19), evidently not because Jerusalem was the next planned stage of his missionary activity; he moved to Jerusalem because he had to leave Damascus in a hurry, because he had returned to Jerusalem since his conversion, because he wanted to make the acquaintance of the apostle Peter (Gal 1:18). He explained the gospel in the synagogues of Jerusalem because he happened to be in the city, and because he wanted to be true to his calling to bring the good news about Jesus, Israel's Messiah and Savior, to 'the Jew first and also the Greek' (Rom 1:16; cf. 9:1-3). He had to leave Jerusalem in a hurry as his life was in danger from determined opponents who wanted to eliminate him. The next phase of Paul's missionary work was Syria and Cilicia (Gal 1:26), where he as active for about twelve years between AD 34-42. He preached in Tarsus (Acts 9:30; 11:25-26) and presumably in many other cities of Cilicia. There were several reasons why Tarsus was a logical choice for the continuation of his missionary work: Tarsus was his home town, which means that he would have had relatives and friends in the city who would not only be a natural first audience for his preaching but also a helpful base of operations for reaching other cities in the region. His Tarsian citizenship gave him protection, a welcome relief after his experiences in Damascus and in Jerusalem. Since Tarsus was the most significant city in the region after Antioch in Syria, and since the city had a Jewish community, there

---

in Lystra.

[46] Cf. James M. Scott, *Paul and the Nations: The Old Testament and Early Jewish Background of Paul's Mission to the Nations with Special Reference to the Destination of Galatians* (WUNT, 84: Tübingen: Mohr-Siebeck, 2002 [1995]), 135-80, with reference to the continued importance of the table of nations in Genesis 10 for Jewish geography.

[47] Cf. Rainer Riesner, *Paul's Early Period: Chronology, Mission Strategy, Theology* (Grand Rapids: Eerdmans, 1998), 245-53.

[48] For the following see Schnabel, *Paul the Missionary*, 258-87.

[49] Cf. Martin Hengel and Anna Maria Schwemer, *Paul Between Damascus and Antioch: The Unknown Years* (London/Louisville: SCM/Westminster John Knox, 1997), 110-13.

were plenty of opportunities to preach the gospel. The next phase of Paul's missionary work was Antioch, the capital of the province of Syria (Acts 11:26-30; 13:1). Paul left Cilicia and moved to Antioch, perhaps because his work in the province over the last twelve years had come to a certain conclusion, perhaps because the congregations of followers of Jesus which he had established had become mature, no longer needing outside help, certainly because Barnabas was evidently able to convince him that he was urgently needed in Antioch, perhaps because of the numerous opportunities in the third largest city in the empire, or perhaps because the situation in Antioch had become critical in terms of the growth of the church, in terms of disputes between Jewish and Gentile believers, and in terms of disputes with the Roman authorities of the province who coined the term 'Christians' (Χριστιανοί; Acts 11:26).[50]

The next phase of Paul's missionary work focuses on cities on Cyprus and in the southern part of the province of Galatia. Paul leaves Antioch after a divine intervention (Acts 13:2), which is significant since it is the only direct directive that the Holy Spirit gives to a local congregation in Acts.[51] If the reference to the fasting of the prophets and teachers of the congregation refers to a deliberate search for God's guidance,[52] the leaders of the congregation may already have considered the possibility of initiating a new missionary move into areas which had not yet been reached with the gospel. The move to the province of Cyprus in AD 45 is probably linked with the fact that Barnabas was a native of Cyprus (Acts 4:36), and with the possibility that some of the Jerusalem believers who had to flee after the persecution that followed Stephen's murder in AD 31/32 and who engaged in missionary work in cities on the Phoenician coast and on Cyprus (Acts 11:19) had started congregations on the island that Barnabas and Paul sought to consolidate. They start in Salamis (Acts 13:5) because the city would have been the first port of call for the ship that brought the missionaries from Antioch to Cyprus, because it was an important city even after Paphos had replaced it as capital, and because it had a Jewish community. The verb used in Acts 13:6 (διέρχομαι) suggests that as Paul, Barnabas, and John Mark went from Salamis to Paphos, they preached the gospel in the cities on the southern coast of Cyprus as well, i.e. in Kition, Amathus, and Kourion. The next phase of Paul's missionary work took him from Paphos, the seat of the governor of the province who was converted, to

---

[50] Cf. Hengel and Schwemer, *Paul*, 179-80, 218; on the term 'Christians' see ibid. 453 n. 1171. It is possible that Paul's ecstatic experience mentioned in 2 Cor 12:2, dating to ca. AD 42, played a role in his move from Tarsus to Antioch; cf. Riesner, *Paul's Early Period*, 272, 320.

[51] For the Spirit directing the actions of individuals see Acts 8:29; 10:19-20; 21:22; 28:25, 27.

[52] Cf. I. Howard Marshall, *The Acts of the Apostles. An Introduction and Commentary* (TNTC: Leicester: InterVarsity Press, 1980), 216; also James D. G. Dunn, *The Acts of the Apostles* (EpComm: London: Epworth, 1996), 173, with reference to Neh 1:34; Lk 2:37.

Pisidian Antioch in the region of Phrygia which belonged to the province of Galatia. Why did Paul travel from Paphos to Pisidian Antioch, bypassing larger and more significant cities such as Perge, the capital of the province of Pamphylia, or in Side, Attaleia, Sillyon, Lyrba, and Cotenna, or in Selge, Termessos, and Sagalassos, or in Kremna, Komama, Pogla, Andeda, Sibidunda, Olbasa, Lysinia, Ilyas, Eudoxiopolis, Apollonia and Tymandos? One explanation for Paul's move from Paphos to Pisidian Antioch in the Anatolian highlands is the suggestion that Paul had contracted malaria and that he sought relief in the higher altitudes of southern Galatia.[53] A second explanation, which does not exclude the likelihood of the first, points to the connections between Sergius Paullus, the converted governor of Cyprus (Acts 13:12) and the family of the Sergii Paullii in Pisidian Antioch. Paul's journey to Pisidian Antioch may have been suggested by Sergius Paulus who proposed "that he make it his next port of call, no doubt providing him with letters of introduction to aid his passage and his stay."[54] When Paul and Barnabas were forced to leave the city by the city magistrates, which suggests that the effort to reach the leading families of Pisidian Antioch with the gospel did lead to conversions or even sympathy, they travelled east on the main road in the region, the Via Sebaste, preaching in the cities of Iconium, Lystra, and Derbe. Instead of continuing to Tarsus, only 220 kilometers from Derbe, they decide to retrace their steps (330 kilometers to Perge) in order to consolidate their earlier missionary work in several cities in southern Galatia, before they came to Perge, the capital of the province of Pamphylia, where they preached the gospel and evidently established a congregation (Acts 14:25).

The next phase of Paul's missionary work begins with a long overland journey from Syrian Antioch via Tarsus on the Via Sebaste. Paul wants to preach the gospel in cities in the province of Asia (Acts 16:6), which is the region immediately to the west of Galatia. While Paul may have aimed at reaching Ephesus,[55] it is equally plausible to assume that he wanted to preach

---

[53] Cf. William M. Ramsay, *St. Paul the Traveller and the Roman Citizen* (London: Hodder & Stoughton, 1896), 92-97; F.F. Bruce, *Commentary on Galatians* (NIGTC: Grand Rapids: Eerdmans, 1982), 208-9, with reference to Gal 4:13: Paul came to Galatia "because of a physical infirmity" (Gal 4:13, NRSV).

[54] Mitchell, *Anatolia*, vol. 2, 7. Cf. Riesner, *Paul's Early Period*, 124-25; Cilliers Breytenbach, *Paulus und Barnabas in der Provinz Galatien. Studien zu Apostelgeschichte 13f.; 16,6; 18,23 und den Adressaten des Galaterbriefes* (AGAJU, 38: Leiden: Brill, 1996), 38-45; Schnabel, *Early Christian Mission*, vol. 2, 1085-86. The latest discussion of the Sergii Paulii and their relationship to Pisidian Antioch is the French study of Michel Christol and Thomas Drew-Bear, 'Les Sergii Paulli et Antioche', in T. Drew-Bear, M. Tashalan, and C.J. Thomas (eds), *Actes du Ier congres international sur Antioche de Pisidie* (Collection archéologie et histoire de l'antiquité, 5: Lyon / Paris: Université Lumière-Lyon / Boccard, 2002), 177-91.

[55] Cf. F.F. Bruce, *The Book of the Acts* (Revised edition, NICNT: Grand Rapids: Eerdmans, 1988), 306; Ben Witherington, *The Acts of the Apostles: A Socio-Rhetorical Commentary* (Grand Rapids: Eerdmans, 1998), 477; Schnabel, *Early Christian Mission*, vol. 2, 1131.

the gospel in Apameia which was an assize center and had a large Jewish community, in the cities in the Lykos Valley in the region of the upper Maeander River, i.e. in Laodicea, Hierapolis, Colossae, Tripolis ad Maeandrum, Antiochia ad Maeandrum, Nysa, Tralles, Magnesia, Priene, and Miletus, or in cities along a more northerly route, i.e. in Eumeneia, Sebaste, Akmonia, Temenouthyrai, Blaundos before reaching the valley of the Hermos River with the cities of Philadelphia and Sardis, and then in Thyatira, Pergamum, and Smyrna.[56] When the Lord intervened and instructed Paul not to start missionary work in the province of Asia, he planned to visit cities in the province of Pontus-Bithynia, which was north of the provinces of Asia and Galatia, the only region apart from Asia that he had not reached in central and western Asia Minor. Evidently Paul planned to preach the gospel in Nicea, Nicomedia, and Chalcedon.[57] The move across the Macedonicum Mare, the northern part of the Aegean Sea, to Greece was not motivated by a strategic decision to reach cities in Europe, but by a dream-vision (Acts 16:9) whose significance was discussed by Paul and his co-workers before they embarked on a ship that took them to Neapolis and then to Philippi (Acts 16:10). The choice of Philippi and Thessalonica as cities in which to preach the gospel was due to the fact that they were located on the main road in the region, the Via Egnatia, and, more importantly, because Philippi was a Roman colony with a proud recent history, because Thessalonica was the capital of the province of Macedonia, and because both cities had a Jewish community. When Paul was forced to leave Thessalonica, he could have continued on the Via Egnatia and preached the gospel in Pella, Edessa, Dyrrhachium, and Apollonia, the last two cities important ports on the Adriatic Sea. Or he could have travelled south to cities in the province of Achaia. Instead, he went to Berea, a small town situated at the south-western end of the Macedonian Plain at the foot of the Bermion Mountains. The reason why he went to this out of the way place may be connected with contacts that members of the Jewish community in Thessalonica, some of whom had become Christian believers, had with the Jewish community in Berea: it was the new Jewish converts in Thessalonica who "sent Paul and Silas off to Berea" (Acts 17:1).

The next phase of Paul's missionary work takes place in Athens and in Corinth in the province of Achaia, in the years AD 50-51. Luke's narrative does not give us any insight into Paul's thinking at this time; his geographical references make it impossible to discern a strategy on Paul's part. Many have argued, or rather assumed, that Paul was in Athens only as a visitor, and that he started to preach the gospel only when he became exasperated about the idols that were on display in the city. This is hardly convincing; while Athens may have had more temples and more statues of Greek, Roman, and Egyptian deities on display than other towns, the scope and the process of idol worship was no different from what he had seen growing up in Tarsus or preaching in

[56] Cf. Schnabel, *Paul the Missionary*, 267-70.
[57] For details see Schnabel, *Early Christian Mission*, vol. 1, 842-48.

Antioch. In the statement, "so he argued in the synagogue with the Jews and the Godfearers and in the agora day by day with those who happened to be there" (Acts 17:17), which follows after the observation that, "while Paul was waiting for them in Athens, his spirit was provoked when he saw that the city was full of cult images" (Acts 17:16), the coordination conjunction translated as 'so' (μὲν οὖν) signals continuation while introducing a new development in the narrative.[58] Luke's long narrative of Paul's Athens visit in Acts 17:16-34, and the summary statement in Acts 17:17 which reports Paul's preaching activity in the local synagogues and in the Agora, indicates that Paul pursued planned missionary work in Athens as he did in other cities. Athens was certainly a suitable city for missionary work, even though its heyday was long in the past: Athens still was an important cultural and intellectual center in the Mediterranean world, and it had a Jewish community.[59] Corinth was the capital of the province of Achaia, it was a thriving city which had been re-established as a Roman colony by Julius Caesar in 44 BC, it was strategically located, and it had a Jewish community. Luke's comment that, "he stayed there for a year and six months, teaching the word of God among them" (Acts 18:11), which follows after the dream-vision in which the Lord had encouraged Paul to stay in Corinth (Acts 18:9-10), probably does not indicate a change to a new missionary strategy in which Paul, rather than leaving cities when opposition arises, stays in a given city despite continued opposition (here of the Jews).[60] As Luke is silent about Paul's plans, and as the reference to the Lord's word of encouragement is neither linked with the Jewish opposition to Paul in the spring of AD 50 nor with the Gallio incident in the summer of AD 51, it is impossible to know why Paul needed divine encouragement. When Paul concludes his missionary work in Corinth and travels to Syria via Ephesus, we have the unique situation that the Jews in the synagogue of Ephesus want Paul to stay and explain his message to them more fully, he declines, with the promises of a visit "if God wills" in the not too distant future (Acts 18:21). While Luke does not explain Paul's refusal to accept the invitation to stay in Ephesus,[61] he underlines his (and Paul's) conviction that his movements as a

---

[58] BDAG s.v. μέν 2e; cf. C.K. Barrett, *The Acts of the Apostles* (ICC: Edinburgh: T & T Clark, 1994-98), 828. See Beverly R. Gaventa, *The Acts of the Apostles* (Abingdon New Testament Commentaries: Nashville: Abingdon Press, 2003), 248, who correctly points out that the "so" that NRSV (and other translations) have at the beginning of v. 17 should not be allowed to "misleadingly suggest that Paul goes to the synagogue in reaction to Athenian idolatry."

[59] Jews had lived in Athens since the fourth century B.C. See Irina A. Levinskaya, *The Book of Acts in its Diaspora Setting* (The Book of Acts in Its First-Century Setting, Volume 5: Grand Rapids: Eerdmans, 1996), 158-62; David Noy, Alexander Panayotov, and Hanswulf Bloedhorn, *Inscriptiones Judaicae Orientis. Vol. I: Eastern Europe* (TSAJ, 101: Tübingen: Mohr Siebeck, 2004), 144-64.

[60] Cf. Philip H. Towner, 'Mission Practice and Theology under Construction (Acts 18-20),' in I .H. Marshall and D. Peterson (eds), *Witness to the Gospel: The Theology of Acts* (Grand Rapids: Eerdmans, 1998), 417-36.

[61] A plausible but unproven suggestion surmises that, "Paul, profoundly disturbed by

preacher and teacher depend on God.[62] This invitation, combined with Paul's earlier plans to reach cities in the province of Asia and with the political and cultural importance of the city, makes Paul's subsequent move to Ephesus a logical choice. He works in Ephesus for three years, from AD 52-55.

If Paul's work in Illyricum (Rom 15:19) in the autumn of AD 56 (before staying in Corinth until the opening of navigation on the Mediterranean Sea in the spring of AD 56) was motivated by the desire to gain experience of preaching the gospel in a predominantly Latin speaking environment in preparation for his missionary work in Spain (Rom 15:23-28), this would have been the one instance where 'global' aspects of Paul's strategy, understood in geographical terms, directly impacted his local movements. Paul was able to explain the gospel to the Sanhedrin in Jerusalem (Acts 23:1-10), to two Roman governors, Marcus Antonius Felix (Acts 24:1-27) and Porcius Festus (Acts 25:6-12), and to the Jewish king Marcus Julius Agrippa II (Acts 26:2-32) while he was in Caesarea for two years between AD 57-59, this was neither the result of a global strategy nor of local methods but developments in which he was caught up as a prisoner.

The conclusion of this survey of Paul's movements, evaluated from the perspective of his geographical movements, seems obvious. Paul did not follow a grand geographical strategy but used the best opportunities available at a particular time to reach people with the gospel, wherever they lived, preaching before as many Jews and Gentiles as possible. As Paul wanted to reach Jews, he had to visit cities where Jewish diaspora communities existed. If he wanted to reach as many people as possible, he had to work in the cities. However, the view that Paul's method of evangelizing a province, "was not to preach in every place in it himself, but to establish centres of Christian life in two or three important places from which the knowledge might spread into the country round" needs to be carefully evaluated. First, most of the cities in which Paul was active were organized as a *polis* in which the citizens governed their own affairs,[63] which means that a 'radiation effect' of developments emanating from a particular urban center would generally end at the borders of the territory (*chora*) which the city controlled. Second, as Greek cities competed with each

opposition that had already made itself felt in Galatia and may have begun to affect Corinth and other centres also, made his way to Jerusalem to find out how far the Jerusalem authorities were behind the trouble-makers, and if possible to stop the trouble at its source. This might account for the speed of his journey – he was not at this point concerned to visit churches *en route* but to get to his destination as quickly as possible – and also for Luke's silence; he did not wish to dig up old troubles" (Barrett, *Acts*, vol. 2, 881).

[62] The phrase translated "if God wills" (τοῦ θεοῦ θέλοντος; Lat. *Deo volente*) was common in antiquity, cf. Josephus, *A.J.* 2.333, 347; 7.373; in the New Testament: 1 Cor 4:19; 16:7; Heb 6:3; Jas 4:15; cf. Rom 1:10; also Plato, *Alc. maj.* 135D; *Phaedo* 80D; Epictetus 1.1.17; also in a papyrus from the second century AD (BGU II 423).

[63] Cf. Peter J. Rhodes, 'Polis II', in H. Cancik and H. Schneider (eds), *Brill's New Pauly* (Leiden: Brill, 2007), vol. 11, cols. 470-73; Oswyn Murray and Simon Price, *The Greek City: From Homer to Alexander* (Oxford: Clarendon, 1991).

other for pre-eminence in the province, the 'radiation effect' of a church in a particular city would not necessarily have impacted other cities. Third, new developments that began in a local Jewish community would not necessarily impress the non-Jewish citizens of other urban centers in the province. Fourth, since social identity was closely connected with the city in which one was born and in which one lived, and since evidence for a provincial (e.g. Galatians), regional (e.g. Lycaonians) and ethnic (e.g. Ionians) identity is rather limited, the Christian message would not have naturally been disseminated from a particular city to other areas. Fifth, important characteristics of urban life in the Roman world were more obstructive than helpful for the missionary penetration of a province, among them the aspirations of the individual cities to move up in the hierarchy of the cities of the province and the claims to honor and fame based on the past and present attainment of their citizens.[64] Such priorities were in fundamental conflict with the gospel and the values it engendered, focused as they were on the death by crucifixion of Jesus, a Jewish provincial, and on the "poor in spirit" whom Jesus promised participation in the kingdom of God. As Paul asserts, the majority of believers in the congregations were "foolish", i.e. uneducated, "weak", i.e. without influence in the affairs of the city, "low and despised" and regarded as being "nothing" by the wise, the powerful, and the noble of birth (1 Cor 1:26-28). Sixth, while the cities were certainly centers of communication, they were also "the base for supervision"[65] of a distrustful provincial Roman administration. Establishing congregations in urban centers certainly had strategic value, but it did not guarantee that the gospel would spread from the cities into the countryside.

Paul's missionary work in Pisidian Antioch (Acts 13:13-52) is a good example of the apostle's 'local' methods, allowing us to observe the realities of missionary work. First, he reaches out to Jews and Gentiles, to average citizens and the elites. Paul visits the synagogue because he is a Jew for Jews "in order to win Jews" (1 Cor 9:20). In the synagogue he meets Jews, proselytes, Godfearers, and Gentile women who belong to the local elite and who sympathize with the Jewish faith. He preaches to the Gentiles who form the majority of people living in the city, particularly once the leaders of the Jewish community make further synagogue visits impossible. Since most people living in Greek cities were average people, freeborn and freedmen who were trying to make a living the best they could, and since a large number of slaves lived in the cities, most people in his audience were ordinary, poor, or disenfranchised. The president of the synagogue was probably wealthy, as were the Gentile women of high standing whom Paul met in the synagogue. The members of the local elite who eventually force Paul to leave Antioch may have included members of the family of the Sergii Paullii whom Paul probably contacted

---

[64] Cf. John E. Stambaugh, *The Ancient Roman City* (Baltimore: Johns Hopkins University Press, 1988).

[65] Nicholas Purcell, 'Urbanism II. Roman,' in S. Hornblower and A. J. S. Spawforth (eds), *Oxford Classical Dictionary* (Third edition: Oxford: Oxford University Press, 1996), 1573.

shortly after his arrival from Paphos. Paul did not organize specialized audiences but proclaimed the gospel to anyone who was willing to listen, whether they were educated or uneducated, powerful or ordinary, freeborn or slaves, men or women.[66] Second, Paul reads and interprets the Scriptures, which in Acts is a foundational reality not only in the church but also in missionary work.[67] Paul uses traditional Jewish methods of interpretation (e.g. *gezerah shavah*) which his Jewish audience was familiar with. He develops his explanation of the significance of Jesus not from the life of Jesus (which he could have done) but from the Scriptures which the Jews acknowledged to be authoritative. When Paul preaches, he does not deduce the truth about God, about sinners, about salvation, about Jesus as Savior logically or experientially from first principles or from contemporary social or philosophical thinking, but from Scripture as the revealed word of God. Third, Paul explains the significance of Jesus. His explanation of the Scriptures focuses on the significance of Jesus. The message that Paul proclaims is the good news about Jesus and the blessings that God bestows on Jews and Gentiles as a result of Jesus' death and resurrection. Fourth, as regards the 'success' of his preaching before Jews and Gentiles, Paul certainly argues with Scripture and with the witness of those who have seen Jesus after his resurrection, but he relies on the sovereignty of God who caused people to come to faith in Jesus.[68] Missionaries and evangelists do not rely on rhetorical brilliance nor on convincing argumentation when they explain the 'scandal of the cross' but on God who is present in the proclamation of his word and who convinces people of the truth of the gospel through the power of his Spirit.[69] Fifth, Paul instructs the new believers. Paul's letters show that his instruction of new believers had a theological focus and an ethical orientation.[70] He explains God's revelation in Israel's history and, climactically, in the life, death, and resurrection of Jesus. He explains the significance of Jesus as the crucified and risen Messiah and Savior. He explains the utter sinfulness of mankind. He explains the role and function of the Mosaic Law. He explains the reality of the life of believers in Jesus whom God's Spirit transforms. And he explains the relevance of these truths for the everyday of the believers who lived in cities in which hedonistic lifestyles were tolerated and propagated by the cultural and social elites.

---

[66] Cf. 1 Cor 1:26-29; 9:22; Gal 3:28; Rom 1:14-16; Col 3:11.

[67] On the importance of the Scriptures in missionary work see Peter Beyerhaus, *Er sandte sein Wort. Theologie der christlichen Mission. Band 1: Die Bibel in der Mission* (TVG/Heilsgeschichtliche Missionstheologie 1: Wuppertal/Bad Liebenzell: Brockhaus/VLM, 1996).

[68] Acts 13:48; 14:27; 15:12; 21:19; cf. 1 Thess 2:13; 1 Cor 3:5-9; 2 Cor 5:18-21.

[69] Cf. Eckhard J. Schnabel, *Der Erste Brief des Paulus an die Korinther* (Historisch-Theologische Auslegung: Wuppertal: R. Brockhaus, 2006), 111-59. See also James I. Packer, *Evangelism and the Sovereignty of God* (Downers Grove: InterVarsity Press, 1961).

[70] Cf. Schnabel, *Paul the Missionary*, 190-201, 236-48, 419-22.

Conclusion

Clarifying global strategies is as important as it is simple, at least it was for the earliest missionaries. As they practiced 'following Jesus' they aimed at reaching all people who were willing to listen to them, irrespective of traditional religious, ethnic, social, or cultural barriers. As commissioned by Jesus, the global strategy of Peter and Paul was to proclaim the good news of Jesus, Israel's Messiah and Savior of humankind, to Jews, proselytes, Samaritans, Godfearers, and Gentiles, whether they were men or women, whether they were Ethiopians, Romans, Syrians, Cilicians, Cypriotes, Phrygians, Lycaonians, Pamphylians, Macedonians, Greeks, or Ionians. While the preaching of the gospel was adapted specifically to the various audiences in the synagogues, in the marketplaces, in local or provincial courts, the central truth of Jesus, the crucified and risen Savior who forgives sins and rescues from God's judgment, always remains central. They did not remove the 'scandal of particularity', created by their conviction that the life, death, and resurrection of Jesus, a Jewish teaching who was active in one time and place, had unequalled, unique, authoritative significance for all times, for all people, and for all places.[71]

The unwavering commitment to Jesus' commission to be his witnesses in Jerusalem and in all regions where human beings live (global strategy) was implemented with a consistent flexibility of methods. Peter and Paul were willing to endure opposition, beatings, imprisonment, and even death for their commitment to Jesus Christ and for their commitment to proclaim the good news of Jesus as Messiah, Savior, and Lord. Since they were not eager to suffer, they were willing to leave cities in a hurry and open up new areas of missionary work in other places. Geographical movement followed natural and available connections and commonalities, geographical proximity, and political necessity. Sometimes, but only rarely, was it directed by divine intervention. Missionary work is hard work. Jesus was sometimes tired (Jn 4:6), his disciples were at times in need of rest (Mk 6:31). Paul speaks of his great labors, his imprisonments, his floggings, having often been near death, his beatings, the occasions when he was stoned and shipwrecked and adrift at sea, his frequent journeys, the danger from rivers, the danger from bandits, the danger from the Jewish people, the danger from Gentiles, dangers in the city, dangers in the wilderness, dangers from false brothers; he speaks of his toil and hardship, the many sleepless nights, the times when he was hungry and thirsty, cold and

---

[71] Cf. Mark Vernon, in his review of Trevor Williams, *The Ultimacy of Jesus: The Language and Logic of Christian Commitment* (Aureus Studies in Post-Foundational Theology: St Bride's Major, Glamorgan: Aureus, 2009) in the *Times Literary Supplement* (February 19, 2010, 26-27). Williams relies in his apologetic on theologians informed by existentialist philosophy such as Paul Tillich. Vernon concludes his review with the assertion that despite Williams' arguments, "for non-Christians, though, the scandal of particularity remains." This is precisely that while Peter and Paul argued from Scripture, from eyewitness observations, and from general culture, they relied on the power of God and of his Holy Spirit to convince people of the truth of the gospel.

without proper clothing; he speaks of the daily pressure because of his anxiety for all the churches, and of his weakness (2 Cor 11:23-30). Paul does not boast in his success, in the many people he has led to faith in Jesus, in the numerous congregations that he has established; rather, he boasts of his weaknesses so that the power of Jesus Christ, who has caused people to come to faith and congregations be established, is given its proper due (2 Cor 12:9). This is precisely where global strategies which result from Jesus' commission and local methods which result from the faithfulness of Jesus' witnesses meet: in the acknowledgment that we are given the grace to be, "content with weaknesses, insults, hardships, persecutions, and calamities for the sake of Christ" because whenever we, Jesus' witnesses, are weak, then we are strong (2 Cor 12:10), because we allow the power of the risen Messiah, which is the power of the Holy Spirit, to work through our weaknesses in the hearts and minds and lives of people who hear the gospel and to come to faith in Jesus Christ.

Global Strategies and Local Methods of Missionary Work in the Early Church: Jesus, Peter and Paul
A Response to Eckhard Schnabel

Hans Kvalbein

When a Professor is asked to give a response to another Professor, you normally expect him to argue for different opinions and trying to find weak points in the views of the colleague. In Germany I have heard a definition of a Professor: "Ein Professor ist ein Mann anderer Meinung" ("A professor is a man of another opinion").

If you have such expectations to my response, I have to disappoint you at once. In some details I may have different views from Eckhard Schnabel, but basically I agree with him and above all I am thankful for his great contribution to clarifying the importance of mission in the New Testament. His two-volume work on *Early Christian Mission*[1] will stand as a classical source of insight to this broad field for many decades, and his more recent book on *Paul the Missionary*[2] is a treasure of information and reflection on Paul's strategy and methods in his missionary work.

In my response I therefore just want to point out some accents in his presentation which I see as especially important for the understanding of mission in the New Testament and today.

The Broad Biblical Foundation for Mission

Mission is no new invention first coming up in New Testament times. It has its basis in the Old Testament, as a consequence of God's activity as creator and of the story of sin, when man and woman turned their back to God and became God's rebels instead of his co-workers. Mission is God's activity to seek and save the lost and to restore the fellowship between God and his fallen humankind. The promise to Abraham and the covenant with him is not a

---

[1] Eckhard J. Schnabel, *Early Mission, Volume 1: Jesus and the Twelve* (Downers Grove: InterVarsity Press, 2004); *Early Christian Mission, Volume 2: Paul and the Early Church* (Downers Grove: InterVarsity Press, 2004).

[2] Eckhard J. Schnabel, *Paul the Missionary: Realities, Strategies and Methods* (Downers Grove: IVP Academic, 2008).

particularistic act separating Abraham and his descendants from the Gentiles, but a universalistic promise aiming at blessing for all families on earth. This universalistic scope is confirmed by the prophets, especially by Isaiah in his servant songs, where God's justice and salvation should be brought to the ends of the earth. One of the most beautiful expressions of this universalistic hope is given in poetic form in Psalm 67, where the Aaronitic blessing (Num 6:22-27) is applied to all the nations so they can be glad and sing for joy and praise the Lord.

These promises form the background for the New Testament mission texts. In the gospels they start with Jesus' call to the disciples to follow him and become fishers of men. The disciples are called to share Jesus' mission to go to the "lost sheep of the house of Israel", but also to share his life conditions as the Son of Man who has nowhere to lay his head. Matthew, Luke and John give in different forms a commission to the disciples at the end of their gospels and as a culmination of the story of Jesus' life on earth. Mission from Jerusalem to the ends of the earth is the story line in the book of Acts. Mission is the driving force in its portraits of Peter and Paul, and mission is the great concern in the letters of Paul.

But even if mission is such a central and basic topic in the Bible, it is not self-evident that biblical scholars are supporters of missionary work today. It is sad to say that many of my colleagues as biblical and New Testament scholars keep a rather cool distance to mission and evangelization. Eckhard Schnabel is not one of them. He combines a firm devotion to biblical scholarship with a warm commitment to missional work today. The last chapter in his book on Paul the Missionary is devoted to 'The Task of Missionary Work in the Twenty-first Century' and shows that mission for him is not only an interesting phenomenon in the past, but also a burning concern for people who want to follow Jesus and be his disciples today. To say it simply: contemporary mission is the logical consequence of the message of the Bible.

Think Globally – Act Locally

"Without a local focus, global strategies remain mere talk." Schnabel points out by many examples that the intention to reach out to the ends of the earth must not be an excuse to withdraw from the local challenges right where you are. Jesus himself moved from village to village in Galilee, proclaiming the kingdom of God both to the crowds and in conversations with groups and individuals. He speaks to anyone who is willing to listen. He is not welcomed by everybody, and his message causes doubts and even fierce opposition. In his commissioning speeches he clearly presupposes that the disciples will be welcomed in some houses, but rejected by others. Missionary activity cannot avoid conflicts and should not expect to be appreciated by everybody. The disciples are advised to avoid conflicts as far as they are able to, but they should be open and consistent in their presentation of the gospel and share the good news with the people they meet. The mission of Jesus is a 'neighbor-mission', with the expanded meaning of the word 'neighbor' which was so characteristic for Jesus.

This commitment to local work right where you are, is demonstrated first by the apostle Peter as example. Schnabel puts together the pieces of information we have about him from the book of Acts and from the letters of Paul and Peter, and summarizes in three pregnant sentences:

> There is no place that Peter is not willing to go.
>
> There is nothing that Peter is not willing to do.
>
> There is nobody that Peter is not willing to speak to.

These sentences of course have a global horizon. At the same time they are linked to local work. Conversion and discipleship are local events concerning individuals and groups in a specific time and a specific place.

It is always impressive to realize the enormous geographic extension of the apostle Paul, the missionary par excellence in the New Testament. From Jerusalem via Antioch, Ephesus, Corinth, Rome to Spain – these horizons of the life of Paul include thousands of kilometers of journeys by foot and sea voyages. For a single man it may seem impossible to overcome such distances when we consider the lack of access to aircraft, cars and motorized boats at that time. Paul must have been an enormously powerful and strong mission strategist? Schnabel warns us against such a conclusion. "Paul did not follow a grand geographical strategy but used the best and the obvious opportunities available at a particular time to reach people with the gospel, wherever they lived, preaching before as many Jews and Gentiles as possible." So even in the case of Paul we may observe that an obligation to local work has priority before the grand, global strategies.

Particularity – Universality

The Christian message is a particular message about a single man, Jesus Christ, who was also God's Son and our Savior, who came from a small nation at the fringe of the Roman Empire, a people of descendants from Abraham. That the salvation of the world is connected to this particular man from this particular people, to Jesus as Israel's Messiah, has always been a scandal. In the New Testament this scandal is not hidden or explained away. It is their conviction that exactly this particularity of the gospel is the reason for its universality. This one man is the savior of the world, and there is no other name under heaven by which we can be saved. This conviction gave the first Christians courage and power to endure resistance and suffering. And it gave them their motivation to share this one, particular gospel with everyone they met at any place they were. God has proved Jesus to be his Son and the Savior of the world by his powerful resurrection from the dead. It is very meaningful to have a conference on mission like this so close to our celebration of Easter, the annual feast of Jesus' death and resurrection. He is not dead, he has risen and he lives today. And that is the reason for his claim to have all authority in heaven and on earth and his global commission to make disciples of all nations. And this discipleship, to which we are called even today, is to be lived out in our own neighborhood. The global commission always implies a local commitment.

Schnabel has rightly pointed to the 'scandal of particularity' as a problem in New Testament times, when the small Jewish sect of Christians claimed Jesus as the Messiah of Israel and the Savior of the world. This scandal was deeply felt in the cross-cultural and the multireligious Hellenistic-Roman world of the first Christians. And it is felt even more today, when we experience a revival and revitalization of the world religions and a decline of the inherited Christianity of the Western world.

Schnabel has also pointed to the hardships the first missionaries met. Paul did not boast of his success as a missionary, but pointed to his own great labors, to his imprisonments, exhausting travels, anxieties and to his bodily weakness. The power of the gospel has to be promoted through our weakness. Mission is not a triumphant crusade, but a commitment to our Lord and Savior in humility and in serving love.

By pointing to these aspects of the missionary work of the Early Church, I feel that Schnabel has given us some important considerations to our celebration of the Mission Conference in Edinburgh a hundred years ago. That conference was colored by great optimism. "The evangelization of the world in our generation," was the great slogan at that time. But you cannot avoid the impression that this optimism was linked to the great achievements of Western colonialism, and that the idea of global mission was easily combined with a kind of triumphant thinking which is not in accordance with the gospel of the cross and the message of Jesus.

We share the view of the Edinburgh conference that the Great Commission implies a global commitment to the gospel. It is for everybody, crossing national, racial, cultural and other frontiers. But we don't want to see mission as a kind of triumphal crusade. The Great Commission is a call to serve Christ locally and in humility, opening our hearts for those who need our help and support in our own neighborhood. "Without a local focus, global strategies remain mere talk."

The Church as Both Local and Global: A Missiological Perspective

Tormod Engelsviken

Introduction

The theological understanding of the church as local and global, and in particular the understanding of the church in mission, missional ecclesiology, is a topic of great importance and increasing interest. There are several reasons for this.[1]

Firstly, the historically unprecedented growth of the church in the non-Western world toward the end of the twentieth century, and the shift of the centre of gravity of the church from the North to the South have drawn attention to the church as a global reality.

Secondly, through the various networks of mission, ecumenism and international aid, both related to the ecumenical and evangelical movements, and supported by the increasing globalisation and internationalization in general, local churches all over the world have come into closer contact with each other and become aware of the various societal and cultural contexts in which the church exists. Thus the relationship between the global and the local aspect of being church is becoming increasingly urgent.

Thirdly, there are a growing number of new models for church and mission making claims that challenge the historical forms and understandings of the church.

Fourthly, and maybe most importantly, the church played a crucial role in the New Testament and the formative years of the Christian movement, and the church needs to reflect anew on its own nature and mission in the light of twenty-first century contexts that in many respects resemble those of the early church.

In his foreword to the book *Globalizing Theology: Belief and Practice in an Era of World Christianity*, Wilbert R. Shenk says that,

---

[1] These points and some of the ecclesiological material in this essay may also be found in Tormod Engelsviken, 'Church/Ecclesiology', in John Corrie (ed), *Dictionary of Mission Theology. Evangelical Foundations* (Nottingham: InterVarsity Press, 2007), 51-55.

> ...to engage in 'globalizing theology' today means that we must guard the commitment to the particular and the local while taking account of the fact that we live with an intensified awareness of the global. If theology is to serve the church throughout the world, it must reflect this bifocal way of seeing; this becomes the vantage point from which we must rethink and revise theology conceptually, methodologically and programmatically.[2]

This essay is a humble attempt to look at the church in this 'bifocal' way, in its two dimensions as local and as global or universal. This approach is justified by the new situation in which we find ourselves at the beginning of the twenty-first century with an increasingly globalized world where the local still plays an important role. Yet, as we shall see, it can also be justified theologically as the church exists, and has to be understood and studied, both as a local and a universal reality. The essay is not an attempt to deal with all aspects of ecclesiology but rather with one specific dimension of it, namely mission. This is not, however, a narrow perspective. The fact that the church is sent to the world by God (*missio Dei)* and therefore is missional is a very fundamental statement about the church that should influence all other aspects and activities of the church. Although many of us use it all the time, the phrase 'church *and* mission' may be misleading since the church *is* mission. To be missional belongs to the very essence of the church. It is therefore the local church and universal church as missional church that will be our two foci.

A Tentative Definition of Mission

It has been pointed out – and demonstrated – by David Bosch that defining mission is an almost impossible task.[3] Yet, before looking more closely at the understanding of the church as local and global, I would like to propose a tentative definition of mission that may guide us in our deliberations:

> Mission is the sending of the church – in its local and global expression – to the world, a sending which has it origin in the Triune God (Jn 20:21-22) and consists in the task of proclaiming the gospel of God in word and deed (Rom 15:16-20) so that humans everywhere, without regard to ethnicity, gender, social status, class, caste or religion, may be reconciled with God through faith in Christ as their Lord and Savior, and be joined to the church by baptism. The mission is by nature transcending boundaries by aiming at reaching new people; geographically, culturally and temporally (new generations), people who have not yet heard or understood the gospel (Rom 15:20).[4]

---

[2] Wilbert R. Shenk, 'Foreword', in Craig Ott and Harold A. Netland (eds), *Globalizing Theology. Belief and Practice in an Era of World Christianity* (Grand Rapids, MI.: Baker Academic, 2006), 11.

[3] David J. Bosch, *Transforming Mission. Paradigm Shifts in the Theology of Mission* (Maryknoll, N.Y.: Orbis Books, 1991), 8-11.

[4] This definition is a translated and slightly expanded version of the definition given in Jan-Martin Berentsen, Tormod Engelsviken and Knud Jørgensen, 'Innledning', in Jan-Martin Berentsen, Tormod Engelsviken and Knud Jørgensen (eds), *Missiologi i dag*

Social service and social action (prophetic diaconia or advocacy) in order to prevent and alleviate human suffering, interfaith dialogue in order to facilitate e.g. understanding, reconciliation or joint social action may be *an integral part* of mission even without the specific aim of converting people to Christianity. However, these ministries *alone* do not constitute mission, as mission according to the model of Jesus should always be *holistic*, reaching people in all dimensions; spiritual, physical and social.

If the church as sent by God to the world is by nature missional, both the church as a fellowship and each individual Christian have the task of being a witness for Christ, persuading people to receive Christ in faith.

The Local Church

In describing what the church is I refer to an old tradition that goes back to the church fathers, e.g. Ignatius and Tertullian, and which recently has been convincingly argued by the Norwegian systematic theologian Harald Hegstad. He takes his point of departure in the words of Jesus in Mt 18:20: "Where two or three come together in my name, there am I with them."[5] This means that the church is a *fellowship* of human beings, two being the lowest number that can establish a fellowship. This fellowship is *coming together*. What is unique about this coming together is that it is done in the *name of Jesus*. This means that it is done on behalf of Jesus or confessing Jesus. In this fellowship *Jesus himself will be present*. That is his promise to the disciples. The church is therefore people coming together in the name of Jesus, believing in Jesus. Hegstad writes, "To believe in the church is to believe in the promise of the presence of Jesus when people gather in his name."[6]

In some ways this understanding of the church corresponds to the Lutheran understanding of the church as expressed in the Augsburg Confession, Art. VII (CA VII): "The church is the assembly of saints (Latin: *Communio sanctorum*; German: *die Versammlung aller Gläubigen)* in which the gospel is taught purely and the sacraments are administered rightly."[7] The emphasis is also here on the fact that the church is a fellowship that consists of people. Then there are two qualifications; firstly with regard to who the people are who come together in this fellowship, namely the 'holy' or the 'believers', secondly with regard to what they are gathered for or around, namely the preaching of the gospel and the administration of the sacraments. A third qualification is also added: the *pure* teaching of the gospel and the *right* administration of the sacraments.

The title of Hegstad's book *Den Virkelige Kirke (The Real Church*) indicates a major emphasis. To Hegstad the real church is the *visible* church, the people

---

(Oslo: Universitetsforlaget, 2nd edition, 2004), 16.

[5] See too Harald Hegstad, *Den Virkelige Kirke. Bidrag til Ekklesiologien* (Trondheim: Tapir Akademisk Forlag, 2009), 19ff.

[6] Hegstad, *Den Virkelige Kirke*, 21 (translation mine).

[7] Robert Kolb and Timothy J. Wengert (eds), *The Book of Concord. The Confessions of the Evangelical Lutheran Church* (Minneapolis, MN: 2000), 43.

who visibly gather in the name of Jesus and where the risen Christ is present. "There exists only one church, namely the church that is concretely and experientially present in the world."[8] I would, however, raise one slight objection to Hegstad's identification of the real church with the visible church. It is true that the fellowship of those who gather in the name of Jesus is visible; both the fact that human beings gather and the fact that they do it in the name of Jesus are visible. However, when Hegstad says that, "the church becomes church by humans gathering in the name of Jesus, believing that Jesus himself through the Spirit is present among them," he seems to me not to notice the difference between 'gathering in the name of Jesus' and 'believing' as far as visibility is concerned. While gathering in the name of Jesus is visible, the faith of those who gather and the presence of the risen Christ are not visible. It is therefore not possible to see or observe who really belong to the true church, namely those who belong to the kingdom of God through faith in Christ. Therefore there needs to be some caution with regard to simply identifying the real church with the visible church. The real church, the people of God, can only consist of those who have sincere faith, who are saved, and therefore also have the promise of God's future salvation.[9] In this world, prior to the return of our Lord, the visible church will be a mixture of people who belong to the real church and people who do not belong to the real church, but only to the church in an outward sense[10] (*ecclesia large dicta* as opposed to *ecclesia proprie dicta*).

It is important to emphasize this in view of the fact that the empirical church in history has been guilty of serious sins and mistakes. These may have been done by people belonging to the real church or by people belonging to the church only in an outward sense. In the latter case the real church may not be held responsible. Examples of this can be seen when political or other powers take control of the church and act in its name, or when the majority of the church are nominal Christians and therefore do no belong to the real church.

One important consequence of Hegstad's insistence that the visible, empirical church is the real church is the rejection of the frequently held idea that the real or true church is an invisible entity which is (only) holy and perfect while the visible church is sinful and imperfect. The church is, like its members, *both* holy and sinful at the same time (*simul justus et peccator*). It has made and still makes serious mistakes, and has to confess not only the sins of its individual members but also the collective sins of the church. Rather than operating with a distinction between the visible and the invisible (or hidden) church, Hegstad would emphasize the eschatological perspective. Only as the kingdom of God is fully realized at the return of Christ, will also the church become perfect. Until then it is a sign and anticipation of the future salvation of God's creation, sharing both God's redemption and the sinfulness and brokenness of creation.

---

[8] Hegstad, *Den Virkelige Kirke*, 10.

[9] Cf. Mt 7:21-23.

[10] Cf. CA VIII, Kolb and Wengert, *The Book of Concord*, 43.

Seen in the light of our topic, the real church where people gather in the name of Jesus, is primarily the local church. Hegstad writes, "A consequence of the emphasis on the church as a distinct and concrete fellowship has been an increased consciousness of the role of the local congregation."[11] This again has important consequences for mission, both through an emphasis on church growth and church development that place the local congregation in focus, and through the insistence that this local church as the real church is sent to the world, and therefore is a missional church. We cannot bypass the local church, either in the direction of parachurch organisations or in the direction of the global church in order to fulfil the missionary calling of the church. Mission has to be anchored in the local church.

The Global Church

Our understanding of the global church must be based on our understanding of the local church. The local church is the basic form of the church.[12] There is no qualitative difference between the local and the global church. The global church is the sum of all local churches in the whole world. And since Jesus is the resurrected and ascended Lord of the whole cosmos he is present in all the local churches of the global church, as is the Spirit that is granted to all Christians.

The actual size of the global church is impossible to calculate. Although the global church is visible in the same way as the local church, it is impossible for humans to know the full extent of it. Statistics can give us a certain indication. A recent figure is 2,292,454,000 Christians in the world, or 33.2% of the world's total population of 6.9 billion.[13] This staggering number can of course be broken down in various ways. The annual statistics in the January issue of the *International Bulletin of Missionary Research* (IBMR) gives a good indication. It seems, however, that the number of active, confessing Christians may be less than 1 billion.

In his essay 'Christianity across twenty centuries', Andrew F. Walls points out that the twentieth century is the most remarkable in Christian history apart from the first century:

> When it began, Christianity appeared to most people, whether well disposed or not, to be *a* Western religion and *the* Western religion. The great majority of people in the West professed it, and the overwhelming majority of those who professed it lived in Europe or Northern America. When the century ended, the majority of professed Christians were living in Africa, Asia, Latin America or the Pacific region.[14]

---

[11] Hegstad, *Den virkelige kirke*, 16.

[12] Hegstad, *Den virkelige kirke*, 175.

[13] Todd M. Johnson and Kenneth R. Ross (eds), *Atlas of Global Christianity 1910-2010* (Edinburgh: Edinburgh University Press 2009), 18.

[14] Andrew F. Walls, 'Christianity across twenty centuries', in Johnson and Ross, *Atlas*, 48.

An interesting graph is used in the Johnson and Ross atlas to illustrate the development of the church in the Global South in relation to the Global North. Until 923 AD the majority of Christians lived in what today is seen as the Global South. Then the percentage sank and remained under 50% until 1981 when the majority again was living in the Global South. Today more than 70% of the global church is situated in the Global South and the percentage is rising.[15] Christianity has again become a predominantly 'non-Western' religion.

Walls emphasizes also what he calls the "serial character of Christian advance." There are no single Christian countries, territories or cultures, or permanent Christian areas. In areas where Christianity once dominated, it may have been eradicated or it continues to exist only on the margins, while new peoples and cultures have embraced it and seen a tremendous growth.[16]

We often think of the growth of the church into a global church as a continuous, steady expansion through missionary work, generally with the West as the point of departure. In recent years church historians have, however, emphasized two important facts: firstly, the ancient church grew not only in the direction of the west, but also towards the east and the south. Philip Jenkins maintains that the Euro-American emphasis is unnatural when seen on a broader background of Christian history. He points out that there existed in fact an earlier global Christianity. For most of its history Christianity was a "tricontinental religion, with powerful representation in Europe, Africa, and Asia," which lasted until the fourteenth century.[17]

Secondly, the reason why the West for a few hundred years later was the centre of gravity for Christianity was not due to a special affinity for the Christian faith on the part of the European continent, "but by default: Europe was the continent where it was not destroyed."[18] Interestingly, Jenkins has named the first chapter of his book *The Lost History of Christianity* 'The End of Global Christianity'.[19] He calls for a memory of the vigorous churches in Africa and the Middle East, and argues that many aspects of Christianity that we conceive of as modern were in fact "the norm in the distant past: globalisation, the encounter with other faiths, and the dilemmas of living under hostile regimes."[20] This should make us aware of an unwarranted bias in the contemporary thinking about mission, namely that Christian mission and the globalisation of the church is merely a modern phenomenon that is tied up with Western expansion, colonialism and imperialism. They far precede the modern period, although, of course, Western imperial politics, culture and forms of Christianity have greatly influenced the expansion and globalisation of the church in the modern period when the West had the hegemony.

---

[15] Johnson and Ross, *Atlas,* 51.
[16] Walls, in Johnson and Ross, *Atlas*, 48.
[17] Philip Jenkins, *The Lost History of Christianity* (New York, N.Y.: HarperOne, 2008), 3.
[18] *Ibid.*, 3.
[19] *Ibid.*, 1-44.
[20] *Ibid.*, 4.

Jenkins laments the lack of interest among theologians for the destruction of churches and Christian communities.[21] There are practical reasons for this as decline and destruction are more difficult to document than growth and expansion. Yet, knowing the history of the vanished churches and the reasons for their destruction can teach us today about the relationship between Christianity and other religions, and not least about the situation in the West, and particularly Europe, where secularization and decline of the church coincide with a great influx of Muslim immigrants. The expansion of Islam was the major factor in the decline of the churches in North Africa and the Middle East. This is not to say that all traces of Christianity were removed from these areas. There are important surviving churches, such as the Coptic Church in Egypt, while in other places the church is almost extinct.

The fate of the destroyed churches should warn us of a naïve, triumphalistic understanding of Christian mission, expansion and globalisation. Persecution, oppression, discrimination, secularisation etc. are serious threats to the church's existence and growth even today in many parts of the world. It cannot be taken for granted the churches may not also in the future decline or even disappear.

The global church today exists in an almost overwhelming diversity, reflecting of course the diversity of the local churches. This diversity is due in part to the cross-cultural expansion of the church. As the church crosses cultural boundaries, the gospel has to be translated into new languages, and new theologies and practices have to be developed on the basis of local languages and cultures with their particular worldviews. In addition, various ecclesial traditions representing both historical and more recent denominational identities are also spread around the globe, adding to diversity and sometimes causing serious division.

Sebastian and Kirsteen Kim claim that there are six ways in which Christianity today may be described as a 'world religion': topographically, theologically, geographically, socio-politically, historically, and structurally.[22] We cannot of course discuss all these dimensions here, but would like to emphasize that Christianity is a religion which today is spread across the globe in a way as never before, being practiced in local churches of great variety (topographical, geographical). The global spread and the local reality of the church in all its variety are among the empirical facts that are open to scientific investigation and are studied by a number of sciences, including social sciences, such as sociology of religion and anthropology of religion. Kim and Kim also point out that world Christianity today is not a result of attempts by powerful churches to replicate themselves but are the result of indigenous response and grassroots movements.[23] Structurally Christianity is transnational and Christians around the world are connected to one another through many

[21] *Ibid.*, 28ff.

[22] Sebastian Kim and Kirsteen Kim, *Christianity as a World Religion* (London: Continuum, 2008), 1-2.

[23] *Ibid.*, *Christianity*, 2.

different structures or networks.[24] Christianity is also a world religion theologically since it claims to be "universally applicable and locally inclusive."[25] This open invitation and global vision of the church is also underlined by Kenneth Cragg when he writes,

> Not, clearly, a universally successful salvation; for that would be to override the precious freedom of the soul; but a universally accessible salvation where accident of birth... would not determine life in Christ. "Thou hast opened the kingdom of heaven to all believers" – to Jew and Greek, with their different reasons, an impossible largesse. For faith, unlike race or elegance, remains within the reach of all.[26]

We want to take another brief look at the theological dimension, the fundamental universality of the church, the global vision. The universal perspective in the Scriptures, and specifically the New Testament is dealt with elsewhere.[27] It is, however, interesting to see how this global vision has influenced the mission of the church down through the ages.

The church historian Oskar Skarsaune points out that both in the ancient and the medieval church the universal vision of the New Testament is carried forward, especially in connection with the understanding of the apostolate. But even when *apostle* was not longer used as a term for missionaries, the missionary function did not cease. Skarsaune quotes the church father Origen, who says, "The Christians do not fail to do what they can to spread the word everywhere in the world."[28] This universal vision is also confirmed by other church fathers.

The reformer Martin Luther has been criticized for lack of interest in mission. Yet he may clearly express the view that the double universalism of mission, to the end of time and to the ends of the world, is still valid. His explanation of the second petition in Lord's prayer in the Large Catechism has a clear universal perspective: "This we ask, both in order that we who have accepted it remain faithful and grow daily in it and also in order that it may find approval and gain followers among other people and advance with power throughout the world."[29]

Jumping to the more recent past we may mention as an example that the founder of missiology as an academic discipline in Norway, Olav Guttorm Myklebust, who served as the first professor of mission studies at MF Norwegian School of Theology, held a lecture at a conference in Durban, South Africa, in 1938, in which he raised the very fundamental question: "Do we have the right to 'force' our faith upon other people? ... Can we in this world of

---

[24] *Ibid.*, *Christianity*, 2.
[25] *Ibid.*, *Christianity*, 2.
[26] Kenneth Cragg, *The Christian and Other Religion* (London: Mowbrays, 1977), 57.
[27] Cf. Eckhard J.Schnabel's chapter in this book.
[28] Oskar Skarsaune, 'Misjonstenkningen i oldtiden og middelalderen', in Berentsen *et al.*, *Missiologi i Dag*, 89; cf. Origen: *Contra Celsum* III, 9.
[29] Jan-Martin Berentsen, 'Misjonstenkningen 1500-1900', in Berentsen *et al.*, *Missiologi i Dag*, 107-108; Kolb and Wengert, *Book of Concord*, 447.

relativity… seriously maintain the thought of the church as steward of an absolute truth?" He answers the questions himself, "There is only one name through which we are saved – Christ… but if the foundation of our salvation is not religion or philosophy or politics, but the work of God in Christ, there is an undeniable duty for every Christian to participate in bringing the message to all that is called human."[30] In this early article by Myklebust the missionary task of the church is seen as universal. The theological reason for this universality is God's revelation in Christ and his work of redemption. The universality of the mission of the church has a Trinitarian basis, in God's universal plan of salvation, in the sending of Christ and the universal scope of his redemptive work and the universal pouring out of the Spirit.[31]

Global Variety and Universal Truth

We have already stated that the global church that has come into existence in an unprecedented way in the late twentieth and early twenty-first centuries, has enormous variety. Many missiologists have argued that this variety reflects a characteristic feature of Christianity closely related to its universality: it crosses boundaries, particularly cultural ones, and in doing so is translated in a wide sense into the language, thought form and lifestyles of ever new people. This does not reduce the content of Christian theology but enriches it. Walls expresses this view in the following way,

> Another generalisation from Christian history is that the transmission of the faith involves translation, and translation leads to theological expansion. Translation is fundamental to the Christian understanding of revelation, and thus of how God deals with humanity… The central affirmation about the Incarnation is itself about a sort of translation. Christ is God translated into humanity, not as a loan word, but as part of the functioning system of the language.[32]

Languages and cultures are always particular, never universal. This raises the question how a universal message, a universal truth, can be carried by particular languages and cultures. Modern linguistic theory has also pointed out that we do not have access to reality except through language. Any access to God may be mediated through words, Christ being God's ultimate revelation, Logos, the Word (Jn 1:1,14).

The translation of the message started already in the New Testament when the gospel and the church were taken from the Jewish cultural context to the

---

[30] Quoted in Olav Guttorm Myklebust, *Det Store Oppdrag* (Oslo: Privat trykk, 1988), 16-17. See a more detailed discussion of the global perspective in mission in Tormod Engelsviken, 'Det globale perspektiv i misjonen', in Bernt T. Oftestad and Nils Aksel Røsæg (eds*), Mellom Kirke og Akademia. Det Teologiske Menighetsfakultet 100 År, 1908-2008* (Trondheim: Tapir Akademisk Forlag, 2008), 391-403.

[31] A further presentation of the Trinitarian basis and universal scope of mission can be found in Jan-Martin Berentsen, Tormod Engelsviken and Knud Jørgensen, 'Grunntrekk i misjonens teologi', in Berentsen *et al., Missiologi i Dag*, 173-186.

[32] Walls, 'Christianity', in Johnson and Ross, *Atlas*, 49.

Hellenistic. The Hebrew or Aramaic idiom was replaced by Hellenistic idiom. Walls writes:

> Christ had so far been translated into the specific humanity of Jewish Palestine. Christ must now be retranslated into the flesh of Hellenistic East Mediterranean society.... The message about Christ had to penetrate beyond language, in the sense of the translation of words; it has to pass into the local systems of thinking and choosing, the networks of relationships that make up identity.[33]

The term contextualization or inculturation are the terms most frequently used today to describe this form of comprehensive translation, at least as seen in the so-called 'translation model' of contextualization. The view that "contextualization is a theological imperative"[34] is generally agreed upon. The recognized fact that the Christian gospel cannot be expressed in a non-contextualized form; that all theology is contextual since language and culture are particular, seems to raise an important question, which in my opinion has not be satisfactorily answered in today's missiology. What is the message that should be contextualized? How can there be a universal and absolute truth when all contextualized expressions of it seem to be local and relative?

There seems to be a common assumption among missiologists dealing with contextualization that a contextualized form of Christianity is a relative, non-universal form of Christianity. In Bevans' description of the 'translation model' he argues that those who favour this model insist that that the gospel is an unchangeable message. When Bevans is critical of this model he seems to assume that those who favour the model believe that the gospel can be expressed in a 'supracultural' or 'supracontextual' way, which is not possible. Another assumption seems to be that any contextual form of the message cannot be universal or normative for all.

I would argue, however, that there are contextual forms of the Christian message that are universally valid: the biblical contextualization of God's revelation in word and deed and in the incarnate Son of God, Jesus Christ, is universal and therefore normative for all other contextualizations, even though they took place within Hebrew and Hellenistic culture. The translation model, as I understand it, means that one contextualized form of the message – not a supracultural, supracontextual essential form of the message, is translated into another contextualized form. The biblical contextualizations have taken place under the guidance of the Spirit of God and represent God's special revelation in history. They come to us through the Scriptures and give the Scriptures their unique authority in the church.

As far as they are genuine expositions of the original contextualization in the Scriptures, creeds and confessions as well as other theological statements may also have universal validity and authority. This may apply to the ancient creeds such as the Nicene Creed and the Apostles' Creed. In another place I have

---

33 *Ibid.*

34 Stephen B. Bevans, *Models of Contextual Theology* (Maryknoll, N.Y.: Orbis Books, 1992), 15.

argued that it also applies to the Lutheran Confessions, such as the Augsburg Confession in so far as (*quatenus*) and because (*quia*) they are a presentation and explication of the gospel and a trustworthy summary of the faith of the (universal) Christian church. This does not of course preclude that also other contextualized expressions of Christian doctrine may be universally authoritative.[35] Neither does it mean that we have to transfer these contextualisations verbatim into other contexts. The universally valid contextual forms of the message need themselves to be contextualized in a never ending process.

This view of a universally valid expression of the Christian faith in the midst of the enormous theological and ecclesial diversity in the global church, raises further the question of the *content* of this expression. In light of this, one may ask: What are the necessary and universally valid elements in a universal theology, and how can they be a criterion for evaluating the church on different levels, local and global? Is there a common identity, a real continuity through the centuries regardless of shifting cultures and contexts? How may the one nature and mission of the church be realized in different historical contexts? In answering these questions the main focus should not be the organization of the church or the characteristics of the national or denominational churches, but the local church, the 'church here with us', and the universal, global church in the world. As we have seen, a local and a global perspective are necessary in missional ecclesiology. What are the main features of the mission that resulted in the establishment of the local churches and therefore also of the global church?

The church was the result of a mission that initially was directed towards Jews but later included Gentiles and aimed at 'all nations'. The central feature of this missionary movement was the preaching of the Gospel of the kingdom of God in word and deed with a call for conversion and an invitation to faith in Jesus Christ, with the promise of forgiveness of sin and eternal life (Mk 1:15; Acts10:43, Jn 3:16). It was also an invitation to be incorporated in the church as the people of God. The church consisted of those who responded to this call in repentance and faith and were included in the church through baptism (Acts 2:38-41).

As the people of God, belonging to his kingdom, the church is called to live in loving communion with God. It is a pilgrim people on the way through this world towards the final goal of the church which is perfect communion with God, 'face to face', and to serve and worship him forever in his new creation (Rev 7:9-17; 21:1-5; Rom 8:22-23). This is the ultimate goal of the whole of God' saving activity in the world (salvation history).

---

[35] See to the contextualization of the Lutheran Confession, Tormod Engelsviken, 'Kontekstualisering av den lutherske bekjennelse', in Torleiv Austad, Tormod Engelsviken and Lars Østnor (eds), *Kirkens Bekjennelse i Historisk og Aktuelt Perspektiv. Festskrift til Kjell Olav Sannes* (Trondheim: Tapir Akademisk Forlag, 2010), 173-186.

As the people of God the church is a sign and an instrument of this salvation, which is already available in Christ but will be perfectly realized only in the future at the return of Christ in power when he will establish his eternal kingdom. To accomplish this task the church is sent by God to the world. In this sense the church is, as we have already seen, missional by nature, by being sent. This sending or mission (*missio Dei,* the mission of God) with the message of salvation takes place on the background of the lostness of people without Christ, variously described as death, sin, guilt, slavery, alienation, etc. (e.g. Eph 2:1-3,12). In its mission the church not only calls individuals to faith but it also plants new congregations and forms new churches made up of those who have come to faith (*plantatio ecclesiae*). The growth and multiplication of the church is one of the main goals of mission.

In its mission the church has primarily a ministry of witness through the proclamation of the gospel in various forms (Greek: *martyria,* Acts 1,8), through the communion of the people of God with one another (Greek: *koinonia*), through various forms of service towards other members of the body of Christ and towards the world (Greek: *diakonia*), and through prayer and worship of God (Greek: *leiturgia*). It may also include God's affirmation of the gospel through accompanying signs (Greek: *semeia,* signs, Rom 15:20; Acts 14:3).

The 'priestly' nature of the people of God in conveying salvation to the world is most succinctly expressed in 1. Pet. 2:9, where to "declare the praises (or great works) of him who called you out of the darkness" belongs to the very reason why the church is a "chosen people, a royal priesthood, a people belonging to God." Based on this text and others one has rightly spoken of the 'priesthood of all believers' or a 'general priesthood'. One could with equal right speak of a general missionary obligation or the 'mission of all believers'.

The theological reason why the sending of the church is not only an external or accidental attribute of the church but belongs to the nature of the church, is not to be found only in the command and commission of Jesus. It has an even deeper foundation in the nature of the Triune God to whom the church belongs, and his eternal salvation-historical purpose. God is a missionary God, a sending God, who down through human history has sent his word and his servants to the fallen world with a message of salvation, finally accomplished and revealed in the incarnation, life, work, death, resurrection and exaltation of his Son Jesus Christ, who will return in power to renew the whole creation and establish the kingdom of God for ever. Forgiveness of sins and new life are bestowed on all who repent and believe in Jesus Christ (Luk 24:26-27; Jn 3:16; Acts 2:38)). Because salvation is not automatic or universal, but tied to the reception of the gospel message, "a message through which you and all your household will be saved" (Acts 11:14), the knowledge of this message becomes necessary for salvation. The apostle Paul's logical reasoning in Rom 10:13-15 shows how the sending (mission) of messengers to proclaim this message actually is a precondition for people's salvation.

From the time of the Roman Emperor Constantine in the fourth century up until modern times, and even today, the church, especially in the West, has often been allied with political power. This 'Constantinian period' with the idea of a *corpus Christianum* has in recent years come under attack as representing a distorted form of church contradicting the very nature of the church as seen in the Scriptures and the early church. While the folk church or state church system in the past has provided an opportunity to reach the whole people with the gospel, and thus can be given a certain missiological justification, it has been argued in my view convincingly that due to increasing secularisation, pluralization and a reductionist theology, it has become untenable and should be replaced by new forms of the church in mission. Most of the churches in the Global South that form a majority within the global Christian church are minority churches in their own context, not representing the rich and powerful, but more often the poor, the powerless, and the marginalized.

Both the diversity and the expansion of the global church coincide with the phenomenon called globalisation. Robert Schreiter draws on Peter Beyer and Roland Robertson when he defines globalisation: "Globalisation is the extension of the effects of modernity to the entire world, and the compression of time and space, all occurring at the same time."[36] Schreiter points out that this spreading of modernization takes place through its first product, Western culture, and that this creates powerful homogenizing systems. Although they are homogenizing, these systems do not, however, end up homogenizing local cultures altogether. As local cultures reinterpret elements of what Schreiter calls a 'hyperculture' the globalisation process creates plural modernities. In some cultures, e.g. in China, modernity may actually help spur a revival of Christianity.[37] I think something similar may be said about Africa, where modernity may further Christianity (and Islam) as African primal religions at least in their traditional forms are seen by many as obsolete. Modernization may have a secularizing effect in Europe, while in other parts of the world it may contribute to a religious revival. Both of these effects of modernization are obviously very significant for missiology.

The 'Heart' or Essence of the Gospel

The spread and diversity of the global church raise the question of Christian identity. What is the essence of the gospel and the characteristic features of Christianity, without which a local church does not represent the *Christian* church? One is reluctant today to use terms such as heretic or syncretistic. Yet the question of whether a local church belongs inside or outside the real Christian global church may be increasingly relevant in a religiously pluralistic era. The term Christian may actually be used to describe not only differing

[36] Robert J. Schreiter, *The New Catholicity. Theology Between the Global and the Local* (Maryknoll, N.Y.: Orbis Books, 1997), 8.
[37] Schreiter, *The New Catholicity*, 10-11.

denominations or Christian traditions but different religions. Churches such as Jehovah's Witnesses or the Mormon Church may belong in this category. But the question may also be raised with regard to other churches such as the Kimbanguist church or some representatives of the originally American prosperity gospel.

The World Council of Churches has in its basis a reference to the Trinity, to Jesus Christ as God and Savior and to the Holy Scriptures. Agreement with this basis is a requirement for membership.

In addition, adherence to the ancient creeds, implicitly or explicitly, particularly the Nicene Creed, has been seen as necessary in order to be called Christian. Yet this may represent only a minimum.

An interesting attempt was made in the Lausanne consultation on gospel and culture in Bermuda in 1978 to define 'the heart of the gospel':

> We recognize as central the themes of God as Creator, the universality of sin, Jesus Christ as Son of God, Lord of all, and Savior through his atoning death and risen life, the necessity of conversion, the coming of the Holy Spirit and his transforming power, the fellowship and mission of the Christian church, and the hope of Christ's return.[38]

The consultation statement goes on to say that, "while these are basic elements of the gospel, it is necessary to add that no theological statement is culture-free. Therefore, all theological formulations must be judged by the Bible itself, which stands above them all." Even in this description of the heart of the gospel some will miss important elements, such as an explicit reference to the Trinity, to faith (it may be included in the term 'conversion'), to the sacraments of baptism and holy communion, and the authority of the Scriptures.

My intention here is not to enter into an extensive discussion of what should be regarded as the unchanging 'heart of the gospel'. My main point is to make it clear that in the midst of an enormous emphasis on contextualization and the responses to the gospel in a great variety of contextual theologies and church practices, there is a necessity to focus on the common elements, that which create a genuine common Christian identity and are faithfully reflecting God's revelation as given in the Bible.

The Marks of the Church

The nature of the church has theologically been described with the so-called attributes, or characteristic marks of the church (*notae ecclesiae*). The church according to the Nicene Creed has four marks. It is one, holy, catholic and apostolic. All of these marks are essential for the mission of the church and may be interpreted in a missiological perspective.

---

38 *The Willowbank Report* (Wheaton, Ill: Lausanne Committee for World Evangelization, 1978), 12-13.

The *unity* of the church is a theological reality grounded in the one Triune God, the one faith, the one body, the one baptism and the one hope of the church. Yet the unity should be visibly realized and demonstrated in the life of the church. Christian unity is a strong testimony to the world. This is expressed in Jesus' prayer: "May they be one in us so that the world may believe that you have sent me" (Jn 17:21). Ecumenical endeavours to demonstrate and enhance Christian unity are therefore a Christian obligation. Such endeavours do not, however, preclude disagreement and even confrontation on truth issues, neither does it imply one uniform church structure. For historical, contextual and missiological reasons the church may, as we have seen, appear in a variety of forms. 'Unity in reconciled diversity' may express this reality. Evangelicals will emphasize that there are limits to diversity, and that visible unity in fellowship, work and witness is dependent upon sharing the same biblical faith (*The Lausanne Covenant*, Par. 7).

The *holiness* of the church should not be seen as an empirical quality, as ethical perfection, but as an expression of the fact that the church is God's saved people set apart from the world. Its holiness is a divine gift due to the sanctifying work of Christ and the Holy Spirit (1 Cor 1:30-31; Acts 20:28,32). In this sense all Christians are saints (1 Cor 1:2). The church is the *communio sanctorum*, the fellowship of holy people (The Apostles' Creed). This holiness should, however, be increasingly realized in the lives of Christians and Christian communities through a process of renewal and transformation (Rom 12:1-2). As a holy, loving people serving God and the needy the church exerts an attraction on the world and invites people to give praise to God (Mt 5:16).

The *catholicity* of the church means that it is universal, consisting of members from the whole world, from all peoples and cultures. As we have already seen, in most of its history the church has been universal in its intention; in our time this universality is realized in an empirical way. The catholicity of the church may come to expression in slogans such as, "The whole church taking the whole gospel to the whole world" (cf. e.g. *The Lausanne Covenant*, Par. 6).

Schreiter has called for a 'new catholicity' as a theological response to the challenge of globalisation. This catholicity will firstly be characterized by wholeness. "One must posit a certain commensurability of cultures, in the sense that all cultures may receive the Word of God and be able in some measure to communicate with one another, despite real and legitimate differences."[39] Secondly, it should be aware of fragmented and partial experience of culture by many people throughout the world. He asks for a "new theology of culture."[40] In addition to wholeness there is also a need for fullness of faith, with orthodoxy. This quest for fullness must also include orthopraxis, to identify different goals (*teloi*) for humanity. The Pauline vision of reconciliation as the "new creation" (2 Cor 5:17) may offer such a *telos.*[41] Schreiter concludes,

---

[39] Schreiter, *The New Catholicity*, 128-129.
[40] *Ibid.*, 130.
[41] *Ibid.*, 131.

> A new catholicity, then, is marked by a wholeness of inclusion and fullness of faith in a pattern of intercultural exchange and communication. To the extent that this catholicity can be realized, it may provide a paradigm for what a universal theology may look like today, able to encompass both sameness and difference, rooted in an orthopraxis providing *teloi* for a globalized society.[42]

The *apostolicity* of the church primarily means that the church is built on the faith and words of the apostles as expressed in the New Testament (Eph 2:19-22). All churches that share the apostolic faith according to the biblical testimony also share in the apostolicity of the church, regardless of differing views of 'apostolic succession' relating primarily to the bishop's office. The church is also apostolic because it is sent in mission and evangelism. 'Apostle' means a messenger, a 'sent one', being derived from the Greek *apostello,* send. As apostolic the church is also a missional church, sent to the world, and itself sending witnesses to the world with the gospel.

The Protestant Reformation in the sixteenth century took up, as we have already seen, the questions of the marks of the church. The Lutheran church has in a classical way expressed its understanding of the church as the assembly of saints (or believers), where the gospel is preached purely and the sacraments administered rightly (CA, VII). This means that the church is seen as a fellowship of human beings, and not primarily as an institution. The church is visibly existing in this world, with God-given means of grace as characteristics or signs. The means of grace (the word and the sacraments) are in the Lutheran understanding so important because God through them creates faith and thus builds his church. The 'saints' in the church are not perfect, sinless people, but people whose sins have been forgiven through faith in Jesus Christ and who are in a process of sanctification. The Reformed tradition has a similar understanding of the church but is more than the Lutheran tradition occupied with the structure of the church, its (four) offices, and church discipline as one of the marks of the church.

The so-called Radical Reformation or what is often today called the 'free church' or 'believers' church' movement, would emphasize separation of the church from the political powers in opposition to the state church system that was to become the historical model of the magisterial reformation. The church consists of voluntary members who have joined the church through personal conversion and 'believers' baptism' as opposed to the folk church where all citizens are church members through infant baptism. This movement would also add more characteristics of the church, such as ethical holiness and church discipline, the mission and witness of all members, and brotherly love and service.[43]

In revival movements of the eighteenth and nineteenth century, such as Pietism, Puritanism, and Methodism the spiritual and ecclesial ideals of the

[42] *Ibid.*, 132-133.

[43] See too the free church model John Howard Yoder and Michael G. Cartwright (eds), *The Royal Priesthood. Essays Ecclesiological and Ecumenical* (Scottdale, PA.: Herald Press, 1998).

Reformation came closer to realization through the establishment of *ecclesiolae in ecclesia,* smaller fellowships of converted, believing Christians within the larger framework of state or folk churches. In these fellowships the priesthood of all believers in terms of new life (sanctification), Bible study, prayer, testimony, mission and even organization could be developed in a way that made these revival Christians an instrument of spiritual renewal and evangelical mission.

In the nineteenth century almost all Protestant churches in the West, folk churches as well as free churches, got its own mission work, with the express aim of establishing independent churches in all parts of the world. The principles of self-supporting, self-propagating and self-governing churches were seen by many as expressions and requirements of independence.

In the Pentecostal and Charismatic movements of the twentieth century a special emphasis has been placed on the work of the Holy Spirit in equipping the church and its members for ministry and mission through the experience of the baptism/fullness of the Spirit with resulting empowerment and exercise of spiritual gifts (charismata), including speaking in tongues, prophecy and healing. They would insist that one of the marks of the church is that it is charismatic. In this connection miraculous 'signs' are seen as another mark of the true church in mission. By insisting that the missional church is charismatic, the Pentecostal/charismatic movements have significantly contributed to the recovery of a biblical missional ecclesiology.[44]

After the colonial period which ended around 1960, most churches in the Global South have become independent, missional churches, and a new era of mission in and from the South has begun. Today, the churches in the South, even when they are the result of the missionary endeavours of mainline denominations in the past, have many of the characteristics of the 'believers' church' movement, and of the Pentecostal/Charismatic movement.

Although there are certain marks and functions of the church that are necessary for its life and growth, no specific church structure or organization is prescribed as universally valid in the New Testament. Nevertheless, empirical studies of growing and missional churches both in the North and the South tend to show certain common characteristic features of theology, spirituality and structure.[45] They emphasize what may be called biblical, evangelical Christianity, often with a strong charismatic dimension, and with an integrated holistic missional perspective on the nature and task of the church. The churches foster a missional spirituality and motivation with close human relations through teaching, preaching and testimonies, through prayer and intercession, through social ministry, and personal care, through sacrificial

---

[44] See Veli-Matti Kärkkäinen, *An Introduction to Ecclesiology. Ecumenical, Historical and Global Perspectives* (Downers Grove, Ill.: IVP Press, 2002).

[45] See e.g. a case study of missional charismatic churches in Malaysia in Tormod Engelsviken, 'Den misjonale kirke og utfordringen fra kirken i sør', in Tormod Engelsviken and Kjell Olav Sannes (eds*), Hva vil det si å være kirke? Kirkens vesen og oppdrag* (Trondheim: Tapir Akademisk Forlag, 2004), 69-92.

giving and living, and through the ministries of the gifts of the Spirit. They also show the importance of developing contextually appropriate structures, forms of service and liturgy in order for the missionary task of the church to be fulfilled both locally and globally. 'Fresh expressions of the church' or 'emerging churches' are among the labels being used to characterize some new contextual forms of the church in mission, churches that draw on biblical principles, merge ancient and modern spirituality, exhibit great creativity and allow radical change in historical forms in order to enable the church for contextual mission in the twenty-first century.[46]

The Glocal Church

Charles van Engen has in an important article argued that, "In the twenty-first century, the church of Jesus Christ needs to be self-consciously what it in fact already is: a *glocal* church." This means that, "it is active simultaneously in global and local mission that dynamically fosters the glocal interaction between the global and the local."[47]

Carrying this perspective forward I would argue that the present local church whether it lives in the North or the South should have a double vision, a vision for both the local and the global. In the past it has sometimes been an either-or. Some local churches have been primarily, or exclusively, occupied with the local challenges, neglecting the global vision for bringing the gospel to the ends of the earth or having fellowship with the global church. On the other hand some congregations or organizations have been almost exclusively occupied with those far away and being limited with regard to serving people locally. Partly due to globalisation there are today new opportunities to practice a glocal vision. Traditional mission as sending out of missionaries is still very relevant, but the role of the missionaries may change. They may in new ways become brokers or bridge builders between the local and the global church and their cultures. As more and more people are able to travel long distances, exchange between churches and personal contacts between ordinary church members may lead to enhanced understanding and new forms of ministry. Global mission or ecumenical networks such as the World Council of Churches, the World Evangelical Alliance and the Lausanne Movement, and confessional communions such as the Lutheran World Federation may also facilitate contact and exchange between local churches all over the world, as well as facilitate a necessary global discourse on theology and mission. The list could be made longer, to include migration, exchange and training of clergy and other church

---

[46] See Eddie Gibbs and Ryan K. Bolger, *Emerging Churches* (Grand Rapids, MI.: Baker Academic*); Mission-Shaped Church: Church Planting and Fresh Expressions of the Church in a Changing Context* (London: Church House Publishing, 2004).

[47] Charles E. Van Engen, 'The Glocal Church: Locality and Catholicity in a Globalizing World', in Craig Ott and Harold A. Netland (eds), *Globalizing Theology: Belief and Practice in an Era of World Christianity* (Grand Rapids, MI.: Baker Academic, 2006), 157.

workers in other cultural contexts, tentmakers etc. to indicate the enormous possibilities of combining a local and global vision.

I would like to close by quoting van Engen again as he ponders the missional significance of the glocal church:

> A truly catholic local group of believers is in fact the local manifestation of the universal glocal church… These glocal believers – no matter where they are in the world – are therefore commissioned to be "witnesses in Jerusalem, *and* in all Judea *and* in Samaria, *and* to the ends of the earth" (Acts 1:8) simultaneously. Thus, a healthy glocal group of believers in this new century must be involved, at the same time, in God's mission locally and globally, that is glocally…. May we all learn to become in practice who we are: one glocal church of Jesus Christ."[48]

---

[48] Van Engen, 'The Glocal Church', in Ott and Netland (eds), *Globalizing Theology*, 179.

A Response to Tormod Engelsviken: Early Asian Mission to Asia

Egil Grandhagen[1]

When did the church become global? The question is, of course, impossible to answer in an appropriate way. It depends on how we define 'global'. In case we choose a geographical approach, we sometimes get the impression that the church became global during the time of the Reformation when Roman Catholic missionaries in great numbers invaded Asia and the two Americas. Or, that it happened during the so called 'Great Century', the nineteenth century, when the Protestant missionary movement went to Africa and the great countries of Asia, e.g. India and China.

This description, however, is a serious devaluation of the missionary power of the ancient church. Western missiologists and church historians have outlined the missionary movement of the first Christian centuries in the following way. The first century Christians brought the gospel to Asia Minor and to Europe. During the fourth century Christianity became the dominant religion of the Roman Empire. Later Constantine could proclaim Christianity to be the official religion of his Empire. Then, from about 1200, the church of the West sends its first missionaries to Asia. The evangelization of the non-European continents is seen as a movement from North to South.

I appreciate that Engelsviken, in accordance with Philip Jenkins in his book *The Lost History of Christianity*, calls for a reappraisal of the vigorous churches of the Middle East and Africa from the first century on up to the Muslim invasion. The history of missions is not a movement from the Middle East to Europe, and from Europe as departing point to the 'heathen' continents. The history of missions has its starting point in Jerusalem, and from there it moves into all four directions. When Paul went from Asia Minor to Macedonia and introduced the Good News to our continent, Jewish Christians from the Palestinian area most likely preached the Gospel in large Jewish synagogues in Alexandria. At a very early stage of history Christians went south into Nubia and present Eritrea and Ethiopia. From the Red Sea coast there were trade routes across the Indian Ocean to the Malabar Coast of India. There are signs indicating a Christian presence there by the end of the second century.

---

[1] Editors' note: Prof. Grandhagen fell sick shortly after the symposium and has not had an opportunity to work on his response. The general bibliography has been put together by the editors after consultation with Grandhagen.

From the Syrian churches missionaries went east to Edessa, which was a significant crossroads near the end of the Silk Road. Edessa was the capital of a small kingdom on the border between the Roman and Persian Empires, called Osroëne, which one hundred years later became the first Christian state! Most likely there was a group of Christians in Edessa as early as before the end of the first century. Tradition strongly affirms one of the seventy disciples of our Lord, Teophilos, to be the founder of that church. His Syrian name was Addai, and the Church of the East has for almost 2,000 years had a memory about the poor disciple who came to their area and preached the gospel for the very first time. Edessa became the cradle of one of the largest churches of all Christianity. It is located where the Eufrates makes a left turn right before it flows down the Mesopotamian Valley. During the second and third centuries this beautiful area became the first stronghold of Christianity in the Persian part of Asia, just as North Africa and Asia Minor did within the Roman Empire.

This means that those bringing the Good News of Jesus Christ eastwards into Asia, were all Asians. And those who brought the gospel further West and South from Àlexandria, were most likely all Africans. The power and vision of this missionary outreach were remarkable – as were the results. Great theologians and church leaders were African: Tertullian, Origen, Clement, Cyrill, Athanasios and Augustine to name a few.

The church in Western Europe soon experienced great difficulties. The Western part of the Roman Empire was turned upside down by the immigration, if not to say the invasion, of Gothic and Germanic tribes. The Western Roman Empire collapsed under this pressure and the church suddenly woke up finding itself a religious minority in their old lands. The immigrants were partly Arian Christians, partly stark pagans. Suddenly, the church in the Western Roman Empire found herself fully occupied bringing the Arian heretics back to orthodox Catholic faith, and to evangelize the pagans within their own borders. All the energy of the Western European Church was directed towards what we would name 'inner mission'! The Persian Church, however, is now fully occupied in spreading the gospel further East. In the year 225 AD there were 13 bishoprics in Mesopotamia, two in the Persian Mainland and one in Arabia. An ancient author around 200 AD mentions that there are Christians among the Parthans, Medians, Persians, Bactrians and Gelians. In 315 AD the bishops within the Persian area gathered for the first church synod. A bishop was elected as the leader of the whole church to maintain the relationship to the Zoroastrian government.

In 410 AD, 40 bishops gathered in the Persian capital Seleukia Ctesiphon for the constitutional meeting of the church. At this meeting the church of the East was formally organized and administratively separated from the patriarchate in Antioch. At the same time the meeting stressed that this church is part of the universal church by accepting the Nicene-Constantinopolitan Creed. Later the resolutions of Chalcedon 451 were accepted as well.

The church of the East never became a state church. The Christians were all the time a minority. By the Milan edict in 313 the persecutions ended in the

Roman Empire. Christianity in the West then went into the 'Constantinian period'. Asia never did see a Constantine. From 313 onwards the Christians in Persia were suspected of siding with the enemy, and the persecutions started. First almost the entire leadership of the church was killed. Then the Zoroastrian state targeted the Christians who had converted from the religion of the state, Zoroastrianism. Finally, by the year 448, 153,000 Christians were massacred in Kirkut during some few days. The persecutions during the Sassanid Persians were most likely the worst that the world has ever seen against a religious minority.

One more element of the ancient Persian church is to be noted. They established a theological education in Edessa (later moved to Nisibis) which had surprising dimensions. The school had more than 1,000 students, keeping a high academic standard. It had outstanding teachers as Narsai and Abraham. The school recruited a large number of church leaders and missionaries for the church.

The church of the East was able to communicate the gospel to a large number of cultures and religious groups. They met amazing response among the Semitic Mesopotamians, the Zoroastrian Persians, Shamanist Central Asian nomads, the Taoist and Buddhist Chinese, and Arabs and Indians. They adequately communicated the Good News to the Muslims who often discriminated them because of their inferior *dhimmi-status*. Nevertheless numbers of Muslims were converted to Christianity. Contextualization was practised by the church long before the time of modernity!

This means that from the time of the ancient church up to the Muslim conquests by the end of the eighth century, the church was widely spread on three continents. In Asia the church flourished until the breakdown of the Mongolian Empire during the fourteenth century. Jenkins is right when he argues that many aspects of Christianity that we conceive of as modern, were in fact "the norm in the distant past: globalisation, the encounter with other faiths and the dilemmas of living under hostile regimes." This tells us that the global church is not merely a modern phenomenon. The ancient and medieval church was global as well. It was far less diverse than the church after the time of Reformation, and it has displayed models of communication across cultural barriers that surprise us even today. And they knew more about persecution than the church of our time.

The question to be asked is this: Why has this become 'the lost history of Christianity'? Is this the Euro-American mind which loves to think that all important movements start from the West?

By the way, the first European missionary to Asia was the Franciscan monk John of Plano Carpino. Pope Innocent IV sent him in the year 1245 to the Great Khan of the Mongols. After almost a year of suffering on horseback through Sibiria, he finally reached the tent of the Mongol leader in Karakorum. But to his surprise he observed an even bigger tent before the tent of the Great Khan, with a Syrian cross on the top. After a while he was told that it was the church of the Christians. A number of generals in the army were Christians. The wife of Tolui, the youngest son of Gengis Khan was a dedicated Christian.

The missionary from Europe was not the first one to proclaim the Gospel in Asia, and he went back confused and disappointed. His European worldview did not work.[2]

---

[2] Sources used when working on this response have been P. Jenkins, *The Lost History of Christianity* (New York: HarperOne, 2008); A. Mingana, 'The Early Spread of Christianity in Central Asia and the Far East,' *Bulletin of the John Rylands Library*, 9, no. 2 (1925), 297-371; S. H. Moffett, *A History of Christianity in Asia, bd. I* (New York: Orbis, 1998); O. Skarsaune, 'Korset i lotusblomsten. Den glemte kristendomshistorien i Asia,' *Årbok 1997. Det Norske Videnskaps-akademi* (Oslo, 2001), 276-294; N.N. Thelle, *Kristendommen i China under T'ang, Yuan, Ming og Ch'in. Studier i Chinas misjonshistories tre første perioder* (København: Gads Forlag, 1949); W.A. Wigram, *An Introduction to the History of the Assyrian Church: Or the Church of the Sassanid Persian Empire* (Whitefish: Kessinger Publishing, 1910/2004).

Religion and Globalisation: An Anthropological Perspective

Asle Jøssang

Through the centuries, the world has become gradually more interconnected by means of exploration and travel, commerce, wars, colonialism and migration. It is only in recent years, however, that the term 'globalisation' has captured our attention as a catchword for describing both "the compressing of the world and the intensification of our conscious awareness of the world as a totality."[1] Impressive developments in electronic communication and means of transport, in transnational flows of capital, goods, people, information, and symbols have bounded the world together in ways that reach even the most remote human settlements.

Early theorists on globalisation such as Marshall McLuhan,[2] envisioned how the shrinkage of the world into a 'global village' would create the conditions for common rèferences and generate harmonious homogenization. In recent years, however, opposite developments are increasingly capturing our attention. The spreading of artefacts and symbols do not produce uniform meanings locally, even though there are instances that may come very close. In fact, the very fact of bringing elements into close proximity with each other generate increased tensions and conflicts. Studying globalisation from the bottom up, instead of top down as did McLuhan, brings real, empirically based variables into the equation, and nuances our understanding of what is really going on. The anthropological perspective termed *glocalization* is an important contribution in this regard. It states that significances and meanings are always created locally as reactions and adaptations to the flow of things, ideas and phenomena that come from the outside. Their actual realizations are always local and embedded in locally constituted life-worlds and relations of power.[3]

---

[1] Roland Robertson, *Globalisation: Social Theory and Global Theory* (London: Sage Publications, 1992), 8.

[2] Marshall McLuhan, *Understanding Media: The Extension of Man* (Toronto: McGraw Hill, 1964).

[3] E.g. Ted Lewellen, *Anthropology of Globalisation: Cultural Anthropology Enters the 21st Century* (Westport: Bergin & Garvey, 2002), 186.
Thomas Hylland Eriksen, 'Introduction', in Thomas Hylland Eriksen (ed), *Globalisation: Studies in Anthropology* (London: Pluto Press, 2003), 4.

In this paper, I will view the phenomena of globalisation in terms of glocalization, and will especially look into an aspect that is of particular interest to church and mission: the growing awareness of the place and role of religion in the world.[4] The resurgence of religion has forced scholars to retract or at least nuance their theories of secularization about the gradual disappearance of religion because of modernization. A famous case is that of the dean of the sociologists of religion, Peter L. Berger, who introduced the new term *desecularization.*[5] While avoiding repeating the mistake of generalizing theory, Berger's primary perspective is on the role of religion in providing meaning in people's lives. Seeking meaning for life in religion is now recognized to be fully compatible with dominating the intellectual and material instruments of socio-economic progress. A case in point is the growing importance of conservative Protestantism in middle class USA in recent decades. My attention, however, will focus on the significance of religion among the people who seek protection against the "undermining of the taken-for-granted" existence.[6] Using ethnographic data from Latin America, I will look into the resurgence of popular religion and especially the growth of Protestantism in terms of what can be called *disharmonious glocalization.*

Characteristics of Globalisation

Studies on globalisation coincide in pointing out how communicational technologies and structures are key driving forces in causing the world to 'shrink'. Distances in space and time have become irrelevant as information and substances travel at lightning speed. We are witnessing increased interconnection and standardization of production systems, financial and commercial networks. Population groups get and keep in contact with each other as never before through factors such as migration, tourism and electronic communication. Globalized structures are also increasingly vulnerable against damaging effects on a vast scale as witnessed recently through the financial crisis and the spreading of pandemics. While disembeddedness and dislocation take place as phenomena and substances spread out from initiating points, re-embeddedness is what happens when they reach specific points of destinations where effects and meanings are conditioned by local variables.

Studies vary as to what to make of the significance of globalisation. These brief features mentioned so far, actually blend views from two competing scholarly groups.[7] In one group we find the sceptics,[8] while the optimistic

[4] J. Micklethwait and A.Wooldridge, *God is Back: How the Global Revival of Faith is Changing the World.* (New York: The Penguin Press, 2009).

[5] Peter L. Berger, 'The Desecularization of the World: A Global Overview', in Peter L. Berger (ed), *The Desecularization of the World: Resurgent Religion and World Politics* (Washington D.C.: Ethics and Public Policy Center, 1999).

[6] Berger, *The Desecularization of the World*, 11.

[7] Thomas Hylland Eriksen, *Globalisering, åtte nøkkelbegreper* (Oslo: Universitets-forlaget, 2008), 19-25.

globalists form the other.[9] The sceptics argue that while we are witnessing an increasing process of internationalization, the traditional bounded entities such as national states still remain the strongest political units. The other camp, the globalists, argues that the forces of globalisation increasingly challenge national sovereignties. The sceptics emphasize the significance of regional economic blocks such as NAFTA and the EU, the globalists point to how the world economy, generated by multilateral and transnational politics, is evolving into one, single arena. The sceptics stick to classical theories of differences between North and South in terms of distribution of power and wealth, and to the continued, and even increased, significance of national identities, cultures and religions. The globalists, on the other hand, stress increased diffusions, hybridities, and the evolvement of cosmopolitical experiences and attitudes as result of increasing interactions across boundaries.

Eriksen[10] suggests that there is no reason to take a clear position for one or the other. Both sceptic and globalist views can variously shed light upon the understanding of which paths globalisation take. It seems quite obvious, for instance, that the growing global solidarity of environment protection movements and human rights organizations benefit from the instrumental means of increased travel, global communication, and transnational mass media, and this seems to support the view of the evolving of common, cosmopolitical attitudes. That said, it is impossible to neglect how divisions based on religion, ethnicity and nationalisms are on the increase, and that boundaries are very much present in imaginations, perceptions, and in practices.

Glocalization: Both Hybridities and Boundaries

In any circumstance, however, *glocalization* is a very useful and relevant point of entrance to studying which paths globalisation takes. No results of global capitalism, internet, and political Islam etc. are produced apart from what are generated locally. They are mediated by situated human experiences and interpretation, which are shaped by local socio-cultural and religious contexts. The 'glocal' view helps us to understand why certain reactions evolve into cosmopolitical adaptations, while others seem to provoke increased opposition and fragmentation, or, as we shall see forthwith, how some people groups need to seek shelter under the protective canopies of their known worldviews.

This seeming contradiction between fluid cosmopolitanism on the one hand and the creation of boundaries on the other needs to be looked into.

---

[8] E.g. Ramón Pajuelo and Pablo Sandoval, *Globalización y Diversidad Cultural: Una Mirada Desde America Latina* (Lima: Instituto de Estudios Peruanos, 2004); Alex Perry, *Falling off the Edge: Globalisation, World Peace and Other Lies* (London: Pan Books, 2010).

[9] Thomas Friedman, *The World is Flat: A Brief History of the Twenty-first Century* (New York: Farrar, Straus & Giroux, 2005).

[10] Eriksen, *Globalisering, åtte nøkkelbegreper*.

'Syncretism', 'bricolage', 'creolization', and 'hybridity' are among anthropological concepts used to describe cultural mixing, which all agree is a constant feature in all human societies. External inputs are received from the point of view of the receptor's cultural horizon, which mediates what is considered to be feasible, viable, workable and trustworthy. The receptor's idiosyncratic worldview is the active agent in producing new meanings by accommodating the new into the known in conceivable ways.

Then 'known' and the 'new' are themselves results of previous amalgamations. There are, in other words, no zones of intrinsic purity, as hybridity is a continuously dynamic process. Instead of hybridity versus purity, it is "hybridity all the way down".[11] Sciences of human cognition affirm this view by pointing out how learning inevitably is a gradual and evolutionary process of continuous domestication of the new by crossing what Lakoff and Johnson[12] call "metaphorical bridges" – that is, by connecting to something familiar in the new, as when an explorer describes a newly discovered animal by reference to a known one, or when Jesus is compared to a shepherd in order to convey an aspect of his being.

The fact that developments on the international scene rather seem to lead to an increase of boundary making such as ethnic and religious divisions, does not refute the basic premise of cultural mixing. With cultural mixing being a given at the level of the apparatus of cultural learning, we have to look to other dimensions of life such as socio-economic means, positions, and politics to find reasons as to why some instances develop into unproblematic mixings, while others develop into divisions and conflicts.

Cultural mixings evolve more fluidly in circumstances that are perceived to be non-threatening and non-competitive. Elitist strata within international societies, for instance, which are capable of dominating or making use of the instruments of globalisation to their own advantage, may experience and focus on the virtues of cosmopolitanism. The elites are "ecumenical collectors of culture", while at the bottom we tend to find "Balkanization and tribalization as poor people must form sharp defensive boundaries to protect themselves from the effects of globalisation."[13] Although elites and resourceful actors may sometimes utilize local culture and religion for political purposes of opposing foreign influences, a widespread tendency is that political and economic hindrances create have-nots who seek solace and justification in their worldviews, and even generate the necessary rationale to react back with violence. In all areas of life there is always something, if need be, which can be

---

[11] Manuel A. Vásquez and Marie Friedmann Marqueardt, *Globalizing the Sacred: Religion Across the Americas* (New Brunswick: Rutgers University Press, 2003), 59.

[12] George Lakoff and Mark Johnson, *Philosophies in the Flesh: The Embodied Mind and the Challenge to Western Thought* (New York: Basic Books, 1999).

[13] Jonathan Friedman, 'Global Crisis, the Struggle for Cultural Identity, and the Intellectual Porkbarrelling: Cosmopolitans versus Locals, Ethnics, and Nationals in an Era of De-homogenization', in Pnina Werbner and Tariq Mohood (eds), *Debating Cultural Hybridity*, (London: Zed Books. 1997), 85.

selected from the cultural repertoire and be activated and over communicated into a difference. Articulating a difference helps to create defence mechanisms, get into a better position in terms of competing for resources, and keeps perceived threats at bay more effectively.

In the continuation of this paper, I will look at globalisation from the point of view of the disadvantaged, from what we can call the underside of globalisation. As Perry puts it: "For millions of people, globalisation is a story of enduring poverty and widening segregation. It is not difficult to understand why the overriding experience of it is not one of a rising sense of well-being."[14] I will especially study the *epistemological* aspect of glocalization, which means focusing on how people make sense of their experiences of marginalization and loss, what conditions their understanding, and how they react accordingly. This is especially revealing to pursue in so-called holistic societies in which economic, political, cultural and religious aspects weave together into an integrated understanding, and where the spiritual and non-spiritual aspects of life are not differentiated. Sometimes, the new comes with such a force or seems to be too radical to grasp that the conditions for bridging become clogged up. Under such onslaughts, revitalization of the known world is often sought for protective reasons.

Disharmonious Glocalization

Max Weber realized that the material side of the expanding capitalist system, which is the core driving force of globalisation, cannot be separated from cultural concepts facilitating its very creation and expansion. The so-called "disenchantment of the world",[15] that is; freeing the instrumental means from religious rationale, was an important condition for transforming conceptual categories such as the ideas of time and space in order to remain in intellectual control of the developments. In the Western hemisphere, the technical and conceptual dimensions have evolved together in a linear and integrated fashion passing through modernization and accompanying secularization processes. For most Westerners, this has been a fairly unproblematic and smooth process. Innovations have not come as shocking surprises, but have come 'naturally', being conceived as plausible and rational. That is the experience of riding on the top of the wave of globalisation.

From such a point of view, breaking limits of time and space leading to increased disembeddedness and deterritorialization is largely a fascination about what the latest technological wonders can do. To indigenous peasants living in the Andean mountains, for instance, who live under different epistemological conditions, the experience of an encroaching outside world is very different. It is about having to deal with the threatening sensation that the

---

[14] Perry, *Falling Off the Edge*, 27.

[15] Max Weber, *The Protestant Ethic and the Spirit of Capitalism* (New York: Scribner, 1958); Vazquez and Friedmann Marqueardt, *Globalizing the Sacred*, 15.

mountain deity, the *apu*, who normally is in charge of the well-being of all living beings in a given territory, is seemingly losing power and control. It is to be thrown into an anomic crisis.

Anomaly is a term used to describe what happens when fundamental systems of meaning are challenged by something unconceivable and extraordinary, to the point of threatening the known understanding of existence. There are several ways of dealing with anomalies, such as trying to physically eliminate it, avoid it by labelling it as dangerous, ridicule and try to render it powerless through redefinition, or try to reinterpret its meaning by stretching one's worldview in order to accommodate it. *Theodicy* is a termed coined by Weber to refer to how religious explanations are employed in trying to provide meaning for meaning-threatening experiences.[16]

It needs to be mentioned that harmonious insertion into globalisation is not, of course, a simple question of having a secular worldview. Some of the most successful economies in the world that are inserted into the globalized system are located in strongly non-secularized regions such as the Islamic Middle Eastern emirates, the Buddhist South East Asian economic 'tigers', not to mention China and Japan. An important variable to consider in the Asian equation seems to be political control of the means of production, which is a different situation from that experienced in Africa and in Latin America. This paper does not pretend to provide a universally valid theory of globalisation, but focuses on situations in which people experience an anomic situation, being at a loss as to what to think and what to do.

The sociologist of religion, Bernice Martin, draws attention towards the importance of seeing globalisation in the larger epistemological framework of its making. In reference to Latin America, she writes that, "a swift transition is occurring from premodern to postmodern conditions with barely any classically modernist phase intervening."[17] This means that a large majority of the population still live in what Weber would describe as an 'enchanted' world while the material means introduced from the outside are premised on other conditions. Their experience is to have been traumatically catapulted into a crude post-industrialist livelihood situation far beyond one's control and where the still taken for granted holistic worldview seems to come short.

Events in Bolivia illustrate how measures initiated far away turn into what we can call disharmonious glocalization. A telling case is the so-called 'Water War' in Cochabamba. In 1999, the American based transnational company Bechtel was granted commercial control of the water supply to city and surrounding areas by the elitist government at the time. The company raised costs, and this sparked a popular uproar and demonstrations that eventually caused the company to cancel the contract and leave Bolivia. While urbanized

---

[16] Meredith McGuire, *Religion: The Social Context* (Belmont: Wadsworth Publishing Co., 3rd edition, 2008).

[17] Bernice Martin, 'From pre- to postmodernism in Latin America: the case of Pentecostalism', in Paul Heeles (ed), *Religion, Modernity and Postmodernity* (Oxford: Blackwell Publishers, 1998), 108.

and middle-class population groups saw this as an economic and political struggle in a globalized context, the motivation of the surrounding peasant agriculturalists was to force the company to give back 'God's water', which under no circumstance should be stolen and commercialized.[18]

Sometimes the threatening forces from the outside world are staved off; often times, however, people are helpless victims of a mysterious, unseen hand somewhere faraway, as when the anonymously owned transnational Bata shoe manufacturer headquartered in Toronto suddenly decided to lay off hundreds of workers at its Cochabamba plant in Bolivia. Cheaper labor was available on the other side of the planet. This decision was executed on a rational post-structuralist basis in the boardrooms of Toronto, but was received as divine punishment by Quechua migrant workers in Cochabamba, who interpret every misfortune in life in holistic terms of harmony and balance. The divine beings show their approval or disapproval through material means, and, not surprisingly, being laid-off was a bad turn in terms of existential standing.[19]

The Strive to Recover Holistic Harmony

In the opinion of many researchers in Bolivia, there is a persistent correlation between the experience of gloomy and bewildering times and increase in religious activity.[20] Popular pilgrimage sites are visited as never before, and a recurring motive among the pilgrims is to seek extraordinary miracle from a *santo* or *vírgen* (saint or virgin) famous for their powers. Typically, the way to seek help is to make up for some perceived shortcoming, which the unexpected bad experiences one has had to endure are signs of. Through ritual redressing, cosmological balance can be restored, and well-being (*bienestar*) will subsequently return.

These are instances of anomic experiences in which the people involved react according to their acquired plausible structures. Theodicial stretching takes place as people try to make sense of their misfortunes by applying their remedies of ritual redressing in increased doses. Taking the rounds to the famous pilgrimage sites is such a strategy; the more sacrifice this involves in high costs of travel etc., the better are the chances of restoring balance and

---

[18] Jim Shultz, 'The Cochabamba Water War', in Jim Shultz and Melissa Crane Draper (eds), *Dignity and Defiance: Stories from Bolivia's Challenge to Globalisation* (Berkeley: University of California Press, 2009).

[19] Tom Kruse, personal communication, 2002.

[20] E.g. Manuel A. Vásquez, 'Religious Pluralism, Identity, and Globalisation in Latin America', *Religious Studies Review* 26, (1999), 333-341, see also Susana Andrade, *Protestantismo indígena: Procesos de conversión religiosa en la provinica de Chimborazo, Ecuador* (Quito: Abya Yala. 2004); Allison Spedding, *Gracias a Dios y a los achachilas. Ensayos de sociología de la religión en los Andes* (La Paz: Plural Editores, 2004); and Denise Y. Arnold, *Entre los muertos y los diablos y el desarrollo en los Andes* (La Paz: ISEAT, 2008).

obtain blessings. Sometimes, desperation leaves no room for all the ritual redressing and the faithful beg for extraordinary *milagros* (miracles) to take place in their lives.

It is in this context of anomic crisis and theodicial stretching that the extraordinary growth of Protestantism in Latin America may be understood.

Having endured a slow growth rate for decades, Protestantism has enjoyed a remarkable rapid growth in recent years, reaching now about half the population in countries where its numbers are greatest, such as in Guatemala. The sector of Protestantism experiencing most growth is by far 'grass-root' Pentecostal churches, which are informally organized and have close proximity to the constituents' needs and interests.[21] The churches are there to receive and attend to people who have exhausted all their traditional means of rectifying their situations, and now turn to the more powerful means administered and facilitated by Protestantism. Through its mission history, Protestantism has been closely associated especially with United States – that great epitome of wellbeing and success, the attraction above all others for migrants, and therefore generally associated with progress and modernism.[22] From a holistic point if view, this image translates into seeing Protestantism as a powerful tool for betterment in life.

Initially, conversion to Protestantism is not about switching from a distinct worldview to another, but is about incorporating new means into one's innate worldview. It is about theodicial stretching by means of metaphorical bridging; transposing one's innate meaning system on to a new set of instrumental means. A case in point is a man I once met in a Pentecostal congregation in Sucre who said he was taking the rounds among the Protestant congregations in search of who had access "to the most powerful Christ", much as he had previously done when visiting famous pilgrimage shrines. Research on processes of conversion clearly showed basic continuations of pre-conversion understandings, and the transposition of these on to Protestant symbols and practices by means of metaphorical bridging. The reason conversion is perceived to be radically discontinuous, however, is that the transposition is camouflaged by the heavy emphasis on radical change of behaviour.[23]

Conversion to Protestantism, then, brings an increased measure of control over individual and communal destiny and expands the options realistically available in their everyday lives. Converts are very clear that their faith and their church together revolutionize their lives and prospects. A key feature of Protestantism in Latin America is its emphasis on 'parting ways with the world' and to live according to strict moral codes. Much like what the puritan

---

[21] Timothy J. Steigenga and Edward L. Clear, *Conversion of a Continent: Contemporary Religious Change in Latin America* (New Brunswick: Rutgers University Press, 2007), 8.

[22] Vazquez and Friedmann Marquardt, *Globalizing the Sacred*, 25.

[23] A. F. Jøssang, 'Searching for a More Powerful Christ: An Anthropology of Religious Conversion in Bolivia', (PhD thesis, University of Oslo, 2009).

Calvinists and incipient capitalists experienced in Europe,[24] this produces changed personal economies and the possibility of saving money, since one is not allowed to spend on 'vices'. Several researchers view conversion to Protestantism as a strategic, utilitarian move to get ahead socially and economically.[25]

I think, however, that such a reading is too shallow. From a holistic point of view, conversion is a ritual undertaking in order to obtain favours (*bendiciones*) from God. To abstain from vices, attend church regularly, to tithe etc., are all sacrifices for ritual purposes. To honour God by complying with the church's expectancies, is to do one's part in the reciprocal relationship with the divine, which, when balanced, brings harmony and well-being. Given so many problems in life, there seems to be so much to make up for, and one is in urgent need of finding the best means available of redressing the hapless situation. An effective recruitment point to Protestantism lies in family and neighbors seeing how the new puritanical life style of the *hermanos* (brothers and sisters in Christ) bring about real improvement. Economic betterment, however, is not an aim in itself isolated from other aspects of life, but is fused into a total understanding of well-being.

One powerful assumption of Latin American religiosity is the view that the primary business of religion is to seek out and clear away whatever hinders the wellbeing of the persons, whether the hindrance is located in their own sin, in external malevolence, in the actions of negative spirits or whatever. The new popular Protestantism is thus intensely relevant to *this-wordly* concerns, and to explain its remarkable growth in Latin America is to view it in the light of disharmonious glocalization. As Martin puts it, "being Protestant is often precisely what makes the practical difference between riding the wave of social change or being swamped by it."[26]

Concluding Remarks

A current focus on globalisation is on how the amazing technological advances have managed to bind all corners of the world. Nothing takes place anywhere in the world, which is not somehow connected to, and thus affected by, something happening far away. There are different views, however, as to the significance of this 'shrinkage'. In this paper, I have tried to show how the anthropological perspective of *glocalization* helps us see significance as being created locally, and being conditioned by local circumstances and variables. From this point of view, we are able to explain why some individuals, people groups and societies

---

[24] Weber, *The Protestant Ethic and the Spirit of Capitalism.*

[25] E.g. Sheldon Annis, *God and Production in a Guatemalan Town* (Austin: University of Texas Press, 1987), Elizabeth Brusco, *The Reformation of Machismo, Evangelical Conversion and Gender in Colombia* (Austin: University of Texas Press, 1995), and Andrew Chestnut, *Born Again in Brazil: The Pentecostal Boom and the Pathogens of Poverty* (New Brunswick: Rutgers University Press, 1995).

[26] Martin, 'From pre- to postmodernism in Latin America', 110.

benefit successfully from globalisation because they are in socio-economic, political and even epistemological position to do so. Likewise, it is possible to explain why other individuals, groups and societies experience globalisation in terms of defeat, and react to it with bewilderment and fear.

These are the topsides and undersides of globalisation, and in this paper my primary concern has been with the latter. I have particularly focused on how people who live in holistic, non-secular societies experience the insecurities, impoverishment and confusion of being on the losing end of globalisation. The experience is doubly heavy because not only do they experience the material misfortunes and hardships of being unwitting victims of external factors, but they are also culturally conditioned to take upon themselves the blame for their misfortunes by interpreting them as *castigo*, divine punishment. Being caught in such an epistemological loop, the prescribed, plausible solution is not only to seek solace in the religious explanations, but to try to rectify the anomic situation through increased religious practice.

The growth of popular Protestantism in Latin America can be seen in this light of trying to regain control over bewildering circumstances when other means seem not to help. Protestantism has a reputation for being a powerful means of turning around difficult life situations, and is appropriated for this reason. This is theodicial stretching. Basically, it reflects the way human beings relate to the outside world by transposing their naturalized worldviews to new situations, and when that worldview is holistic and non-secular, naturally, it implies engaging religion to that purpose.

International missions form part of globalisation in the sense of introducing elements from the outside. As Christianity has spread throughout the world, it has become easy to be euphoric and speak of the 'global church'. However appropriate this may be in certain contexts, it actually clouds the dynamics of local appropriation. The Christian faith is always received locally, and the ensuing church is always *glocal*. Often, foreign led mission work has generated disharmonious situations that have resulted in existential confusions, leading people to back off or to create their own indigenous churches. An increased sensitivity to glocalization will help mission agencies become more sensitive to situate theology and practice within larger epistemological frameworks, thus helping people living on the undersides to ease into the inevitable encroachments of globalisation. Such an approach generates an environment of confidence and trust, which, in turn, makes people more sensitive to open themselves to new horizons beyond their situated lives; to knowledges that 'never occurred to the human heart'.

Religion and Globalisation: An Anthropological Perspective
A Response to Asle Jøssang

Øyvind Dahl

With his well-written paper Asle F. Jøssang has brought us straight into the main topic of this symposium: 'Mission and Globalisation'. My response, as former professor of Social Anthropology and Intercultural Communication, will be a comment and a supplement to Jøssang's presentation.

Jøssang correctly contends that 'globalisation' has become a catchword in recent times. Globalisation is manifold and complex and has so many aspects that it is not easy to describe in few words. The effects of innovating communication technology, global financial transactions, transplanetary politics eroding national states, and cultural interchanges are observed almost everywhere. In search for a common denominator professor Jan Aart Scholte has identified 'supraterritoriality' as the most important aspect of the term globalisation.

> Globalisation is the spread of transplanetary and supraterritorial connections between people.... With globalisation people become more able – physically, legally, linguistically, culturally and psychologically – to engage with each other wherever on the planet Earth they might be.[1]

Many observers have noted that globalisation involves "collapse of space and time."[2] The globalisation has consequences for everyday life, not only for us in the developing North, but also in far-distant countries and cultures in the South.

Since the focus in this session is on anthropology and globalisation I will first discuss the consequences of globalisation for the anthropological profession and then come back to Jøssang's paper on glocalization and mission.

---

[1] Jan Aart Scholte, *Globalisation: A Critical Introduction* (Basingstoke: Palgrave Macmillian, 2005), 59.

[2] Tony Schirato and Jen Webb, *Understanding Globalisation* (London: Sage Publications, 2003).

Crises for the Notion of Culture

For anthropologists the globalisation processes have triggered a discussion of the very core concept for the study of anthropology: the understanding of culture itself. What is culture in the era of globalisation?

A case will bring forth the dilemma. A Norwegian student can sit on the tram in Oslo and 'chat' by the help of her mobile phone with an Australian friend in Sydney, or with a Brazilian student in Rio de Janeiro, who has the same admiration for the same pop idol. They can even exchange photos and music links. The youths have developed a language of 'chatting' and a special jargon, which works well for the communication purposes of the young. They like the same hip-hop music, watch the same (American) movies, drink the same Coca Cola, and eat the same burger at McDonald's wherever they live in the world. What 'culture' do these young people belong to? On the same day the Australian student can surf the waves of Manly Beach in Sydney; the Norwegian can ski in Nordmarka[3] or visit her own grandmother who does not know her way around a cell phone. Do the grandmother and the student *have* the same culture? Or is it the student and her friend in Sydney who *have* the same or share the same culture? The supraterritorial aspect of the globalisation has brought the geographical and bounded concept of culture into a crisis.

It was easier before, when anthropologists could travel to remote islands and tribes, and come back concentrating on writing a monograph on 'My Tribe' – an essentialist description of an exotic culture, seen through his Western glasses. Cultures were something people had and could be described. We were members of Norwegian culture; Samoans 'had' Samoan culture.

In an essay which the Norwegian Professor of Anthropology Thomas Hylland Eriksen characteristically calls 'The Lost Cultural Archipelago', he states, "Culture, or cultures, if one prefers, are not indivisible parcels of customs that one has or has not. Humans are cultural amalgams."[4] It is no longer possible to confine cultures either geographically or thematically. People are, may be more than ever before, cultural hybrids. Probably it has always been so, but it has become essentially conspicuous when globalisation has upset all our former notions. Jøssang states that there are no zones of intrinsic purity, as hybridity is a continuous dynamic process. "Instead of hybridity versus purity, it is 'hybridity all the way down'."[5]

In his book *Kulturterrorismen* Eriksen voices his critique of the traditional *essentialist functionalist* concept of culture in several statements: "We have been trained to think about culture as a thing that belongs to a people, which

---

[3] Manly Beach is the famous beach for surfing in Sydney, Nordmarka refers to the popular skiing area in the surroundings of Oslo.

[4] Thomas Hylland Eriksen, *Kulturelle Veikryss: Essays om Kreolisering* (Oslo: Universitetsforlaget, 1994), 14. All translations are mine.

[5] Vázques and Friedmann Marquardt, *Globalizing the Sacred: Religion across the Americas* (New Brunswick: Rutgers University Press, 2003), 59, quoted in Jøssang's paper.

has physical borders and which builds on the past."[6] However, "Culture is obviously variable, ambiguous, and changeable."[7] "Culture is a process and by nature unlimited."[8]

In the realm of globalisation, culture is not something that a person *has*, but something the person *makes relevant* in the encounter with other persons. This phenomenological understanding of culture represents a paradigm shift in relation to classical anthropology.[9] Culture is neither in the social surroundings independent of people, nor is it possessed by a group of people. Cultures are not islands or boxes in which we can sort human beings and on this basis predict their habits and actions.

The *essentialist concept of culture* can no longer describe the changing situation in a globalized world. Cultures are hybrids, they are creolised, and embodied in the subject, but at the same time shared with other subjects, thus representing an inter-subjective common sense. A *phenomenological understanding of culture* is concerned with human experience in everyday life. Its task is to describe human experience as it is lived – to account for social reality from the point of view of the actors involved. Consciousness as 'web of meaning' is a phenomenon of subjective experience; nonetheless, as Peter Berger writes, "it can be objectively described because its socially significant elements are constantly being shared with others."[10]

A more dynamic process-oriented phenomenological understanding of cultures (in plural) for our contemporary globalized world could be summed up as follows:

- Cultures are not closed, homogeneous entities;
- The location of culture is no longer a fixed geographical space;
- Cultures are constituted by multiple locations reflecting the movement of peoples, capital and symbolic systems;
- Cultures are *arenas of contest* where different conceptions, discourses, and practices meet, compete and struggle;
- Cultures are socially constructed and are constantly negotiated in human encounters;
- Individuals are constructors of these cultures through their life narratives, which are constantly revised and narrated again and again.

---

[6] Thomas Hylland Eriksen, *Kulturterrorismen: et oppgjør med tanken om kulturell renhet* (Oslo: Spartacus, 1993), 10.

[7] Eriksen, *Kulturterrorismen* , 13.

[8] Eriksen, *Kulturterrorismen*, 19.

[9] Marita Svane, *Interkulturel Dynamik i Kulturmødet: en fænomenologisk, individorienteret analyse og forståelse* (Aalborg Universitet, 2004), 97.

[10] Peter L. Berger, Brigitte Berger, and Hansfried Kellner, *The Homeless Mind: Modernization and Consciousness* (Middlesex: Penguin Books, 1973), 19.

Culture in a Globalized Age

A phenomenological way of interpreting the global scene is to admit that culture is individually experienced and lived collectively. It is embodied, part of the personality, but can only be learned in relationship to others. The person *is part of* culture, by incorporating tradition, history, narrative, time, and language. Culture understood this way becomes part of the personality and dependent on time and place. But this is not the whole picture since culture cannot be lived individually. People interpret their role in society and attach meaning to events and to own experiences in relationship with others, whether they live in Grorud or in Antananarivo.[11] Thereby they constantly construct new cultures. People communicate using words, acts and omission of acts. Therefore, communication is the key to culture in this constructivist sense of the word. Eriksen contends that, "culture makes communication possible."[12] But this statement can also be turned around saying that, "communication makes culture possible." It is through communication that common sense about the meaning of words, signs and symbols is made possible and this common sense is a prerequisite for sharing of culture. If communication makes culture possible it is because culture is constructed in the social encounter of people. If culture makes communication possible it is because groups of people share (more or less) the same meanings of words, signs and symbols. Culture and communication represent two sides of the same coin.

The cultural encounter is, according to this phenomenological interpretation, not a meeting between abstract concepts of culture. The encounter is necessarily a meeting between different individuals of flesh and blood with different frames of interpretation – or frames of reference – with different interpretations of existence. It is not a meeting of two different homogeneous, essentialist cultures defined for groups of people. "Cultures never communicate – people do."[13] What is new in the globalized world is that these cultures are not necessarily geographically located and do not necessarily have geographical borders. Instead, cultures, or shared codes and meanings, exist in social networks, which can also be supraterritorial networks. The Norwegian student mentioned above may share concepts and meanings with her Australian friend as well as with her grandmother, but these concepts and meanings are not necessarily the same in all situations, they are dependent of the actual connection – in other words – the interpersonal communication in a certain relationship at a certain time.

---

[11] Grorud is a suburb of Oslo, Antananarivo the capital of Madagascar.

[12] Eriksen, *Kulturelle veikryss*, 32.

[13] Øyvind Dahl, *Møter Mellom Mennesker: interkulturell kommunikasjon* (Oslo: Gyldendal akademisk, 2001), 4.

Globalisation and Glocalization

Jøssang describes the indigenous peasants living in the Andean mountains experiencing the encroaching outside world in their everyday life. Their local reaction is 'stretching their worldview' to accommodate it to new situations. The peasants experiencing global meaning-threatening discourses search for local meaning-restoring reactions, and Jøssang uses the term 'glocalization' to describe this local reaction to global trends. The description is well chosen because global trends of technology, economy, politics and culture are always responded to locally.[14]

One of the important contributions of Jøssang, is the emphasis on studies of globalisation 'from the bottom up' instead of 'top down'. He contends that there are 'topsides' and 'undersides' of globalisation. Globalisation can be seen as a world-wide game. Those who see the opportunities and have the knowledge are winners of the game. Production, commerce, finance, property and labor are all an international market. Because all globalisation inputs must be reacted to locally the local continues to thrive and develop. Globalisation does not necessarily reduce cultural diversity. However, globalisation has fatal consequences for those who are excluded from the system – those who live on the 'underside' – to use Jøssang's terminology. They experience the material misfortunes and are victims of external factors they cannot control.

For many people this is today's reality. Better than in the past they know how life could be. Modern communication tells them that. But deeper than before they realize that such a life is not within reach. They have no land to work on, no job, no credit, no education, no basic services, no security of income, no food security, no rights, but ever more squalor, an ever greater chance to be affected by HIV/aids, a house without electricity, water and sanitation. Despite unprecedented world economic progress during the last decade, for about two billion people there is only the experience of sinking further and further into quicksand. During the World Summit on Sustainable Development in Johannesburg in 2002 president M'beki from South Africa called this Global Apartheid. The gap between rich and poor in the world can no longer be explained in terms of a strikingly unequal distribution of income and wealth which could be modified through world economic growth and a better distribution of the fruits of growth. The gap appears to have become permanent. It is a game of power.

Consequences for Mission

Mission is both commission and transmission. The church has since the days of missionary Paul considered this task as global. The gospel is meant for "the whole world" (Mk 16:15). The love of God concerns all humans wherever they

---

[14] The term glocalization was coined by Roland Robertson to express the dual processes of globalisation and localization, see Zygmunt Bauman, *Globalisation: The Human Consequences* (Cambridge: Polity Press, 1998), 70.

live. In that sense mission was supraterritorial long before the modern globalisation processes. The globalisation can be seen as both opportunities and threats for the mission of the church. New mobility and contacts through diverse communication media offer new opportunities and create arenas where the church can meet different groups of people without being bounded by geographical borders and territorial distances. But there is no quick and easy access. If culture is understood as arenas where competing discourses meet and struggle, both at the individual and the societal level, the church is also an actor on such scenes in competition with other trends and actors.

The globalized world is a cultural arena where contesting trends and influences meet and struggle. The world culture is not integrated and harmonious, neither on the global level nor on the local level. Conflicting trends and values meet and compete. The new generations in the twenty-first century seem to be quite open for new challenges. Encountering the uprooting that follows globalisation people are searching for new footholds. In the western world where people probably are most exposed to the effects and challenges of globalisation and secularization we have seen an uprooting from traditional loyalties also in the religious realm. The modern youth are surfing – not navigating – both on the world-wide-web and in their life orientations. The postmodern human is a restless shopper also of spiritual orientations – picking up, consuming, and throwing away for the benefit of new trends. The urban and globalized human is a global nomad composing his or her ideological and religious menu, always searching for new objects of identification without really attaching himself or herself to any lasting commitment.

The challenge of the church in the age of globalisation is to create cultural meetings that bring the global nomads to ask questions about themselves, their identity and goals for life. The globalized church can provide new elements for their lives. Probably the best method for realizing the calling of Jesus Christ today is visualizing in local acts His concern for individuals. Actions speak stronger than many words.

Two Religions with a Global Vision: Violent Conflict or Peaceful Co-Existence?

Chawkat Moucarry

Christianity and Islam are the main monotheistic religions in terms of their following and their presence worldwide. They both originated in the Middle-East but soon expanded far beyond Palestine for the former and the Arabian Peninsula for the latter.

For three hundred years, the Gospel spread peacefully, from Jerusalem to Egypt and Ethiopia in the South, to Mesopotamia up to India in the East, and to Syria, Asia Minor and Europe in the North. During all this time the Christian community was living in pluralistic societies and was regularly persecuted by the Roman Empire. The beginning of the fourth century marked a turning point in church history when Emperor Constantine issued the *Edict of Milan* about religious tolerance (313). In 380 Christianity was declared the official religion of the Empire. Gradually but surely the church aligned itself with the political power of the Empire and its successors. This misconceived alliance proved in the long term to be one of Christianity's major misjudgements. It resulted in Christianity often being associated with violent action against dissident Christians as well as non-Christians, including Muslims.

Islam too made amazing progress in a relatively short time. From a small group of believers in Mecca, Muhammad's birthplace, it developed into a large community, after the Prophet's migration, *hijra*, to Medina in 622. At the same time Muhammad took on new roles. He became a political leader and a military commander. When he died ten years later virtually all Arab tribes had already embraced Islam. Within one hundred years Islamic conquests had reached the Indus River to the East, North Africa and Spain to the West. The year 732 marked the first major battle lost by the Muslim army which was defeated by Charles Martel near Poitiers in central France. Thus, Islam, unlike Christianity, right from the beginning was closely linked with power: from the first Islamic state in Medina up to the Umayyad and the Abbasid Empires, and finally the Ottoman Empire which collapsed in the aftermath of WW1. This linkage also resulted in Muslims often oppressing fellow Muslims and sometimes waging war against non-Muslims.

Lord John Acton made a perceptive comment about the danger of too much power when wielded by sinful human beings: "Power tends to corrupt, and absolute power corrupts absolutely."[1] Because Christianity and Islam claim to be God-given religions, Christian and Muslim leaders believed their power was entrusted to them by God. It was almost inevitable for those leaders who held political roles not to get corrupted and involved in violence. They justified this violence in the name of religion. The way they used and abused God's name for their own purposes provide a particular case of transgressing the third commandment: "You shall not misuse the name of the Lord your God, for the Lord will not hold anyone guiltless who misuses his name" (Exod. 20:7). Paradoxically, the progress of secularisation has one beneficial effect inasmuch as it limits the political influence of the religious establishment.

The purpose of this paper is to highlight that the two largest world religions, Christianity and Islam, claim to have been mandated with a universal mission grounded in their exclusive and conflicting claims. Their self-understanding of this mission has historically led them, more often than not, to confront each other on the world stage. Yet, this century-old confrontation is not unavoidable. It is possible for both Christians and Muslims, who live in an ever-increasing secular world, to interpret their respective faiths in terms that promote not only mutual respect but also cooperation between the two communities for the common good of society at large. The difficult journey on this new path of Christian-Muslim relations does not compromise the essential tenets of either tradition.

Religions of the South

Let us first of all take the measure of the numerical size of the Christian and Muslim communities in the context of global religious landscape. In a few years the world population will reach 7 billion. Most people adhere to one of the following religions:

- Christianity – 2.3 billion – 33%
- Islam – 1.6 billion – 23%
- Hinduism – 900 million – 13%. Hinduism is the dominant religion in India and Nepal.
- Buddhism – 400 million – 6%. Buddhism is the dominant religion in Cambodia, Laos, Mongolia, Myanmar, Sri Lanka, Thailand and Vietnam.
- Chinese religions – 400 million – 6%

These figures show that:

- No single religion can claim to have the majority of the world population.
- We live in a religious world. The number of atheists and agnostics is reckoned to be around 1 billion (14%). Secularisation is dominant in the North but remains a relatively marginal phenomenon in the

[1] Ward, H., and Wild, J. (comps.), *The Lion Christian Quotation Collection* (Oxford: Lion, 1997), 160.

South (Latin America, Africa, and Asia).

- The Christian community is the largest religious community in the world, followed immediately by the Muslim community. Together the two communities represent more than half of the world population. Both communities are found mainly in the South.

Christianity is no longer a Western religion in terms of its adherents. Historically the roots of Christianity are in the Middle East, in particular Palestine, Syria and Egypt.[2] Christianity is the dominant religion in Latin America whereas nearly two-thirds of the Muslim population is found in Asia. In Africa Christianity and Islam are equally represented with Christians mainly in the South of the continent and Muslims in the North.[3]

Some triumphalistic Muslims want us to believe that Islam is the fastest growing religion. Some scaremongering Christian leaders make the same claim for very different reasons: they want to mobilise their people and get them involved in mission. The reality is that Christianity and Islam are growing in very similar proportions. They are competing to win the hearts and minds of people in many countries including Western countries where a secular culture has proved unable to meet the spiritual aspirations of the human heart. In 2025 it is predicted that Muslims will be around 2 billion whereas Christians will be 2.7. The growth of both communities is due mainly to the high birth rate in many countries in the South. This rapid population growth often increases the difficulties of addressing the challenges facing Christian and Muslim societies.

The majority of the Christian community lives in other-faith or secular contexts where they interact with people from other faiths (especially Muslims, Hindus, and Buddhists) or none. By contrast the majority of the Muslim population (80%) live in Muslim-majority countries.

Clearly Islam represents one of the main challenges facing the Christian community. In order to fully appreciate this global challenge we need to consider the main characteristics of this religion, as understood by Muslim leaders and scholars.

Islam as a Global Religion

I do not need here to make the case that Christianity is a global religion, but what about Islam? What makes Islam a global religion apart from the fact that the Muslim community is found on all continents? The answer lies in the sum of at least seven features that characterise this religion according to Islamic

[2] It was in Antioch of Syria that the Disciples of Christ were called Christians for the first time (Acts 11:26). The Church of Antioch was the first international church – its members included Jewish and non-Jewish believers, and the first missionary church that sent Paul and Barnabas on their first missionary journey (Acts 13:1-3).

[3] For a detailed distribution of the Muslim population worldwide, see the report published in October 2009 by the Pew Research Center's Forum on Religion and Public Life, *Mapping the Global Population: A Report on the Size and Distribution of the World's Muslim Population* (pewforum.org/docs/?DocID=450).

sources. These features are applicable to the Christian faith as well, although the way they are articulated in the Christian tradition is different.

An Abrahamic Religion

Abraham is one of Islam's greatest figures. For Muslims he represents the prototype of the Prophet Muhammad. He is the spiritual father of all Muslims (22:78) and a good example for all believers (60:4). He grew up in a polytheistic society before he became a passionate monotheistic believer (6:74-82). He had two sons, Isaac and Ishmael, from two different wives, Sara and Hagar. Both Isaac and Ishmael were prophets (2:136). With his son Ishmael, Abraham built the Ka`aba temple in Mecca and implored God to send his offspring a prophet to show them the way to worship their Creator (2:122-129). Muhammad was sent in response to Abraham's prayer to teach God's religion to the Arab people, Ishmael's descendants, but he was also sent for non-Arabs.

A Rational Religion

Islam is seen by Muslim scholars as *din al-fitra* or a 'natural' religion in the sense that if human beings carefully considered the universe they would naturally believe in the existence of one Creator God, and they would consequently worship him. The reason why many people do not believe and worship the one and true God is that they are misguided by human religions. As a God-given religion Islam confirms God's revelation through creation that is displayed for everyone to ponder upon.

In Islam there are no mysteries comparable to the ones we find in Christianity (e.g. Trinity, Incarnation, Redemption). Why would God reveal things which are beyond our grasp? To the extent that divine revelation in Scriptures (i.e. the Qur'an) is within the scope of human understanding, it is accessible to everyone, at least to those who are familiar with Arabic language.[4] This understanding of Islam as a religion available to and comprehensible by all human beings makes it potentially a global religion.

A Holistic Religion

Islam acknowledges that Judaism and Christianity are both God-given religions. However, neither of them is perfect. Muslims see Judaism as a religion centred on life on earth to the detriment of the afterlife. Because Christianity does not have a political, social or economic agenda, Muslims perceive it as an otherworldly religion. With its comprehensive law, Islam is by contrast concerned about the afterlife as much as about life in this world. It is

[4] The Qur'an is believed to be God's Word only in Arabic. Translations are by definition human products which cannot match the divine text. Therefore they do not have the same status as the Qur'an.

'religion and life on earth', *din wa dunya*. Thus, traditionally, Islam has been simultaneously a religious, political, social and economic system.

Without denying that Islam is an all-embracing religion, some contemporary Muslim reformers challenge the traditional alliance in Islam between 'religion and state', *din wa dawla*. They refer to Mecca where the Prophet exerted no political role. In Medina he became a political leader simply because he was the best man for the job.

A Missionary Religion

The word for mission in Islam, *da'wah*, comes from a verb which literally means 'to invite', 'to call'. Muslim preachers should follow the example of the Prophet who was instructed to preach the Message persuasively and courteously: "Call to the way of your Lord with wisdom and good exhortation; and argue with them in the best possible way" (16:125). Jews and Christians are also invited to embrace Islam (3:20), and Muslims should be equally respectful when debating with them: "Do not argue with the People of the Book but in the best possible way, except in the case of those among them who have been unjust" (29:46; cf. 3:64). If Muslims are prevented from carrying out their mission, then they have the right and the duty to fight their opponents militarily if necessary (9:29).

A Universal Religion

The Prophet Muhammad was an Arab and he preached the Qur'an in Arabic to the Arab people. However, the Qur'an makes it clear that the message he was given was not just for Arabs but for all peoples on earth: "We [God] have sent you as a mercy to the worlds" (21:107; cf. 7:158). Islam is therefore a universal religion which Muslims have been mandated to spread among all nations.

The fact that Islam has been a successful missionary religion is demonstrated by the fact that Arab Muslims represent just over twenty per cent of the *umma*, the Muslim community. Although Arabic remains Islam's liturgical language, there are hundreds of other languages spoken by Muslims worldwide.

A Final Religion

Islam teaches that Judaism and Christianity are both revealed religions. However, Muslim theologians consider that these two religions were valid until Islam was revealed. Just as Christianity superseded Judaism, Islam superseded both Judaism and Christianity. However, not all contemporary Muslim scholars accept this traditional teaching. Some argue that Judaism and Christianity remain legitimate religions but Islam is the final and greatest religion.

The Only Saving Religion

Unlike Judaism and Christianity Islam is believed by Muslims to be God's perfect revelation. This results in Islam being God's final and only saving religion. The Qur'an asserts that "[the only acceptable] religion in God's sight is Islam" (3:19). This means that only Muslims will be saved on the Day of Judgment: "If anyone follows a religion other than Islam, never will it be accepted of him; and in the afterlife he will be in the ranks of those who have lost" (3: 85).

However, we do find in the Qur'an texts that are more open towards other religions. These texts suggest that all monotheistic believers will go to paradise together with Muslims:

> Those who believe [Muslims] and those who are Jews, Christians, and Sabaeans – whoever believes in God and the Last Day and works righteousness – surely their reward is with their Lord. They have neither to fear nor to grieve (2:62; see 5:69).[5]

To the extent that the word 'Islam' is about believing, obeying and worshipping the one and only God, Muslim reformers consider that all monotheistic faiths, especially Judaism and Christianity, preach the message of Islam.

These seven characteristics show that Islam is a radical monotheistic religion and therefore has a lot in common with Christianity in terms of religious beliefs and ethical values. At the same time there is a theological divide between the two religions. Christians and Muslims have numerous misunderstandings about each other, but there are also genuine and insurmountable differences. Both Christianity and Islam claim to be the expression of God's final, perfect, and saving revelation, which reached its climax in the coming of Jesus Christ for Christians and with the revelation of the Qur'an for Muslims.

Not only are there conflicting truth claims between the two faiths but traditional Islamic teaching rejects the core of the Christian faith: the reliability of the Bible, the Trinitarian God, and the divinity, the crucifixion and the resurrection of Jesus Christ. Regrettably this has led many Christians to demonise Islam and to consider this religion as evil and a subtle expression of the Anti-Christ.

The Roots of Christian-Muslim Polarisation

Clearly the theological divide between Christianity and Islam accounts for the persistent opposition between the two communities. However, it is not the only factor; there are other important reasons, some have to do with the past, others with the present.

---

[5] The Sabaeans are a group of Jews who follow the teaching of John the Baptist. They have survived in Iraq although their number is very small.

The Legacy of History

Right from the start Christians and Muslims confronted each other on the battlefield. The Muslim army engaged the Byzantine army in two battles, Mu'ta and Tabuk (east of the river Jordan), respectively in 630 and 631. The early Muslim conquests, *al-futuhat al-islamiyya*, were carried out in many places which had traditionally been Christian territories (Palestine, Syria, Egypt, North Africa, Spain). The ill-famed Crusades were to some degree a (wrong) response to the Seljuk invasion and occupation of Armenia and Asia Minor. Their sinister enterprise is still vivid in the Arab-Muslim psyche. The Ottoman army invaded Eastern Europe and twice besieged Vienna (1529 and 1683). The colonialist movement was led by so-called Christian nations. Between the two World Wars all Islamic countries were occupied by European powers with the exception of Saudi Arabia, Turkey and Afghanistan. We still suffer from this age-old animosity that resulted in difficult and distrustful relationships. The wars in Iraq and Afghanistan rekindled the hostility between the 'Christian West' and 'Muslim world'.

Migration

The number of immigrants in Western Europe has dramatically increased over the last fifty years or so. Many of them have settled in their host countries and have become citizens. The number of Muslim immigrants is significant and in some countries they represent the majority among immigrants. Many people, including some Christians, badly react to what they perceive as a potential threat to Western civilisation. They feel that the growing Muslim population seriously undermines their country's national identity, both cultural and religious. In several countries the foreign population includes political refugees, some of whom hold and propagate extremist views. Unfortunately, in times of economic crisis, foreigners too often become an easy target and a convenient scapegoat. They are blamed for all sorts of problems faced by society at large. Foreigners easily fall victims to xenophobic attitudes, and Muslims in particular have become the object of Islamophobic reactions in many places.

Terrorism

The rise of religious violence committed in the name of Islam before and after the tragic events of September 2001 has reinforced people's hostility towards this religion. Although the number of Muslims involved in terrorist activities is thankfully extremely small, Islam has nevertheless become in the minds of many people, Christians included, associated with violence. Muslims are the first victims of violence committed by extremist Muslims. When former political leaders, who are self-confessed Christians (Bush, Blair), resorted to the War-on-Terror rhetoric and led the wars in Iraq and Afghanistan, they inevitably contributed to reinforcing the idea that Islam is a violent religion. Their desperate efforts to reach out to the Muslim community in their respective countries had little effect. Some influential Christian leaders in Western countries are also responsible for nurturing Islamophobic attitudes among Christians. They are the modern crusaders who engage through polemical arguments in a war of words with Muslims.

Perhaps Muslim leaders should speak up more clearly and loudly against terrorism committed in the name of their religion. Unfortunately some media seem to be more interested in Muslim extremists than in moderate and ordinary ones.

Christian Zionism

Christian Zionism has fuelled the hostility between Muslims and Christians to a degree that Western Christians are unaware of. Christian Zionists show little sympathy for Muslims and are often biased against Islam, which is seen as the major obstacle to the fulfilment of the Zionist dream. As a matter of fact this dream has turned into a nightmare for the Palestinian people, the native people of the land (Jews, Christians and Muslims) since the creation of Israel in 1948.[6]

Christian Zionism, grounded in the dispensational theology of the nineteenth century, has led many Christians in the West to become staunch supporters of Zionism and of the contemporary State of Israel. The vast majority of Christians are not Zionist and they do not support Israel. Because Zionist Christians are often very active, well off and outspoken, especially in the U.S.A., their influence has been disproportionate in comparison with their numerical size within the Christian community.

Christians who support Israel do so for three main reasons. First of all, they understandably have much sympathy for the Jewish people because of the Holocaust in World War II (although the Jews were not the only victims of the Nazi regime). Secondly, they believe God has given 'the Promised Land' to Israel to be their land forever. Finally, they are either unaware of or misinformed about the suffering of the Palestinian people caused by the creation of the state of Israel in 1948.

The theology of 'Christian Zionists' has actually very little to do with the teaching of Christ. Jesus predicted the destruction of Jerusalem and the exile of the Israelites as a result of his rejection by his people – the city was indeed destroyed and its inhabitants driven out by the Romans in 70 AD. Jesus did not make any promises about their return, let alone the restoration of their nationhood (Luke 21:20-24). As for the Old Testament themes of land, chosen people and temple, they are time-bound, pointing beyond themselves to the

---

[6] For a documented study of the suffering endured by the Palestinian people at the hands of the founding fathers of Israel see the remarkable study by the Jewish Israeli historian Ilan Pappé, *The Ethnic Cleansing of Palestine* (Oxford: Oneworld, 2006). See also Michael Prior, *Zionism and the State of Israel: A Moral Inquiry* (London: Routledge, 1999).

coming of the Messiah, Jesus Christ, who fulfilled in his mission all the promises God made to Israel (Jn 2:18-19; 2 Cor 1:20).[7]

Israel's supporters often label those who criticise Israel as anti-Semitic. We need to acknowledge and to combat anti-Semitism. However, anti-Zionism and anti-Semitism are two different things. The Jewish prophets themselves were very critical of the Israelites when they disobeyed God, especially when they oppressed the non-Israelites living among them (Mal. 3:5). Today many courageous Jews criticise Israel for its oppression of Palestinians. Those who support Israel unconditionally make no contribution whatsoever to a just and peaceful settlement between Israelis and Palestinians. They also contribute to deepening the gulf between the Christian and the Muslim communities because of the solidarity that Muslims and Arabs have with the Palestinian people.

Whatever Christians may feel and believe about Israel, their role is to seek justice and peace for the two peoples. They need to show solidarity and support especially for the Palestinians who are the largest homeless and refugee people on earth. Violence breeds violence and brings more suffering to everyone (Mt 26:52). Sadly this has been so much the case in the Arab-Israeli conflict. Thankfully more and more Israelis and Palestinians are getting involved in a non-violent commitment to a just and peaceful solution. They certainly need our support so that Jews and Palestinians may one day enjoy the same rights on the same land, the sooner the better.

Plight of Christian Communities in Muslim-Majority Countries

There is another important reason that lies behind Christian hostility towards Islam and Muslims. It has to do with the plight of Christian communities living in the Middle East and in the Muslim world in general. In Islamic law Jews and Christians are described as 'the People of the Book', *ahl al-kitab*. They have the status of protected minorities, *dhimmis*, which means that their lives and their possessions are protected under an Islamic regime in exchange for the poll tax, *jizya*, they have to pay. This status does not, however, guarantee total equality with Muslim citizens. To be sure the status of *dhimmis* has been abolished in most Islamic countries. Yet some aspects have survived, which means that Christians and Muslims do not have the same rights in most Islamic countries (e.g. a Christian man cannot marry a Muslim woman; Muslims cannot convert to Christianity; leadership roles are reserved for Muslims). To this legal discrimination one must add the social discrimination which is often found among all majority groups. Christians are sometimes suspected of not being loyal to their country. Some consider them as a threat to the cohesion of the Arab and/or the Muslim nation, and suspect them of being covert agents of Western governments and agencies. This seems so unfair given the leading role

---

[7] A well-informed and Biblical analysis of Christian Zionism can be found in Stephen Sizer, *Zion's Christian Soldiers. The Bible, Israel and the Church* (Nottingham: IVP, 2007).

that Arab Christians (in Egypt, Lebanon, Iraq and Syria in particular) have taken in the Arab renaissance, *al-nahda*. Not surprisingly many Arab Christians were key players in the emergence of Arab nationalism.[8]

The authoritarian and oppressive regimes in some Islamic countries (e.g. Iran, Saudi Arabia, Sudan) grievously damage the public image of Islam as a whole. They have a large responsibility in reinforcing people's prejudice against Islam and Muslims. Christian solidarity, like Islamic solidarity, is an obligation. Unfortunately this solidarity is often unnecessarily combined with prejudice against Muslims in general and against Islam itself.

Given the wounded past and the hurting present it is no wonder that Christian-Muslim relations have been strained to the point of regularly breaking into violent clashes in parts of the Muslim world (e.g. Egypt, Indonesia, Nigeria). Yet there are ways to break free from this vicious cycle, and we have witnessed in recent years a growing number of Christians and Muslims who are determined to bridge the gap between the two communities.[9] One such endeavor has recently come out of the Muslim community worldwide.

A Landmark Islamic Initiative

On 13 October 2007 as many as 138 Muslim scholars and leaders published an Open Letter. The signatories represented virtually all Muslim denominations from all over the world. The recipients were the Pope and the leaders of major Christian denominations. The title of the Letter 'A Common Word Between Us and You' derives from the following Qur'anic text which is understood as inviting Christians to join hands with Muslims on 'the most solid theological ground possible', namely the respective teachings of the Qur'an and the Bible:

> Say: O People of the Scripture! Come to a common word between us and you: that we shall worship none but God, and that we shall ascribe no partner unto Him, and that none of us shall take others for lords beside God. And if they turn away, then say: Bear witness that we are they who have surrendered (unto Him). (3:64)[10]

This remarkable document is highly significant in many respects. Two main characteristics should be noted. The first is the judgement made by the Letter's signatories that Christians form a monotheistic community. This is a huge step forward in terms of developing good Christian-Muslim relations and a better understanding of Christian beliefs. For centuries Muslim theologians considered the Christian doctrine about the Trinitarian God (Father-Son-Holy Spirit) as a subtle form of polytheism, *shirk*. Christians were therefore seen as a

---

[8] The Arab Socialist Ba`ath party was founded by two Syrians, a Christian (Michel Aflak) and a Muslim (Salah ad-Din al-Bitar).

[9] One noteworthy example of Christian-Muslim peace-building ministry is represented by 'The Interfaith Mediation Center' headed by two leaders from the Muslim and the Christian communities in Nigeria. Their work has been documented in a remarkable DVD entitled *The Imam and the Pastor* (see fltfilms.org.uk/videos.html).

[10] See the official website for this document at www.acommonword.com.

kind of polytheistic people (and therefore unbelievers). Their Trinitarian faith not only undermined but practically nullified the truth about God's oneness.

The second characteristic of this document is that Muslim scholars have summed up Islamic teaching and practice in '*The Commandments of Love*': loving God and our neighbor. Christians are familiar with this summary that was first made by Jesus Christ himself (Mt 22:34-40). That Muslims have formulated their faith in such terms is no coincidence. In fact, the document makes several quotations from the Bible. One can only rejoice that Muslims have made such an effort to identify in their own tradition those elements which achieve a real rapprochement between the two communities of faith. Not surprisingly many Christians have responded positively to this Islamic initiative.[11]

The twofold command about loving God and our neighbor was given by Jesus when a Jewish expert in the law asked him this question, "Which is the greatest commandment in the Law?" We have in Jesus' response a remarkable summary of God's law given to Moses. This summary provides a sure guide to Christians in particular as to how they should relate to their Creator and to their fellow human beings. It does not, however, spell out what the Gospel of Jesus Christ is all about. This Gospel is first and foremost about God's saving love for humankind which has been supremely demonstrated in Christ, through his life, death and resurrection. In other words our love for God is our fitting response to his love for us, "we love because he first loved us" (1 Jn 4:19). In fact, love is God's overarching attribute:

Whoever does not love does not know God, because God is love. This is love: not that we loved God, but that he loved us and sent his Son as an atoning sacrifice for our sins (1 Jn 4: 8, 10).

A Christian Approach to Islam

As followers of Christ how are we to relate to Islam and Muslims? Christian leaders and scholars have to take the lead in reaching out to the Muslim community. They will be more convincing and efficient if their approach is genuinely inspired by the Bible teaching. For obvious reasons Christians do not find in their Scriptures any specific texts about Islam or Muslims.[12] However, it is possible to find in the Scriptures principles that will guide us as we seek to relate to Islam and Muslims in a distinctively Christian way. I would like to outline four guiding principles.

---

[11] One significant response was the statement issued by the Yale Center for Faith and Culture (see www.yale.edu/faith). Many Christians including this author have signed this response.

[12] Islam as a religion preached by the Prophet Muhammad started six hundred years after Christ. The Qur'an claims that Jesus foretold the coming of Muhammad but does not provide any proof text to back up this allegation (61:6).

Fairness

Jesus summed up the teaching of the Jewish law and the prophets in these words: "In everything, do to others what you would have them do to you" (Mt 7:12). We need to educate the Christian community and to urge them to be fair with Islam and Muslims. This means clearing the misunderstandings that people have about this religion and its followers, challenging their prejudice, providing them with an unbiased presentation of what Islam stands for, highlighting the common ground to Christianity and Islam, etc. We obviously need the help of our Muslim friends in this task as Muslims are in a much better position to speak about their own faith and community.

Treating others the way we would like them to treat us clearly indicates that reciprocity is desirable but not a requirement. As Christians we must be concerned about the plight of our brothers and sisters in Islamic countries, and we have the right to be worried about the way some Muslim extremists deal with Christianity and Christians. However, we should not allow this to poison our own attitude towards Islam and Muslims.

Unconditional Love

The story of the Good Samaritan is one of Jesus' best-known parables (Luke 10:25-37). This story teaches two important lessons which are as much challenging for Christians today as for the Jewish teacher of the law who had asked Jesus, "Who is my neighbor?" The first lesson is that every human being, especially the needy one, is my neighbor. As such I must love them regardless of their creed, culture, colour or class. The second lesson is that human beings who belong to neither my religion nor my ethnic background are able to exhibit godly character that puts to shame many in my own community. I don't need to underscore the relevance of this kind of teaching in terms of how Christians should relate to Muslims and to other religious communities. Whatever people may think of Islam they need to show respect for Muslims, their Prophet and their Scripture. Respecting Muslims does not mean agreeing with their beliefs; it is simply looking at them as our neighbors.

Care for the Stranger

The Mosaic Law provides an amazing teaching about how the Israelites had to deal with the non-Israelites living among them. Let me just quote one text:

> When foreigners reside among you in your land, do not mistreat them. The foreigners residing among you must be treated as your native-born. Love them as yourself, for you were foreigners in Egypt (Lev 19:33-34).

Caring for the non-Israelites had to be expressed in practical ways including providing for their basic physical needs, respecting their human rights (e.g. wages, rest, free-loan), and implementing an impartial justice. Jesus embodied this Old Testament teaching in the way he cared for the Samaritans (Luke 9:51-

56; 10:25-37; 17:11-18; Jn 4:1-26; see Mt 25:35). This teaching is so relevant today with regard to our attitude toward immigrants, including Muslims, who live in Western countries and to the way the Jewish people and the State of Israel should treat the Palestinian people. The irony is that the creation of Israel has made native Palestinians foreigners on their own homeland.[13]

Self-Criticism

Jesus also recommends to his disciples to adopt a critical attitude. He invites them to be critical of other faiths (Mt 7:15-20) as well as of their own faith and life (Mt 7:21-23). As Christians we have to develop a Christian and balanced approach to Islam that is Biblical, well informed, and unbiased. We also need to take a long look at ourselves, at our history and even at our beliefs. This will remind us that we are as sinful and guilty as anyone else. The more we are aware of our own shortcomings the less judgemental we are likely to be and the more lenient with Muslims whose attitude seems offensive to us for whatever reason:

> Why do you look at the speck of sawdust in someone else's eye and pay no attention to the plank in your own eye? You hypocrite, first take the plank out of your own eye, and then you will see clearly to remove the speck from the other person's eye (Mt 7:3, 5).

How do these guiding principles work out? Christian approaches to Islam are very diverse. There seems to be four major paradigms of how Christians relate to people of other faiths in general and to Islam in particular.

The *conflict paradigm* focuses on the conflicting truth claims that divide Christianity and other faiths. The Christian truth claims about the Trinitarian God and the uniqueness of Christ are in the final analysis incompatible with all other religions including Islam, Hinduism and Buddhism. People who adopt this paradigm can easily be tempted by either ignoring Islam altogether or taking a confrontational attitude to Muslims and their religion. When we examine other faiths, we are bound to acknowledge that they all have certain truths which reflect the fact that "God has not left himself without testimony" among the nations (Acts 14:17). This is more evident in the case of Islam because of the impressive Biblical material found in the Qur'an.

The *conciliation paradigm* highlights the real similarities that exist between Christianity and Islam. Christians who adopt this approach seek to understand, appreciate and identify with the communities they serve. There is no doubt that there is a lot of common ground between Christianity and Islam. People who engage in this process sometimes reach the conclusion that the two religions share the same essentials. This conclusion is unwarranted; indeed it does not do

---

[13] A Christian understanding of how to relate to foreigners is provided in Christine D. Pohl, *Making Room. Recovering Hospitality as a Christian Tradition* (Grand Rapids: Eerdmans, 1999). See also Nick Spencer, *Asylum and Immigration. A Christian Perspective on a Polarised Debate* (Milton Keynes: Authentic Media, 2004).

justice to Jesus Christ as Lord and Savior of all. When this paradigm becomes dominant the need, let alone the urgency, of Christian mission gets blurred.

The *compassion paradigm* seeks to reflect in practical ways God's unconditional love for everyone in particular for the neediest and most vulnerable people. As in the parable of the Good Samaritan this down-to-earth demonstration of God's love does not need to be followed by any word. Christians need to reflect their faith through getting involved in social action rather than in endless theological debates. Those who focus on mercy ministry in Islamic contexts have a point in drawing our attention to the fact that compassion is what gives human beings their true identity. However, action needs words to explain the meaning and the distinctive aspects of Christian ministry.

The *cooperation paradigm* looks at Muslims and people of other faiths first and foremost as fellow human beings. It also seeks to enhance our shared moral and religious beliefs. This common ground should be taken seriously through working together for the common good of our societies. The old-age rivalry and opposition between Christians and Muslims need not be. Without denying the exclusive claims of each religion it is possible for both communities to get involved in addressing the challenges facing the community at large. Christian-Muslim dialogue has the best chances to be fruitful when it takes place in the context of personal and social relationships.

These four paradigms are all found within the Christian community. They have their promoters and opponents. They all have their merits. The problem arises when they are taken separately rather than together. Any serious examination of the teachings of Christianity and Islam is bound to find incompatible beliefs between the two faiths (for instance with regard to Jesus Christ and Muhammad). Does this mean that they have nothing in common? Of course not. Monotheism is at the heart of both with all the ethical implications of this central belief. Yet, doctrine is not all what these faiths are about. They call for action, for God's worship and for care for the underprivileged. Faith has to be authenticated through deeds. Christianity and Islam teach that God is the Creator and the Lord of all; they call their followers to acknowledge that all human beings are equal and have the same dignity, rights and duties. We have all been tasked by our Creator to look after his creation and to show compassion to our fellow human beings regardless of their religious or ethnic background. If they respond to this call Christians and Muslims can prove history wrong. Confrontation between the two communities is not inescapable. It is possible, indeed imperative and urgent, for Christians and Muslims to come to a fresh understanding of their respective Scriptures that enable them to remain faithful to their core message and to be agents of justice, peace, change and transformation within their communities and beyond.

Our Five Common Commitments

There have been a lot of discussions about 'the clash of civilisations' in recent years following the publication by Samuel Huntington of a book with the same title.[14] I believe that the real divide is not between Christianity and Islam but between extremists on either side. Mainstream Christians and Muslims are able to come to a common understanding without denying their own faith. In a spirit consonant with the Islamic Open Letter (cited above), I would like to highlight what I would call 'Our Five Common Commitments'. Despite the crucial differences between the Christian and the Muslim faiths, our shared monotheism should enable us to work together for the sake of our communities and beyond. Many, perhaps most Christians and Muslims would agree on these commitments.[15]

We are committed to God – in a world where he is ignored and blasphemed

God is the Creator and sustainer of the world. We owe him our very existence and everything we possess. We are his unique creatures, and we have been made first and foremost for him. It is both our joy and duty to worship him sincerely, to submit willingly to his authority, to serve him humbly and to honour his name in everything we do. We are also to love him as best as we can. We show our gratefulness to him for all his undeserved blessings by dedicating our lives to his service.

We are committed to our families – in a world scarred by family breakdown and immorality

God has created all human beings equal and with the same dignity. Human dignity does not depend on creed, colour, culture or class. The Creator has made us men and women for a purpose which is fulfilled when a man and a woman commit themselves to each other and become husband and wife. The family unit is vital for children to grow in a healthy environment, and for human society to flourish. We aspire to sexual purity before and during marriage life as this represents an expression of God's holiness. This implies sexual chastity for single people and mutual love and faithfulness for couples. Unmarried men and women also fulfil their humanity and can make a significant contribution to human society and God's kingdom.

Human life is sacred from beginning to end. Children are always a blessing from God including those born with physical or mental disabilities. This does not mean that childless couples are guilty or the object of God's displeasure. Parents have the privilege and obligation to love and look after their children.

---

[14] Samuel Huntington, *The Clash of Civilizations and the Remaking of World Order* (New York: Simon and Schuster, 1996).

[15] What follows is extracted from my forthcoming book *Relating to Islam and to Muslim People*.

They are to use their God given authority to protect their children's emotional, physical and spiritual well-being. Children should respect their parents, honour them and acknowledge their parental authority. Adults should show gratefulness to their parents by caring for them and helping them, especially in their old age.

We are committed to freedom of religion and genuine dialogue – in a world of persecution, polemics and inter-religious conflict[16]

There is a special bond between monotheistic believers, in particular Jews, Christians and Muslims. Religious freedom means that everyone has the right to worship according to their own beliefs. We acknowledge that more often than not we have failed to show solidarity for each other. Instead we have fought one another and in so doing dishonoured the name of our Creator. We neither engage in polemics (a war of words) nor do we seek to convert people by dishonest means. We commit ourselves to genuine and respectful dialogue. The aim of Christian-Muslim dialogue is to understand each other's faith as well as to witness to one's own faith. Conversion to either Christianity or Islam might be the outcome of such dialogue. If it happens it will test our religious tolerance and show how committed we are to religious freedom.

We should support all those who are under pressure or who suffer persecution for their faith. This starts with the members of our own community and goes well beyond to include all people regardless of their faith. Freedom of religion, thought and expression goes hand in hand with respect for people of faith and of no faith. In increasingly multi-cultural and multi-ethnic societies, respect for people, their religion and their culture is essential for peaceful and fruitful co-existence.

We are committed to our fellow human beings – in a world where so many are needy, vulnerable and oppressed

All human beings are God's special creatures, loved by him regardless of their faith, ethnic group, social status and gender. Our neighbor is every human being, and in particular those who are vulnerable, needy or oppressed. Our love for our neighbor must reflect God's love for them.

Such love for those in need must be an unconditional love, not dependent on them converting to our own religion. At the same time, there is nothing wrong in presenting our respective faiths in contextually appropriate terms, with the hope that people will find the way back to God. Christians believe Jesus Christ is the Way (Jn 14:6). Muslims are convinced that Islam lead people to "the

---

[16] I am aware that 'freedom of religion' does not sit comfortably with traditional Islamic teaching. I also know that today many Muslims would have no problems signing up to this principle.

Straight Way" (1:6). We all need to demonstrate that our religious convictions are perfectly compatible with respect for freedom of conscience.

Human development is about more than technological, economic or scientific progress. It includes spiritual development enabling people to realize their full potential. This is achieved when people live in a right relationship with their Creator and with one another.

Human life is sustainable when we use the resources of the earth responsibly. God has appointed us as his stewards over the earth, and the environment in which we live has been entrusted to us. We are to manage God's creation with wisdom and respect, to enjoy it and to treat his creatures humanely.

We are committed to the values of God's kingdom – in a world corrupted by evil and injustice.

As Christians and Muslims, we see ourselves as God's witnesses on earth and our mission is to extend his kingdom worldwide. It is clear that we do not share the same story about this kingdom, how to become a member of it or how to expand it. But many of the values of God's kingdom are strikingly similar in Christianity and Islam: justice, equality, solidarity, peace, love, forgiveness, mercy, hope, faith, truth and freedom. So while we cannot agree on many vital theological issues, there are areas in which we can and should work together. These include fighting for peace and justice, seeking reconciliation between divided parties, bringing freedom for the oppressed, food for the hungry, care for the sick, promising future for the children and hope for the forgotten and marginalized.

We believe in life before and after death. Modern civilisation has resulted in values we can all celebrate (freedom, human rights, democracy, rationality, progress, etc.), yet at the same time, our societies are often driven by the love of power and money. Our fallen world is scarred by all sorts of evil (violence, corruption, materialism, individualism, ethnic and religious conflicts). Something has gone wrong. Christianity and Islam see all of this as the result of *sin*, our refusal to follow God and the way he has revealed for us. As creatures we are morally accountable to our Creator. One day we will all have to stand before him as our divine judge and give account for the way we have lived in this life.

God has not given up on humanity. He wants to bring us back to himself, to forgive us and to give us a new hope for this life and the next. He wants everyone to worship him as their supreme Lord and King.

Two Religions with a Global Vision
A Response to Chawkat Moucarry

Terje Østebø

How do we view and value our Muslim fellow being? Is he or she regarded as an independent subject or perceived as the 'other' – reduced to an object for mission or as the antithesis of our 'civilizational values'? A main point in Chawkat Moucarry's paper is to redress perspectives based on an asymmetric subject-object relationship and forward ideas for increased parity and improved Christian-Muslim coexistence. Recognising how Christianity and Islam are both rooted in an exclusive and universal paradigm of world mission and *dawa*, he argues that this self-understanding often has produced conflict and confrontation between the two communities. Such a conflictual pattern is far from unavoidable, and he claims that it is possible for both Christians and Muslims to "interpret their faith in terms that promote not only mutual respect but cooperation between the two communities for the common good of society at large." And moreover, that such a "new path" of Christian-Muslim relations does not necessarily compromise "the essential tenets" of the two religious traditions.

Moucarry's paper offers a well-founded and interesting discussion of the main causes for the strained inter-religious relations, both from a historical and contemporary perspective. Particularly appreciable is his emphasis on what he calls "Christian Zionism" and Christians' support for the state of Israel as impinging on the relationship between Christians and Muslims – an issue often overlooked by many Christians. Equally interesting is his discussion of what would be a fruitful Christian approach to Islam, and the suggestive list of what he calls the "five common commitments" – issues that would be shared and agreed upon by both Christians and Muslims, and as committed to by both communities, would improve inter-religious relations and produce a better world.

Terms and conceptualisations are in general carefully applied, with, perhaps, a few exceptions. I am in particular questioning what the writer means by "extremist" versus "mainstream Christians and Muslims". It is probably not Moucarry's intention, but the choice of words brings to mind the unwarranted dichotomy between "the good and the bad Muslim."[1] Analogous to that, and

[1] Mahmoud Mandani, *Good Muslim, Bad Muslim: America, the Cold War, and the Roots of Terror* (New York: Pantheon, 2004).

more problematic, is the manner in which the writer refers to Christianity and Islam as seemingly self-evident categories, as intelligible and inherently homogeneous. Where Moucarry repeatedly refers to the two religions' scriptures as supporting his arguments, we would benefit from being reminded by Michael Lambek, saying that, "texts are by themselves silent."[2] Texts are always read, interpreted and transmitted – often in incongruent and contracting ways – by positioned adherents. Seeing texts, and textual sanctioned symbols and rituals as situated in time and space, a more fruitful approach would be to view the tenets of Islam and Christianity as products of dynamic processes in which the literal traditions are conceived, sanctioned and debated in relation to disparate historical circumstances. Drawing from the insights of Talal Asad, seeing orthodoxy as inherently discursive,[3] my argument is that Moucarry's use of terms such as "the essential tenets" of the two religious traditions, the "Bible teaching" or the "core message" simplifies a far more complex reality, and represents a perspective which comes close to essentialising two overtly heterogeneous and dynamic traditions.

A case in point is Moucarry's description of the main features of Islam. Said to be according to Islamic sources, and as understood by (unidentified) Muslim leaders and scholars, his description is presented as an objective account – as the way *Islam is.* If we understand Qur'an as 'silent' and the so-called tenets of the religion as part of a discursive tradition, Moucarry's view cannot be anything but his own reading. This is for example noticeable in his understanding of Islam as a religion less concerned with the after-life. Rooted in a Weberian perspective, such a perception arguably overlooks the importance of the varied Sufi traditions which clearly emphasise the spiritual realm.[4]

Moucarry claims that inter-religious conflicts and confrontations are caused by the two religious traditions' emphasis on universal mission and *dawa*. There is substantial empirical evidence to support this notion, and it is clear that the modern Protestant mission movement have accentuated tension between the two religious communities. Not least is this true in numerous localities in Africa, where Muslims increasingly see themselves as victims of aggressive Christian evangelism. It is thus rather surprising that the writer does not include this aspect when discussing the roots of Christian-Muslim polarisation. The text would certainly have benefitted from this; how Christian mission is reproducing its own particular subject-object relationship, prolonging the image

---

[2] Michael Lambek, 'Certain Knowledge, Contestable Authority: Power and Practice on the Islamic Periphery', *American Ethnologist* 17. 1 (1990), 23.

[3] Talal Asad, *The Idea of an Anthropology of Islam* (Washington, D.C.: Center for Contemporary Arab Studies, Georgetown University, 1986).

[4] For a discussion on Weber's views, see Bryan S. Turner, 'Islam, Capitalism and the Weber Theses', *The British Journal of Sociology* 25.2 (1974), 230-43; and for a discussion of the this- and other-worldly in contemporary Islam, see Terje Østebø, 'Une économie salafi de la prière dans la région du Balé en Éthiopie', *Afrique Contemporaine*, 231 (2009), 58.

of the Muslim as the orientalised 'other' and reciprocally generating polemic responses from the Muslim side (such as the writings of Ahmed Deedat).[5] While Moucarry sees the issue of seeking converts as fundamental for both Christian and Islamic communities, he underscores, at the same time, the need for improved inter-religious understanding and respect, for increased Christian-Muslim cooperation – something which should not be in contradiction with each other. While he mentions the disparate opinions of Jesus and Mohammed found among Christians and Muslims as incompatible, he seemingly recognises that truth is to be found in both of the religious traditions. In particular, he underscores the notion of monotheism as an important common ground for inter-religious respect and cooperation, and claims that such a shared understanding would enable mutual respect and peaceful co-existence. It is not clear what is meant by the claim that there is "a special bond between monotheistic believers, in particular Jews, Christians and Muslims". Is this of a metaphysical nature, and does it mean that mutual respect and cooperation is less possible between, let's say; Muslims and Hindus or Christians and atheists? As these questions are part of a broader philosophical debate about the question of universal truth found in different religious traditions, I believe Moucarry would have benefitted from more explicitly situating his arguments in relation to the main positions in this debate.

In congruence with the call to work for mutual cooperation, Moucarry underlines the importance of genuine and respectful dialogue. Yet, here he enters one highly difficult aspect of Christian-Muslim relations, namely that of dialogue in relation to making converts. In Moucarry's view, the aim of such a dialogue would both be to enhance understanding of the other's faith, as well as to bear witness to one's faith to the other – which *might* result in conversion to either Christianity or Islam. Nuanced and pragmatic, Moucarry's perspective is very interesting. It recognises the fact that many Christians and Muslims see the task of seeking adherents as an irreducible imperative, yet tries to revert itself from a view which sees Christian-Muslim relations as exclusively constituted by mission and *dawa*, i.e. the task of seeking converts. Delineating himself from the issue of trying to convert people by dishonest means and emphasising the issue of mission and *dawa* as the *presentation* of one's faith, Moucarry makes an important point when he understands this as one of many possible aspects of inter-religious relations. Not only does this approach guard us from unnecessary tensions, as a result of inappropriate means of action, but it moreover brings us beyond the risk of reducing our fellow human beings to objects for proselytization – something which is very often seen in organised mission and *dawa* movements. This does not mean, however, that the complexity found intrinsic to the question of dialogue in relation to mission and *dawa* is solved. Although there are voices from both the Christian and Muslim communities that see mission and *dawa* as incompatible with genuine dialogue

[5] For an enlightening discussion of Deedat's writings, see David Westerlund, 'Ahmed Deedat's Theology of Religion: Apologetics through Polemics', *Journal of Religion in Africa* 33.3 (2003), 263-278.

and mutual respect, it is likely to assume that the vast majority of the two faiths' adherents would advocate the task of seeking converts as an integrated part of their call in the world. Yet, even in this respect, Moucarry's emphasis on learning to understand and respect each other would be of relevance. Enhanced knowledge of the respective religious traditions could not only be limited to the promotion of equality, justice and peaceful co-existence, but could also be integrated with efforts to generate mutual understanding of the two religious communities exclusive and universal claims of world-wide mission and *dawa*.

Mission to Muslims after Edinburgh 1910
A Century of Lessons for the Missional Church

Jan Opsal[1]

The World Mission Conference in 1910 gave a significant contribution to the globalisation of mission to Muslims as two of the four challenges to the global church were related to the encounter with Islam.[2] During the century that has passed since then, the Christian Church, including the mission movement, has been introduced to a number of lessons to be learned concerning the relationship to Muslims.[3] Ten such lessons are introduced and discussed in this contribution, without claiming that this is in any way a comprehensive list. But the selection has been made in order to identify some significant experiences during the last century that the missional church has made, and hopefully learned from. The ten lessons are lessons of:

- Competition
- Colonialism
- Communication
- Conversion
- Contextualization
- Cooperation
- Conflict
- Controversy

---

[1] In the final post-conference version of his paper, Professor Jan Opsal has taken note of several of Dr Chawkat Moucarry's helpful comments.

[2] World Missionary Conference Edinburgh 1910, *Report of Commission I-VIII / Published for the World Missionary Conference* (Edinburgh: Oliphant, Anderson & Ferrier 1910), 364. The four recommendations were related to China, Equatorial Africa, India and the Mohammedan World, especially the Near East. The fact that two of the four recommendations were related to Islam is remarkable, and may indicate that Samuel M. Zwemer had a significant influence as one of the members of the commission of the conference.

[3] During this period there has been an ongoing discussion on the relationship between 'church' and 'mission'. Our context here is not the place to unfold this discussion, we can deal with our issues without establishing a defined relationship between church and mission, in many cases these terms can be used alternately. The term 'missional church' is combining the perspectives of 'church' and 'mission' and will be used here.

- Creativity
- Counterculturalism

This list of lessons is a contribution to a curriculum of historical practice and experience. Some of the lessons may already be learned, others are yet to be identified and taken seriously by many leaders in the missional church today.

Competition

"The threatening advance of Islam in Equatorial Africa presents to the Church of Christ the decisive question whether the Dark Continent shall become Mohammedan or Christian." This was one of the four fields to which the World Missionary Conference in 1910 with special urgency challenged the church as a whole to concentrate attention and effort.[4]

The German missionary H. Karl Kumm had made a deep impression on the participants in Edinburgh in 1910 as he read a list of 27 African peoples he had visited in the belt between the Sahara desert and the rainforest as he traveled from West Africa to East Africa the year before the conference.[5] This region was called the Sudan after the Arabic term for black. In this region there were few mission stations and Islam was established in the northern part and spreading rapidly to the south. Kumm's appeal was not a new one. Already in the mid-nineteenth century Johan Ludwig Krapf had made the same observation and proposal. An international Sudan mission movement had already started, the Sudan Interior Mission had been established in 1893 and Kumm himself had himself initiated the founding of the Sudan United Mission in 1904. Kumm advocated establishing a chain of mission stations and churches across Africa in order to stem the southward advance of Islam. Both these missions were international missions in a double sense. They established sending groups in several countries and they started mission work in several countries in the Sudan belt. Also other Christian missions took part in the new Sudan mission enterprise.

In this context Islam was seen as a competitor in a race for territorial dominance in Sub-Saharan Africa. The actual emphasis was geographical, although the concern for the salvation of the peoples of the Sudan belt was strongly expressed. The expansion of Islam was seen as a geographical process, being stimulated by the constructions of highways and railways, as well as by colonial administration, according to Kumm.[6]

Another aspect of Kumm's perspectives was the perception that once a person or a people group became Islamized, they were lost to Christianity. He warned that if nothing was done, the 27 peoples could become Islamized in the

---

[4] World Missionary Conference Edinburgh 1910, *Report of Commission I-VIII,* 364.
[5] *Ibid.*, 406-407.
[6] *Ibid.*, 407.

near future, stating: "They are worth the winning, and it will be an eternal shame on our generation if we let those tribes go over to Islam."[7]

Kumm saw Christianity and Islam competing for dominance in Sub-Saharan Africa, and the Sudan belt was to him the most important arena of this competition. The rhetoric of Kumm focused both on the territorial and ethnic dimension of the mission to the Sudan, but his main emphasis was on winning these ethnic groups before they were reached by Islam.

The Sudan mission movement was boosted by the Edinburgh conference. After World War I many initiatives were made to establish Christian ministries in the Sudan belt, and there were at times competition also between different mission societies in securing the most attractive fields for their respective ministries. According to Latourette, the number of Christians in Africa increased more than fivefold during three decades from 1914, in a period where the total population of Africa probably did not increase greatly, if at all.[8]

The perspective of competition between Christianity and Islam can be related to other fields as well during the century that has passed since the Edinburgh conference. But the concept of Christianity and Islam competing for ground, for people and for souls has probably not been this clearly expressed earlier and has certainly not led to such a significant international response in the form of a concentrated mission effort.

Colonialism

At the time of the Edinburgh 1910 conference, most of the missionaries came from the Western world, and most of the Muslim areas were colonized by Christian nations in the West. This situation is reflected in the documents from Edinburgh. One interesting example is this quote from the Vice-Chairman of the Commission, Rev. George Robson from Scotland: "I say with shame that the British administration gives every encouragement to pagans becoming Muslims and hinders Christian missionaries from appealing to Moslems."[9] This quote shows that there was at least not always a close partnership between the colonial administration and the mission movement. But maybe it also shows that some mission leaders thought that the colonial administrations should at least not hinder the missionary work in the colonies.

Edinburgh 1910 did not seem to see colonisation as a problem. The burden of the colonial past is a lesson the mission movement has had to learn later in the century passing since 1910. Missions from the West, especially from the former colonial empires, have had to learn lessons of redefining their relationships to churches and populations in the former colonies, for example in terms of partnership.

---

[7] *Ibid.*, 407.

[8] Kenneth S. Latourette, *A History of the Expansion of Christianity, Volume 7: Advance Through Storm: AD 1914 and after, with concluding generalizations* (Grand Rapids MI: Zondervan Publishing House 1970 [1945]), 249.

[9] World Missionary Conference Edinburgh 1910, *Report of Commission I-VIII*, 406.

During the colonial period, Muslim intellectuals saw a parallel between the crusades and the colonisation of the Middle East and other Muslim areas. The concept was that the colonisation was a new attempt to achieve what failed during the time of the crusades, so the crusades became a hermeneutical key for interpreting colonialism. In this perspective Christian missions were perceived as an integral part of the colonial strategy, a strategy that took different imperialist forms after most colonies became independent around 1960. The Libyan mission organisation Call of Islam Society produced a sticker with this text for use in African contexts: "Islam in Africa is, like in the Orient, at war against a crusade." The sticker maintained that Western engagements in Muslim contexts should be regarded as crusader activities, and be fought. Although this perspective is particularly relevant in the Arab Middle East, the sticker indicates that any mission to Muslims had to be prepared to be perceived as a crusading effort.

Palestinian literature professor Edward Said coined the term Orientalism as a key to understand Western attitudes to the Orient, including the Muslim Middle East.[10] He argued that there was "...a Western style for dominating, restructuring, and having authority over the Orient."[11] Orientalism served in Western literature and scholarship as "...an accepted grid for filtering through the Orient into Western consciousness."[12] Through this filtering grid the West got a distorted image of the Oriental as the Other, an image that reflected the otherness of the Oriental, and as such had less to do with the Orient than with the Western world.[13] According to Said's concept, Orientalism implied that the West construed the Orient as a negative contrast to its own self-image. Said initiated a debate that engaged a broad range of scholarly disciplines,[14] and is now a part of the wider postcolonial field.

Said's perspectives had a particular relevance when it came to the image of Islam in the West. In his book *Covering Islam* he states that, "yet there is a consensus on 'Islam' as a kind of scapegoat for everything we do not happen to like."[15] This perspective on Islam is not a new one, it has been identified from medieval times in Europe.[16] It is interesting that Said brings this perspective up, as he himself was a Middle Easterner, but not a Muslim.

---

[10] Edward Said, *Orientalism* (London:Penguin Books Ltd 1985 [1978]).

[11] *Ibid.*, 3.

[12] *Ibid.*, 6.

[13] *Ibid.*, 12.

[14] A.L. Macfie, *Orientalism: A Reader* (Cairo: Cairo University Press, 2000). This reader contains several key texts of Said himself, of philosophers and scholars that influenced him, and it documents important aspects of the debate he initiated.

[15] Edward Said, *Covering Islam. How the Media and the Experts Determine How We See the Rest of the World* (London: Routledge & Kegan Paul PLC 1981), xv.

[16] See N. Daniel *Islam and the West: The Making of an Image* (Oxford: Oneworld, 2nd edition, 1993) and W.M. Watt, *The Influence of Islam on Medieval Europe* (Islamic Surveys 9, Edinburgh: Edinburgh University Press, 1972) for this perspective.

Developments of the century since Edinburgh 1910 have challenged the mission movement to realize that mission cannot escape the consequences of colonialism. The last few decades have been a learning process in dealing with the recent political past of the West and the way it influences Christian-Muslim relations today. The mission movement is challenged by postcolonial insights in general and by Said's criticism of orientalism in particular to reconsider and evaluate its activities and attitudes with regard to Islam and Muslims.

These might be hard lessons to learn. In many Christian texts on Islam, Islam is often described as 'everything we do not happen to like' – that is as a negative contrast to ourselves. Some Christian ministries still use crusader terminology for its Christian ministry in Muslim contexts, in spite of the strong negative connotations this term carries for most Muslims. A more structural issue is the issue of power, the question of how the mission relates to different dimensions of power in its relations to Muslims.

Communication

The fourth challenge the World Mission Conference presented to the church as a whole, was the Muslim world, was formulated like this:

> The problems of the Mohammedan World, especially in the Near East, which, until recently, received little consideration from the church at large, have been lifted unexpectedly into prominence and urgency, as well as into new relations, by the marvellous changes which have taken place in Turkey and Persia. One of the important tasks before the church at this time is to deal adequately with these problems.[17]

In this statement the decline of power of the Ottoman dynasty in Turkey and the Persian Constitutional Revolution were called "marvellous changes" that lifted the "problems of the Mohammedan World" into "prominence and urgency." The conference clearly felt that this was a time to focus on the Muslim world.

This emphasis was clearly a result of Samuel M. Zwemer being a member of the committee for the World Mission Conference, working closely with John R. Mott in developing the perspectives of the conference. Zwemer himself started working in the Middle East in 1891, and he had been central in the mission conference in Cairo in 1906, after this conference Zwemer wrote: "Throughout vast regions of the Mohammedan world millions of Moslems have never so much as heard of the incarnation and atonement of the Son of God, the Savior of the world."[18] For Zwemer, dealing adequately with the problems of the Muslim world was to communicate the Gospel to the Muslims, and he was

[17] World Missionary Conference Edinburgh 1910, *Report of Commission I-VIII*, 364.

[18] Samuel M. Zwemer, *Islam: A Challenge to Faith: studies on the Mohammedan religion and the needs and opportunities of the Mohammedan world from the standpoint of Christian mission* (New York: Laymen's Missionary Movement, 2nd edition, 1909), 255.

obviously instrumental in convincing the Edinburgh conference that this task was an urgent task for the church as a whole.

Following the World Mission Conference in 1910, Zwemer continued urging the Christian Church to become involved in communicating the Gospel to Muslims, especially through his many books and as an editor of the periodical *The Muslim World.* He inspired a number of mission organisations to take up work among Muslims. He especially challenged them to share the Gospel with Muslims in the heartlands of Islam, the Arabic Middle East.

The task of communicating the Gospel in a non-Christian world was also the focus of Hendrik Kraemer as he presented his book *The Christian Message in a Non-Christian World* as an input to the 1938 World Missionary Conference in Tambaram in India. As he evaluated the challenge of communicating to Muslims, he rejects the idea of building on the similarities between Islam and Christianity, stating that:

> …the entrance to this impregnable religious citadel cannot be opened by presenting Christianity to the Moslem mind as the enrichment of the half-truths as to its belief in God, its veneration for Jesus, its logos speculation, its conception of fraternity, etc., or developing into full growth what is to be found, for instance, in the Qur'an about the Holy Spirit (*ruh*) and the need for an intercessor.[19]

Kraemer's position on this is hardly surprising following his discussion on points of contact with other religions, where he takes the theology of religion of Karl Barth as his starting point and concludes that the point of contact is found in a trustful meeting with the person, not in similarities between the religions.[20] As for the approach to Islam, he states that:

> …the best method undoubtedly is direct personal contact and study of the Bible in a spirit of human sympathy and openness, the Moslem being treated not as a non-Christian, but as a fellow-man with the same fundamental needs, aspirations and frustrations, whose religious experience and insights are as worth while as the missionary's, simply because he is a living human being.[21]

After World War II there was a significant increase in the sending of missionaries to Muslim contexts, and there was an emphasis on the perspectives of Zwemer, Kraemer and others on the task of communicating the Gospel to Muslims. A wide range of books were published in this field, with titles as: *A Christian Approach to Muslims*[22] or *Share Your Faith With a Muslim.*[23] These books dealt with issues of contact points and communication challenges. One example is James P. Dretke's discussion on the common religious terminology of Christianity and Islam as a communication problem,

---

[19] Hendrik Kraemer, *The Christian Message in a Non-Christian World* (London: The Edinburgh House Press, 1938), 355.

[20] *Ibid.*, 130-141.

[21] *Ibid.*, 356.

[22] James P. Dretke, *A Christian Approach to Muslims. Reflections from West Africa* (Pasadena, CA:William Carey Library, 1979).

[23] Charles Marsh, *Share Your Faith with a Muslim* (Kent:STK Books, 1980).

he titles his chapter on this issue: 'Same words – different meanings'.[24] Another type of Christian literature is more apologetic, addressing Muslim questions and objections towards Christianity.[25]

The 1974 Lausanne Congress saw communicating the Gospel as a main task for the whole church: "World evangelization requires the whole church to take the whole gospel to the whole world."[26] The focus on the whole world had to imply everybody: "The goal should be, by all available means and at the earliest possible time, that every person will have the opportunity to hear, understand, and to receive the good news."[27] This emphasis made it more difficult for evangelical missions to prioritize only the most receptive and responsive peoples, as everyone, including Muslims, had a right to hear and understand the good news.

The second Lausanne congress in Manila in 1989 addressed the religious pluralism more explicitly and rejected relativism and syncretism:

> There is only one gospel because there is only one Christ, who because of his death and resurrection is himself the only way of salvation. We therefore reject both the relativism which regards all religions and spiritualities as equally valid approaches to God, and the syncretism which tries to mix faith in Christ with other faiths.[28]

The one gospel is according to the Manila Manifesto to be communicated in an increasingly pluralistic world, and the manifesto states that the uniqueness, indispensability and centrality of Christ should be affirmed.[29] This has clearly implications for the mission to Muslims as well, as Islam is the largest religion outside Christianity. Any statements on the policy of communicating Christ in a pluralist setting would have to be applied to Islam in order to be valid at all.

Conversion

For many decades, the statistical results of the missionary efforts in Muslim contexts were small. But some Muslims responded to the message. Their conversion stories were often dramatic ones, and some of these testimonies were published. Some books told the story of one convert, like Hassan Dehqani-Tafti[30] and Bilquis Sheikh.[31] Others were collections of shorter testimonies, one typical title is *Jesus – More Than a Prophet*, where twelve

---

[24] Dretke, *A Christian Approach to Muslims,* 26-38.

[25] Norman L. Geisler and Abdul Saleeb, *Answering Islam: The Crescent in Light of the Cross* (Michigan: Baker Books, 1993).

[26] Lausanne Covenant, art. 6, www.lausanne.org/covenant, accessed 31.3.2010.

[27] Lausanne Covenant , art. 9.

[28] Manila Manifesto, section A, point 3, www.lausanne.org/manila-1989/manila-manifesto.html, accessed 31.3.2010.

[29] Manila Manifesto, section A.

[30] H.B. Dehqani-Tafti, *The Hard Awakening* (London:Triangle/SPCK 1982).

[31] Bilquis Sheikh, *I Dared to Call Him Father* (Virginia: Kingsway Publications1982).

former Muslims told their stories.[32] A common denominator in these individual stories was the negative reactions of the family and wider social context of the convert. These reactions were also used to explain why relatively few Muslims were responsive to the mission work.

Conversions from Islam to Christianity in Pakistan were studied by the Finnish missionary Seppo Syrjänen, who made use of a multidisciplinary approach to the topic, including theological, psychological, sociological and religio-phenomenological theories.[33] His qualitative study included 36 informants, which was in fact close to the total numbers of known converts from Islam to Christianity in Pakistan in the mid-seventies. Some of them had converted decades ago, whereas many of them had made their decision during the last decade before Syrjänen did his fieldwork.

Most of them had experienced alienation from Islam in one way or another before becoming attracted to Christianity. Three elements played key roles in this attraction, the first one being a supernatural event, experienced by nine of them.[34] The second one was the Bible in one way or another, one striking feature being the frequent occurrence of Mt 11.28 in their testimonies about their conversion. The third element was the significance of a Christian friend. This friend could be a local Christian, an expatriate missionary or a person in a radio program or responding to a Christian correspondence course.

In Indonesia there were much bigger numbers of converts from Islam to Christianity. Avery Willis tries to explain why two million Muslims came to Christ in the Indonesian revival.[35] This movement was triggered by the Indonesian government, trying to prevent communism from getting a foothold in the country. The government promoted a policy called the *pancasila* (five pillars) of Indonesia, the first one being an obligation for all citizens to believe in the one God. Five different religions were acknowledged as having such a belief, and all citizens were required to register their religious affiliation.

In this process, many Indonesians with a Muslim background decided to register as Christians. Willis generated quantitative data on this process and was able to identify a number of reasons for this. The informants could mention several of eleven factors, but they were supposed to mention the most important one first. Most frequently the government was mentioned as a factor in the conversion, closely followed by the church. The church had offered protection to many people with a Muslim background who were harassed by militant Muslims to register as Muslims. After being protected by, and often in a church, many decided to register as Christians, and protection was listed among the seven most frequently mentioned factors. Those who mentioned protection,

---

[32] R.W.F. Wootton, *Jesus – More Than a Prophet* (Bromley: Inter-Varsity press 1982).

[33] Seppo Syrjänen, *In Search of Meaning and Identity: Conversion to Christianity in Pakistani Muslim Culture* (Vammala: The Finnish Society for Missiology and Ecumenics 1987), 24-46.

[34] Syrjänen, *In Search of Meaning and Identity*, 129-141.

[35] Avery T. Willis, *Indonesian Revival: Why Two Million Came to Christ* (South Pasadena, CA., William Carey Library, 1977).

often put this factor first, so the three most important factors were: spiritual need, government and protection.[36] Another striking feature of this study is that miracles rank at the bottom of the lists, both the one with the causes mentioned first and the one listing the most frequently mentioned causes.[37]

Willis investigated the Indonesian revival from a church growth perspective, making use of the theories developed in the church growth movement in order to understand the dynamics of the revival better. He noted that in most of the cases people converted together with family members, so they were not alienated from their family as a result of the conversion. These and other sociological factors were used to explain how the Indonesian revival developed.[38]

The study by Willis demonstrates that conversion needs to be studied in its specific social and historical context, and that both theological and sociological theories and methods are helpful in order to understand the processes influencing such a social movement as the one in Indonesia.

In a South African qualitative study of a total of twenty conversions both ways between Christianity and Islam, the Swiss researcher Andreas Maurer identified both similarities and differences between the two groups of converts.[39] Maurer analyzed five conversion motives, and both the religious and the affectionate motive were expressed by eighteen of the total of twenty converts. But only six of the ten converts to Christianity and none of the Muslims reported the mystical motive, having had a supernatural experience in connection with the conversion. Five of the converts to Islam expressed a sociopolitical motive, which can be understood on the background of Christian support for the apartheid regime in South Africa.[40]

Conversions to Christianity by Fulani Muslims in Nigeria were studied by the former Danish missionary to the country, Mogens S. Mogensen.[41] Mogensen combined both quantitative and qualitative methods as he studied this West African context.

During the last few decades there have been significant numbers of conversions in two other contexts. One is among Iranians, inside and outside Iran. This movement has taken place especially after the Islamic Revolution in Iran in 1979. It is quite ironic that the Islamic Revolution led to more conversions to Christianity than the Constitutional Revolution in 1906, which was seen as a 'marvelous change' in Edinburgh in 1910. Many people who came to dislike the changes after 1979 were alienated from Islam in this way, and they have decided to leave Islam as a consequence. The other context is in

[36] *Ibid.*, 12.
[37] *Ibid.*, 13 and 24.
[38] *Ibid.*, 123.
[39] Abstract of Maurer's dissertation available at www.versoehnung.net/wp-content/uploads/Abstract-Maurer.pdf – accessed 30.3.2010.
[40] Maurer, *Abstract*, 5
[41] Mogens S. Mogensen *Contextual Communication of the Gospel to Pastoral Fulbe in Northern Nigeria* (Ann Arbor: UMI, 2001).

South Asia, where former Muslims are heading numerous groups of new believers.

Contextualization

As the number of converts from Islam to Christianity increased, contextualization became a major issue in the missiological debate concerning mission to Muslims. This was not a new issue, suffice to mention Kraemer's discussion on contact points in 1938. But the church growth movement placed the issue of contextualization in a wider context, assuming that if the missions made the right decisions in terms of methodology, the results would increase.

These perspectives were central in the 1978 North American Conference on Muslim Evangelization at Glen Eyrie, Colorado, organized jointly by the Lausanne Movement and World Vision International. Lausanne President Leighton Ford writes that Don McCurry, the director of the conference and a former missionary in Pakistan, was "…convinced that one of the greatest obstacles to Muslim evangelization was the lack of culturally congenial churches for Muslim converts."[42] World Vision President W. Stanley Mooneyham sees the conference as a history-changing conference, as "…the participants left believing that God is doing a new work among Muslim peoples and that the church must move quickly if it is to be a faithful instrument in his hands."[43]

Don McCurry himself put a strong emphasis on the cultural and contextual relevance of the ministry to Muslims under the headline, "A time for new beginnings."[44] His approach had been developed in the classroom at Fuller School of World Mission, and was aimed at a more efficient ministry to Muslims.[45] Fuller Scholars like Arthur F. Glasser,[46] Charles H. Kraft[47] and Paul Hiebert[48] made central contributions to the conference on the issue of contextualization.

Shortly after the Glen Eyrie conference, Phil Parshall published his book *New Paths in Muslim Evangelism.*[49] This book became a central document in the missiological and methodological discussions on mission to Muslims in the following years. Parshall shared with Don McCurry the conviction that new ways were needed for the mission work to become efficient in Muslim contexts.

---

[42] Don McCurry (ed), *The Gospel and Islam. A 1978 Compendium* (Monrovia, CA: MARC 1979), 5.
[43] *Ibid.*, 7.
[44] *Ibid.*, 16.
[45] *Ibid.*, 18.
[46] *Ibid.*, 129.
[47] *Ibid.*, 114.
[48] *Ibid.*, 58.
[49] Phil Parshall, *New Paths in Muslim Evangelism* (Grand Rapids MI: Baker Book House, 1980).

The issue of contextualization was a controversial one, and many were afraid of syncretism as a result of a high degree of contextualization in Muslim contexts. Some tried to distinguish between contextualizing to a Muslim culture, which was accepted, and contextualizing to the Islamic religion, which was not accepted. Fuller Professor J. Dudley Woodberry demonstrated that this distinction was not an easy one, as contextualization among Muslims could imply 'Reusing common Pillars.'[50] In this article he documented that the first four pillars of Islam have roots in Biblical traditions, so if new Christians from a Muslim background wish to develop similar forms for their Christian worship, they can find Biblical models for such worship.

Issues of contextualization are also central in the book *Muslims & Christians on the Emmaus Road.*[51] The understanding of the Gospel, the forms of witness and the new Christian worship are all evaluated according to the dynamics of contextualization. Former Muslims are making significant contributions to this volume. In other cases, former Muslims have been critical towards the issue of contextualization, advocating a clear departure from everything reminding them of their Muslim past as a consequence of their conversion.

Cooperation

During the latter part of the twentieth century there was a growing concern that Christians and Muslims needed to meet and work together for the common good, especially for peace and mutual understanding.

This was a controversial issue in the 1960s. The World Council of Churches (WCC) brought Christians from the Muslim world together in Broumana in 1966 to discuss issues of dialogue with Muslims.[52] Some of them were disappointed that the topic was not placed at the agenda of the WCC assembly in Stockholm in 1968, but Victor E. W. Hayward concluded that "...experience at the Broumana consultation only confirmed the view that we are not yet ready to take up this question fruitfully at a large assembly."[53] This indicates that in the member churches of WCC there were conflicting views on this issue, and this became very clear as Christians living in Muslim contexts were discussing the relationship to Islam.

But from 1969 and onwards, the WCC organized a series of dialogical meetings between Christians and Muslims, some of them also including people from other faiths as well. These dialogues developed from "friendly conversations" to including on the agenda "divisive and conflictive issues"

---

[50] J. Dudley Woodberry, 'Contextualization among Muslims: reusing common pillars', in Gilliland, Dean S., (eds), *The Word Among Us* (Dallas, TX:Word, 1989).

[51] J. Dudley Woodberry, *Muslims and Christians on the Emmaus Road* (Monrovia CA:MARC, 1989). This book was a result of a second Lausanne/World Vision initiated conference, some ten years after the Glen Eyrie conference.

[52] World Council of Churches, *Christians Meeting Muslims: WCC Papers on Ten Years of Christian-Muslim Dialogue* (Geneva:World Council of Churches, 1977).

[53] *Ibid.*, 14.

according to Tarek Mitri, WCC executive secretary for Interreligious Relations and Dialogue.[54]

One of the more divisive and conflictive issues was brought up in Chambésy in 1976. In this dialogue Christian mission and Islamic da'wah was the topic, and the idea was to draw up a common code of conduct and reach a shared understanding of religious liberty.[55] However, none of this was possible, and the documents from the meeting reflect sharp disagreement on interpretation of the past.

There was also disagreement between Christians on the issue. Sir Norman Anderson discusses whether a Christian response to pluralism should be proclamation or dialogue – or both.[56] He concludes that there is a difference between evangelism and dialogue, but that a clear-cut line cannot be drawn between the two of them.[57] Many evangelicals would accept dialogue only as a tool of evangelization, and they could not agree with the theological implications of the WCC dialogue program. One of the issues being discussed was the issue of whether syncretism may be implicitly or explicitly an element of dialogue and other forms of cooperation.[58] Another aspect of this discussion was whether dialogue or other forms of cooperation would include Christians and Muslims praying together, and if so, in which form.

Missionaries had, however, been engaged in different forms of dialogue for a long time. Both Ramon Llull and Henry Martyn had taken part in public debates with Muslims. These often turned out to increase the antagonism between the two parties, illustrating that a podium is a difficult setting for a dialogue. A more recent example is the dialogue in East Africa between the Muslim Badru Kateregga and the missionary David Shenk.[59] This dialogue proved that it was possible for a Christian and a Muslim to have an open conversation on theological issues and deal with theological agreements and disagreements in a respectful way. The book has been translated into a number of languages and is still available more than three decades after the dialogue took place.

---

[54] Jutta Sperber, *Christians and Muslims: The Dialogue Activities of the World Council of Churches and their Theological Foundation* (Berlin/NewYork: Walter de Gruyter, 2000), v.

[55] Sperber, *Christians and Muslims* , 101.

[56] Sir Norman Anderson, *Christianity and World Religions: The Challenge of Pluralism* (Leicester UK/Downers Grove IL: Inter-Varsity Press 1984 [1970]), 176-194.

[57] *Ibid.*, 192.

[58] Jerald Gort, Hendrik Vroom, Rein Fernhout and Anton Wessels (eds), *Dialogue and Syncretism: An Interdisciplinary Approach* (Grand Rapids, MI: William B. Eerdmans Publishing Company, 1989). In this volume issues of syncretism are discussed related to a number of contexts, demonstrating that 'syncretism' is a difficult term to define and use. Missiologists have often held that syncretism starts where legitimate contextualization ends, but there is no general agreement on where the line between contextualization or dialogue on one hand and syncretism on the other is to be drawn.

[59] Badru Kateregga and David W. Shenk, *Islam and Christianity: A Muslim and a Christian in Dialogue* (Dodoma, Tanzania: Central Tanganyika Press, 1980).

Beside the WCC, the German theologian Hans Küng became a central actor in inter-religious dialogue in the late twentieth century.[60] He opposed the secularist theories of the declining significance of religion and maintained that there would be no peace in the world without peace between the religions, and that there would be no peace between the religions without dialogue between them.

Küng was one of the organizers of the second World Parliament of Religion in Chicago in 1993, one hundred years after the first one. The parliament resulted in a declaration on a global ethic,[61] developed out of a conviction that there was a common ethical ground between the religions and that the followers of different religions could work together to make the world a better place.

During the last few decades, a significant level of trust has been built between Christians and Muslims on a number of local, national and international levels. The level of mistrust was often high before the dialogical programs started.[62] By talking through agreements and disagreements, the participants have often found that it is possible to find a common ground on which to build a constructive conversation (dialogue) and cooperation (diapraxis). Social projects have been developed in contexts where Christians and Muslims live together in poor communities. Muslims in dialogue with Christians in the West have become advocates for Christians facing difficult circumstances in Muslim countries. Christians in dialogue with Muslims have spoken up against harassment of Muslims in Western public spheres.

'A Common Word' - the open letter sent by 138 Muslim leaders in October 2007 to all Christian leaders of the world has been received by many Christian leaders as a sign of hope for Muslim-Christian understanding and cooperation.[63] The letter points out that as Muslims and Christians combined comprise more than half of the population of the world, there will not be peace in the world without peace between Muslims and Christians. The letter suggests that a basis for peace can be found in the ideal of loving God and loving one's neighbor, which is seen as the 'Common Word' by the Muslim leaders, who are extensively quoting Biblical texts in their letter. Several aspects of this letter have given hope for a trustful cooperation between Muslims and Christians for improving the relations between the two communities.

---

[60] Hans Küng, Josef van Ess, Heinrich von Stietencron and Heinz Bechert (eds), *Christianity and World Religions: Paths to Dialogue with Islam, Hinduism and Buddhism* (New York: Doubleday, 1986).

[61] Karl-Josef Kuschel and Hans Küng (eds), *A Global Ethic: The Declaration of the Parliament of the World's Religions* (London: SCM Press, 1993).

[62] Ataullah Siddiqui, *Christian-Muslim Dialogue in the Twentieth Century* (Basingstoke, Hampshire/New York: Palgrave, Macmillan 1997) and Kate Zebiri, *Muslims and Christians Face to Face* (Oxford: Oneworld Publications, 2003 [1997]) give insights in the perspectives of the Muslim participants in these dialogues and efforts.

[63] Miroslav Volf, Ghazi bin Muhammad and Melissa Yarrington (eds), *A Common Word: Muslims and Christians on Loving God and Neighbour* (Grand Rapids MI/Cambridge UK: William B. Eerdmans Publishing Company, 2010). The full text of the letter is included in this publication.

Unfortunately there is also another story, a story not only of distrust, but also of violence. We will deal with this story of violent conflict in the next section.

Conflict

During the last few decades we have also seen a significant number of violent conflicts between Muslims and Christians. In countries like Nigeria, Sudan, Lebanon and Indonesia thousands of people have been killed in such conflicts. But are these conflicts rightly identified as religious conflicts because they are conflicts with Muslims on one side and Christians on the other side?

Many secular sociologists and political scientists are responding negatively to that question, identifying socio-economic and political factors that can explain the conflict between those groups. A negative response to the question above can also be derived from an idealistic concept of religion, holding that true religion does not promote violence, only abuse of religion leads to violence.

Another perspective has been advocated by political scientist Samuel P. Huntington and termed as the theory of the clash of civilizations, a term he borrowed from Bernard Lewis.[64] Huntington introduced the concept in an article in *Foreign Affairs*[65] and elaborated the theory later in his book *The Clash of Civilizations and the Remaking of World Order*.[66] He identifies a conflict between Islam and the West and sees this conflict as a conflict between civilisations:

> The underlying problem for the West is not Islamic fundamentalism. It is Islam, a different civilization whose people are convinced of the superiority of their culture and obsessed with the inferiority of their power. The problem for Islam is not the CIA or the U.S. Department of Defense. It is the West, a different civilization whose people are convinced of the universality of their culture and believe that their superior, if declining, power imposes upon them the obligation to extend that culture throughout the world. These are the basic ingredients that fuel conflict between Islam and the West.[67]

This perspective is developed out of a set of assumptions regarding the relationship between what he identifies as the Western civilization and the Islamic civilization. On one hand he sees the West against the Rest, referring to all the other civilizations combined.[68] On the other hand he identifies the conflict between the West and Islam as a conflict that develops out of the very nature of the West and the very nature of Islam, seeing it as a conflict

---

[64] Samuel P. Huntington, *The Clash of Civilizations and the Remaking of World Order* (New York: Touchstone, 1997[1996]), 213.

[65] Samuel P. Huntington, 'The Clash of Civilizations?', in *Foreign Affairs* (Tampa, FL, 72(3), 1993) 22-49.

[66] Huntington, *The Clash of Civilizations and the Remaking of World Order*.

[67] *Ibid.*, 217-218.

[68] *Ibid.*, 183, 245.

> …between two different versions of what is right and what is wrong and, as a consequence, who is right and who is wrong. So long as Islam remains Islam (which it will) and the West remains the West (which is more dubious), this fundamental conflict between two great civilizations will continue to define their relations in the future even as it has defined them for the past fourteen centuries.[69]

These quotes locate the conflict between Islam and the West as two civilizations. But Huntington relates what he calls the causes of the ongoing pattern of conflict directly to the religions: "The causes of this ongoing pattern of conflict lie not in transitory phenomena such as twelfth-century Christian passion or twentieth-century Muslim fundamentalism. They flow from the nature of the two religions and the civilizations based on them."[70] The causes are according to Huntington related to both differences and similarities between the two religions, such as the difference with regard to the relationship between religion and state, and the similarities of monotheism, universalism and the obligation to convert non-believers to the one true faith.[71] We should note that missionary zeal is seen by Huntington as one of the elements in his conflict explanation theory. We also have to admit that in some cases unwise missionary zeal has triggered social conflicts, even violent ones.

Huntington's arguments have been adapted by many and criticized by others. Those agreeing with Huntington find in his analysis a key to understand the frequent conflicts between Muslim and Christian ethnic groups and between Muslim and Christian countries. Those disagreeing with Huntington find his arguments to be developed more from an ideological conviction than on convincing empirical findings. He is, of course, using historical facts to support his argument. But he is neglecting other facts that do not support his main theory. He claims that 50% of wars involving pairs of states of different religions between 1820 and 1929 were wars between Muslims and Christians.[72] But as Muslims and Christians in that period constituted nearly 50% of the population of the world, this does hardly prove anything, even if the claim is correct.

By arguing for an underlying, invisible cause of conflict between Muslims and Christians, Huntington is downplaying the causes that can be found by an empirical analysis of each individual conflict. It can be argued against Huntington that violent conflicts between Muslims and Christians can be adequately understood by analyzing the empirical issues related to conflicts. Most conflicts are related to issues regarding one or several of these fields: resources, rights and religion. By issues of resources we think of water, land, oil, minerals and other natural resources. By issues of rights we think of democratic, political and human rights, including minority rights. By religious issues we think of oppression and marginalization of religious minorities, religious freedom and equal opportunities regardless of religious affiliation.

---

[69] *Ibid.*, 212.
[70] *Ibid.*, 210.
[71] *Ibid.*, 210-211.
[72] *Ibid.*, 210.

The difference between this position and that of Huntington is that these religious issues can be identified and managed, whereas Huntington claims that there are issues that cannot be changed, because they are essential to the religions and the civilizations he refers to.

Some Christians are also referring to another type of war with Islam, a spiritual warfare. The idea has a Biblical reference in Eph 6, but it has been developed into a comprehensive ideology and methodology in some Christian circles.[73]

Those promoting the concept of spiritual warfare would probably emphasize that they are not fighting against people, but against spiritual powers, like Paul also points out in Eph 6.12. All the same, it can be argued that a certain type of focus on spiritual warfare can create an impression that the main task of the mission is to secure victory in the spiritual warfare. There is a danger that such an approach removes the focus from Muslims as fellow human beings and reduces them to a booty won in a battle fought with demons. There is also a danger that the rhetoric of spiritual warfare related to Islam can stimulate and fuel antagonism between Christians and Muslims, and be used to legitimize hostility and violence from the Christian side in a conflict with Muslim neighbors.

Controversy

A number of issues have already revealed disagreements within the church and also within the mission movement. This can be seen in the context of modernity and late modernity or postmodernity, as plurality is one of the key elements of a modern society. Our issue here is to identify and discuss some selected areas of controversy within the church and the mission movement, like the issue of Christian theology of Islam and of Muslim followers of Jesus. These issues are examples of controversies developing between Christians, controversies that most probably will not be resolved, so the church will most likely have to live with a considerable amount of confusion with regard to its theology on Islam.

Firstly, Christian theologies of Islam differ significantly. The three positions of exclusivism, inclusivism and pluralism that are often outlined,[74] are helpful, but not sufficient to cover the variety of alternatives that we find in different Christian contexts.

---

[73] C. Peter Wagner and F. Douglas Pennoyer (eds), *Wrestling With Dark Angels: Toward a Deeper Understanding of the Supernatural Forces in Spiritual Warfare* (Ventura, CA: Regal Books, 1990) documents discourses from evangelical, Pentecostal and charismatic Christians on issues of spiritual warfare. The volume confirms that there are diverse opinions on this issue, but also that there has been established a dialogue between different Christian traditions in which spiritual warfare terminology is used.

[74] Alan Race, *Christians and Religious Pluralism: Patterns in the Christian Theology of Religion* (London: SCM Press, 1983).

The pluralist position is probably the easiest one to accommodate. A pluralist theology of religions has been promoted by John Hick[75] and Paul Knitter.[76] The basic idea is that all religions are equally valid as ways of salvation. John Hick's book title *God Has Many Names* indicates that the gods of different religions are seen as different expressions of the same reality. The argument that some religions have an impersonal concept of God and other religions have a personal concept of God is answered with the claim that God is so great that he might be conceived as both personal and impersonal, so all religions have seen one aspect of the truth, but no one the whole truth.

The position of Karl Rahner, a Roman Catholic position, is to include in the church pious people belonging to other religions under the pretense that they would have received Christ if they had been given the opportunity. In this version of inclusivism it is the pious individuals that are included – that would be pious Muslims, like for example the Sufis. Many Christian mystics have found themselves spiritually related to the Sufis and spoken of Sufism in inclusive terms. Another version of inclusivism is to include parts of the other religion in one's own theology. We can take Guilio Basetti-Sani as an example of such an inclusivist theology of Islam as he is reading *The Koran in the Light of Christ.*[77] He states in his book that: "If we start with the hypothesis that even the Koran may be inspired, not with actual biblical inspiration, but with supernatural inspiration, the mystery of Christ may also be found in the Koran."[78] In order to find the mystery of Christ in the Qur'an, a Christian key of interpretation is needed, a key that not even Muhammad might have known. "The Christian key, however, gives the inner sense that is really there."[79] The theological assumptions behind these statements are controversial in Christian circles, but they are also seen as offensive by many Muslims, as one obvious implication is that the Qur'an cannot be understood correctly without the Christian key.

If the exclusivist position is defined in line with the Manila Manifesto, hence understood as affirming the uniqueness, indispensability and centrality of Christ,[80] there is still a variety of different theologies of Islam that would concur with this statement. The more radical ones would see Islam as a demonic system with Allah as Satan and Muhammad as Antichrist. Others would see Islam as a non-Christian religion and the similarities between Islam and Christianity more as obstacles than points of contact, a position close to Hendrik Kraemer's. Others again would find significant amounts of truth in Islam and in the Qur'an, truth that could theologically be ascribed to the

---

[75] John Hick, *God Has Many Names* (Philadelphia: The Westminster Press, 1982).

[76] Paul F. Knitter, *No Other Name?* (Maryknoll N.Y.: Orbis Books, 1985).

[77] Guilio Basetti-Sani, *The Koran in the Light of Christ* (Bombay: St. Paul Publications, 1981).

[78] *Ibid.*, 82.

[79] *Ibid.*, 171.

[80] Manila Manifesto, section A, www.lausanne.org/manila-1989/manila-manifesto. html, accessed 31.3.2010.

general revelation or to influence of the Bible, for example with regards to a number of biblical persons being included in Qur'anic narratives.

Other theologies on Islam can hardly be categorized within the exclusivist-inclusivist-pluralist paradigm at all. The late professor Willem Bijlefeld suggested for example that as Islam was a post-Christian religion, Christian theology should postpone any evaluation of Islam.[81] Against Bijlefeld it can be argued that in any practical relationship to Muslims a certain theology on Islam would be implicit. Therefore the formulation of such a theology cannot really be postponed, as relating to Muslims would imply doing theology on Islam, even without words.

Kenneth Cragg suggests that the other religions should be measured with the measure of Christ.[82] Cragg is one of the most influential theologians in this field in the last century. Utilising the measure of Christ implies asking whether other faith-systems have elements that are already 'in Christ' and can be recognized as such.[83]

We have seen that at least half a dozen different positions can be identified when it comes to Christian theologies on Islam. They are reflecting deep disagreements in the global church on the theological foundations for a theology on Islam, but also on the evaluation of what Islam is as a religion.

Secondly, the issue of internal controversy more related to the mission movement, namely the issue of Muslim followers of Jesus. The question is whether a Muslim must leave Islam in order to follow Jesus. Behind this question a number of alternatives are hidden, and we will try to spell out some of them.

Some Muslims have come to know the Biblical message of Jesus, have accepted it and received baptism, but have decided not to tell their families and friends. There might be different reasons for not telling. One of them is fear of negative and even violent reactions against the new faith; in that case the silence may be indefinite. Another reason is that the new follower of Christ is looking for opportunities to win relatives and friends for Jesus, and therefore trying to live the new life in order to demonstrate what it means to be a follower of Jesus. The followers of Jesus in this group have different strategies concerning going to the mosque and taking part in the ritual prayers of Islam there.

Others are still seeing themselves as Muslims, but identifying Jesus as an important person to get to know and follow. Some of them relate to the Jesus of the Bible,[84] others find the Qur'an a sufficient source to identify Jesus as a unique person in the history, and the person to follow.

---

[81] Yvonne Y. Haddad and Wadi Z. Haddad (eds), *Christian-Muslim Encounters* (Gainesville FL: University Press of Florida, 1995).

[82] A. Kenneth Cragg, *The Christian and Other Religion* (London and Oxford: Mowbrays 1977), 50. This paragraph on Kenneth Cragg has been added in line with C. Moucarry's response (editor's note).

[83] *Ibid.*, 64.

[84] Paul-Gordon Chandler, *Pilgrims of Christ on the Muslim Road. Exploring a New Path*

The cases of Muslim followers of Jesus are so manifold that the phenomenon has been called an insider movement within Islam. It has been suggested that this phenomenon could lead the mission movement to adapt this as a strategy, to overcome some of the difficulties faced by converts who are confessing their new faith openly.

The debate on these positions is a heated one, even in evangelical circles. After Joseph Cumming posted an article on this issue on the Lausanne website late in 2009,[85] hundreds of responses came to the website, reflecting very different evaluations of such practices. Most of those taking part in this debate could be categorized in the exclusivist position, but still some of them would dismiss the position of others as illegitimate in a Christian context. It is hard to see a prospect for a consensus developing out of this controversy.

Creativity

In the latter half of the twentieth century many Muslim countries restricted the issuing of visas to Christian missionaries. Because of this Christian missions started looking for new ways to reach Muslims with the Gospel. It was also a fact that professional missionaries were often distrusted by Muslims, who saw the missionaries as modern crusaders, using their superior technology, education and economy to impose Western values on poor Muslim communities. This situation also called for alternative models of ministry.

A number of creative methodologies and strategies have been developed during the last few decades,[86] a couple of them discussed here – tent making ministries and the creative use of media. None of these are exclusively designed for Muslim contexts, but both of them have particular qualities with regard to such contexts.

The tent making concept is developed out of the story in the Acts of the Apostles, where we read that Paul worked as a tentmaker in order not to take a salary from any of the churches he served as a missionary.[87] In that way he became more free and credible in his dealings with the churches – he refers to this fact in his letters, and the issue is also identified in the Old Testament.[88]

Behind this concept is a very simple idea: Christian witnesses in the marketplace can be efficient witnesses. They can go places where a

---

Between Two Faiths (Lanham MD/Plymouth UK: Cowley Publications, 2007) tells the story of Syrian writer Mazhar Mallouhi, who discovered Jesus in the Bible and decided to follow him as a Muslim, see the interview with him, 175-206.

[85] Joseph Cumming, 'Muslim Followers Of Jesus?' A later version of his article, published 23.02.2010 at http://conversation.lausanne.org/en/conversations/detail/10004.

[86] In J. Dudley Woodberry (ed), *From Seed to Fruit: Global Trends, Fruitful Practices, and Emerging Issues Among Muslims* (Pasadena CA: William Carey Library, 2008), a number of authors introduce and analyze a number of practices experienced as fruitful among Muslims.

[87] Acts 18.3.

[88] 2 Cor 11.7, see also Micah 3.5.

professional missionary would not be welcomed. They are not paid by a mission agency, so when they witness, their witness is easily regarded as more authentic than the professional witness, only doing his or her job by witnessing.

In many cases, Christian professionals have been very much sought after, also in Muslim contexts. Many Muslims are worried by the potential influence of Western secularism in their communities, and therefore they feel more comfortable with Christians who are living according to a religious ethic. As a Christian bears witness to his faith in such a situation, the context will be one of friendship and trust, and such a witness will probably not be taken as Christian propaganda.

Some media are transnational in the sense that the media message can hardly be limited by border restrictions. It is especially the creative use of such media that we will discuss in this section, the two cases being internet and satellite TV. Both have changed the potential of global communication and interaction during the last few decades in ways that would have been hard to imagine only forty years ago.

The internet offers a virtual reality where people can communicate directly with other people from around the world. Being able to understand the same language helps the communication process, but online translation services can help to bridge language differences.

For Muslims seeking out information that their religious and political leaders do not approve of, the internet gives an opportunity to find such information without being socially exposed. There are already many examples of Muslims engaging in discussions on the internet on topics that those in power would prefer to silence, often topics related to issues of freedom in one way or another.

Internet use is not without risks, as activities on the net leave electronic tracks that can be traced by the government. But this risk can be reduced by using internet cafés where one does not have to reveal one's identity in order to have internet access. Investigating internet use takes a lot of resources, so the risk is reduced for the individual user if there are many users in the same field.

With satellite TV technology new channels of communication (literally speaking) have been opened. As the satellite is outside the reach of repressive governments, it is hard to close the borders to the messages being transmitted by means of satellite. Signals can be jammed, of course, but often the popular satellites are transmitting a number of programs, so jamming the signals of one satellite would interfere with a number of popular and less controversial programs as well.

Counterculturalism

A century has passed since Edinburgh 1910 and it has been a century of changes. We have seen that sociopolitical and technological developments have affected and challenged mission to Muslims in significant ways. Some of these issues have already been touched upon, but issues of modernity like secularization and multiculturalism should also be considered as we discuss the lessons relevant to mission to Muslims during the last century.

Until recently the social theory of secularization was widely accepted in the scholarly community and it became a paradigm in the discipline of sociology.[89] The theory implied that the religions would gradually lose their social influence and eventually disappear from society as they became privatised. The last few decades have developed differently. Religions have lost some of their previous influence in many societies, especially some political privileges that e.g. Christianity had in many Western societies at the time of Edinburgh 1910. But at the same time many religious movements have developed new ways to influence social life through civil societies and public spheres. José Casanova studied the social influence of religion in Spain, Poland, Brazil and the United States and concluded that there is a deprivatisation of modern religion as it finds new way to gain public roles and influence.[90] Since then other scholars like Peter L. Berger[91] and Jürgen Habermas[92] have changed their position on secularisation and are now recognising more religious influence in public society.

Some Muslims countries have been politically secularised – the changes in Turkey leading to secularisation of the country was noted by the Edinburgh conference in 1910. But in many Muslim countries Islam has become a stronger political force now than it was a century ago. Often Muslim leaders have emphasised that Islam is the key to successfully developing a counterculture to Western secular influence. At the same time, many Christian leaders have been calling their followers to resist the secularization of their life worlds, living by different standards than the secular ones.

Social theorists may see such examples of revitalisation as reactions to modernity, seeing religion trying to stay relevant, hence the secularisation theory is basically confirmed.[93] Others believe that religion has proved that it is here to stay, and social theory will have to develop relevant interpretations of the contemporary world. Casanova points out that some religions are focusing on individual salvation, but not all. "Certain cultural traditions, religious

---

[89] To the following discussion, see David Herbert, *Religion and Civil Society: Rethinking Public Religion in the Contemporary World* (Aldershot, Hampshire: Ashgate Publishing Limited, 2003).

[90] José Casanova, *Public Religions in the Modern World* (Chicago and London: University of Chicago Press, 1994), 211-234.

[91] Peter L. Berger (ed), *The Desecularization of the World: Resurgent Religion and World Politics* (Grand Rapids, MI: The Ethics and Polity Center and Wm B. Eerdmans Publishing Co, 1999).

[92] Jürgen Habermas, 'Religion in the Public Sphere', *European Journal of Philosophy* 14(1), 2006, 1-25.

[93] Thomas Luckmann, 'The New and the Old in Religion', in P. Bourdieu and J.S. Coleman (eds), *Social Theory for a Changing Society* (New York: Russel Sage Foundation, 1991). Luckmann holds that religious intensification as a phenomenon of reaction to modernity will remain a privatised phenomenon and survive for only a limited period.

doctrinal principles, and historical circumstances, by contrast, will induce other religions to enter, at least occasionally, the public sphere."[94] Casanova's notion that some religions due to their own doctrines and developments will develop a public presence and a public influence is worthwhile noting. It is relevant for many forms of Islam as well as of Christianity and implies that encounters between Islam and Christianity will continue to have a public dimension.

Anyway, the socio-political relationship between Christianity and Islam in the world community has been significantly changed during the last century. Muslims are generally more self confident in their relation to Christianity, often seeing Islam as a stronger and more consistent spiritual movement than Christianity. For the church it is a new lesson to see Islam on the one hand as a potential partner against destructive effects of secularisation, and on the other hand as a strong and confident neighbor questioning the relevance of Christian mission to Muslims.

Being neighbors in multicultural societies is also a new experience for mission in the last century. In 1910 virtually all missionaries were sent from fairly homogenous Christian countries in Western Europe and North America, and Muslims were found in other parts of the world. Now there are millions of Muslims living in Western Europe and North America, and a large number of missionaries are coming from countries in the South with a significant Muslim population, like Nigeria. Multiculturalism is therefore another topic in the curriculum for the mission to Muslims.

Multiculturalism has often been described as an outcome of modernization and globalisation. As societies are developing multicultural patterns and policies, many scholars and politicians think that these changes require a deeper change in society. Previously it was often assumed that society needed a common morality and that religion played a central role in producing such a morality. Émile Durkheim developed ideas along these lines and he saw this connection between religion and society to be a basic one.[95] Religion was assumed to have an integrative role in society, serving the purpose of social unity.

Durkheim influenced a large number of other scholars, although his views were also controversial. Today many scholars argue that society does not need to share a religion, but that different religions and other value systems will have to look for a common ground in the form of shared values or rites.[96]

Many Muslim and Christians find themselves in such multicultural settings today, where they have to look for shared values with the other for the common good of society. At the same time they realize that not all their values are shared and they have to find ways of dealing with their differences as well. For

---

[94] Casanova, *Public Religions in the Modern World*, 221.

[95] Émile Durkheim, *The Elementary Forms of Religious Life* (London: George Allen and Unwin, 1982[1912]).

[96] James A. Beckford and Sophie Gilliat, *Religion in Prison. Equal Rites in a Multi-Faith Society* (Cambridge: Cambridge University Press, 1998) argues for a pluralisation of the public sphere in their study on the roles of religion in prison.

many, multiculturalism is not only a fact of a modern society, it has also become an ideology upon which to base a successful multicultural society.

In multicultural settings mission is often seen as reflecting the opposite attitude of multiculturalism. Many regard it as impossible to combine mission work with the promotion of the freedom and tolerance that a multicultural society needs to function. In postmodern society the idea of an absolute truth is rejected, and any activity based on a concept of absolute truth is regarded as an act of intolerance. In this perspective mission to Muslims is surely a countercultural activity in a modern multicultural society, and significantly more so in 2010 than it was in 1910.

In 2010 one of the tasks of the missional church is to develop an understanding of what it means to be a counterculture in a secularised and multicultural society. These lessons of counterculturalism are not easy to learn. But if the missional church is going to work with all people of good will, including Muslims, for the good of society, and at the same time is going to share the Good News with all people loved by God, including Muslims, these lessons have to be learned.

Conclusion

The last century has been a century of crises and of changes. Both crises and changes have affected Christians as well as Muslims. The world is not the same now as it was in 1910. But for those who believe that the love of Christ for all people is the same, the challenge of sharing this love with the Muslims is still relevant. In many ways it has to be done differently now than a century ago as time has presented a number of lessons to be learned by the missional church. We have seen that some of the developments and dynamics of the last century surely require different approaches today than a century ago.

After a century of lessons, the missional challenge of today for the church as a whole could be formulated this way: Communicating Christ in a non-confrontational and contextually relevant way to our Muslim neighbors in the global community in the context of peaceful coexistence.

Mission to Muslims: What Lessons has the Christian Church Learned? A Response to Jan Opsal

Chawkat Moucarry

The paper surveys the complex relationships between Protestant mission and Islam over the last hundred years, using eight 'c' words: competition, communication (understood in terms of communicating the Gospel message to Muslims), conversion, contextualisation, cooperation, conflict, controversy, and creativity (understood in terms of new ways of carrying out mission such as 'tent making' and modern communication media, e.g. internet and satellite TV). The survey is done with a very limited critical engagement with the issues raised by Christian mission in Islamic contexts.

One would have expected to see *compassion* as a key word in Christian-Muslim relations, in particular after the publication in October 2007 of the Open Letter, 'A Common Word Between Us and You', signed by 138 Muslim leaders and scholars. This initiative was in itself an Islamic response to Christian perceptions of Islam in recent years, and in particular to the controversial characterisation of Islam as a violent religion in the Pope's Regensburg lecture in September 2006. The Pope was quoting the Byzantine emperor Manuel II Paleologos in 1391, which takes us back to the aftermath of the crusading movement.

When looking at Christian-Muslim relations since 1910, one cannot ignore the legacy of the past. From an Islamic-Arab perspective the major event of this past is the crusades, which were to a certain degree a misguided response to the Islamic occupation of Christian territories including the Holy Land.[1] This event is still very much a reality in the Arab psyche.[2] Muslim radicals have recently described the invasion of Afghanistan and Iraq as yet another manifestation of the crusading movement which in their view has never admitted defeat. These wars were championed by two political leaders (Bush and Blair) who happened to be self-confessed Christians.

The Open Letter is entitled 'A Common Word between Us and You' in reference to the third Qur'anic Sura, Aal `Imran verse 64, which invites "the

[1] See the remarkable work by the Christian Lebanese historian Amin Maalouf, *The Crusades through Arab Eyes* (London: Saqi Books, 2001).

[2] I still remember the day when as a teenager I was taken to watch the film on Saladin (who took Jerusalem back from the crusaders) with all the school pupils.

People of the Book", Christians in particular, to sign up to a declaration with Muslims based on their respective monotheistic faiths. What is most remarkable in this document is that the signatories deliberately present the message of Islam in the same way Jesus Christ himself summed up the teaching of the Torah and the Prophets in the twofold commandment about loving God and our neighbor (Mt 22:34-40). This ground-breaking initiative has been welcomed by most Christians. One of the first and warmest Christian responses is that of the Yale Center for faith and culture.[3] The 'Common Word' and the many Christian responses it provoked represent a very significant step in terms of Christian-Muslim relationships. If Christians and Muslims lived up to the command of loving one's neighbor as oneself, surely this will open a new and unprecedented era in their relationships.

The paper briefly discusses Christian theologies of Islam. The three traditional approaches to other faiths (exclusivism, inclusivism, pluralism) are considered as helpful but somehow simplistic. One would have expected to find an alternative model for understanding Islam from a Christian perspective. It would have been useful, for example, to suggest some keys for a Christian theology of Islam. The author dismisses the exclusivist position and seems to favour the inclusivist Christian interpretation of Islam by Guilio Basetti-Sani. If many exclusivist approaches to Islam tend to demonise Islam, Basetti-Sani's approach unduly reads Christianity into the Qur'an, which does not do justice to this religion either. Islam needs to be understood on its own terms. In this context, it is rather surprising that the paper makes no mention whatsoever of Kenneth Cragg, one of the most influential Christian scholars and missionaries to Islam. His many books reveal an outstanding engagement with this religion and its followers.

The author refers to Samuel Huntington's *The Clash of Civilizations* and makes some pertinent critical comments about its key thesis which claims that the hostility between the Western world and the Muslim world is based on the irreconcilable values of the two civilizations. The fact that Western civilization is man-centred and Islamic civilization is God-centred need not lead to conflict. It all depends on how the respective values of these civilizations are interpreted. I take the view that the real divide is not between the West and the Rest of the world, but between those who think that the West is the Best and those Muslim extremists who see nothing good outside their own group. In other words, the real conflict is between two fundamentalisms, the secular and the Islamic ones.

The issue is, therefore, how people understand their values and, for people of faith, their Scriptures. Our hermeneutics often depends on the context, both local and international. Those Christians who take Paul's teaching on spiritual warfare in Eph 6 to justify their polemical attitude towards Islam and Muslims represent a case in point. They use this text "to fuel antagonism between Christians and Muslims" and "to legitimize hostility and violence from the

[3] However, a few Christians expressed some misgivings about this document, accusing its signatories of a hidden agenda and duplicity. See for instance the response to this document by Patrick Sookhdeo, the head of the UK-based Barnabas Fund.

Christian side in a conflict with Muslim neighbors." However, a careful reading of this passage clearly shows that the Christian Gospel is "the Gospel of peace" (verse 15), and the only legitimate weapons for God's people to use are "the belt of truth", "the breastplate of righteousness", "the shield of faith", "the helmet of salvation", and (least but not last) "the sword of the Spirit, which is the word of God" (verses 14-17).

This means that the nature of the Christian message, which is about love, forgiveness and reconciliation, requires that this message is shared with peaceful and non-violent means. To the extent that polemics (the Greek stem word means 'war') is a war of words, it is fundamentally incompatible with a Christian approach to Islam. Christian polemicists are the crusaders of our time. However, Eph 6 and other parts of the Scriptures tell us that there is a spiritual dimension to Christian living and mission. The spiritual world exists and we would be unwise to dismiss this reality altogether. Our struggle, our *jihad* if you will, is indeed "not against flesh and blood, but against the rulers, against the authorities, against the powers of this dark world and against the spiritual forces of evil in the heavenly realms" (verse 12). We indeed live in a dark world', which includes the Western and the Muslim worlds as well as 'the Christian world' and every other world. 'The spiritual forces of evil' are at work on every continent, in every country, among every people; they are found in every one, myself included. The Scriptures tell us that we live in a fallen world and every one of us is sinful including people of faith and of none. The seriousness of the human predicament is such that our first enemy is first and foremost inside each one of us. This is why having sent us many prophets, God eventually sent us a Savior to forgive our sins and to set us free from the power of our spiritual enslavement to sin in all its forms.

The one lesson that we as Christians must learn from history is that confrontation is not the way to do mission. The motive for Christian mission is God's compassion and ours, which drive us to seek *as far as possible* conciliation between the Christian faith and the Islamic faith. In other words, dialogue is the way for mission: "In my experience, these two words [dialogue and mission] belong so much to each other that they should never be divorced… Not only are the two words compatible, but they must shape each other."[4]

[4] From my article 'A plea for dialogue between Christians and Muslims', The Lausanne Global Conversation: http://conversation.lausanne.org/en/conversations/detail/10023.

PART B

CASE STUDIES

Global Migration: Mission to Iranians in Scandinavia – Example of a Development Through Immigration

Nasser Fard

Immigration and statistics

As of January 1st 2009, 17652 persons with Iranian background were registered in Norway.[1] Of these 13,001 were first generation immigrants, 2,655 were born in Norway of two Iranian-born parents, 1,824 were Norwegians born of one Iranian parent, and 72 persons had another background related to Iran, e.g. born of Norwegian-born parents in Iran.

Of all immigrants from Iran, we can identify the background of 95%, i.e. 74% have come as refugees, and 19% have come for reasons of family unification or to establish a family. Some very few have come to seek employment, others to study, totalling 1%.

The main reason for migration, then, has been to flee from the worsening political situation in Iran. Up to 2007 40% (or 4,500 persons) were refugees under the United Nations, i.e. United Nations High Commissioner for Refugees (UNHCR). These UNHCR-refugees are therefore the largest group of such refugees living in Norway today. Just about all immigrants from Iran in the period 1990-2003 came as refugees under UN.

Examining the 13,001 first generation immigrants from Iran, most of them have come after 1984. Only 130 have lived in Norway more than 25 years, i.e. those who came before 1984. If we consider immigration from Iran in 5-year blocks, we find the following:

1984 – 1988: 3,285
1989 – 1993: 2,606
1994 – 1998: 1,916

[1] The following figures are taken from the tables of Statistisk Sentralbyrå (Norwegian Bureau of Statistics), e.g. www.ssb.no/innvbef/tab-2009-04-30-01.html. Thanks to Oddvar Hatlehol who has analyzed and assisted me in interpreting these figures, Oddvar Hatlehol, "Iranians in Norway." (Unpublished manuscript, 2009). See also Kristin Henriksen (2007): "Innvandrerbefolkningen med bakgrunn fra Iran," www.ssb.no/emner/02/rapp_200729/rapp_200729.pdf, 95-105, and Oddbjørn Leirvik (2008), "Islam i Norge," http://folk.uio.no/leirvik/tekster/IslamiNorge.html.

1999 – 2003: 3,281
2004 – 2008: 1,783
Iranians are scattered throughout Norway although ⅓ are living in Oslo. The figures of first-generation immigrants prior to Jan 1st, 2008 show the following pattern:

> Oslo 4,124, Bærum 680, Trondheim 554, Bergen 529, Skedsmo 453, Stavanger 412, Drammen 328, Fredrikstad 306, Lørenskog 285, Kristiansand 272, Asker 214, Skien 185, Rælingen 175, Sarpsborg 168, Sandnes 143, Gjøvik 136, Moss 129, Ski 109, Arendal 104 og Hamar 97. The remaining 3,223 persons are scattered throughout other smaller communities.

Kurds from Iran

Many Iranians in Norway are Kurds. In Iran the Shah-regime was overthrown in 1979, and the Islamic republic declared war on the Kurds who demanded local self-government. The war between the Kurds and the Iranian army resulted in thousands being forced from their towns and villages. Many sought refuge in the neighboring countries of Iraq and Turkey living in refugee camps run by the UNHCR. It is from these camps that Norway has for years received a certain number of Kurdish refugees from Iran.

The war between Iraq and Iran in 1979-1984, and the war between Kurds and Turkey (1984) have brought new groups of Kurdish political refugees to Europe and Norway, among them many Kurds from Iran.

Religion among Iranians

The religious background of Iranians is quite complex. The Kurds from the North are Sunni Muslims, while the greater part of Iran are Shi'ite Muslims. Many of those who have fled to Norway from Iran are adherents of the Baha'i' religion, and some belong to Christian minorities. Several of these have come for religious reasons. Those with a Shi'ite Muslim background in Norway often have a more liberal and modern Shi'ite view and practice their religion privately and individually in their homes or with friends in, for example, cultural associations. Tronstad in Norwegian Central Bureau of Statistics comments:

> In the European research (ESS) where Norway takes part, the respondents of 2006 were asked to place themselves on a scale from 0 to 10 where 0 was no religion, while 10 indicated that religion was very important. Norway was ranked among the least religious societies of Europe with a mean score of 3,8. Mean score for ten non-Western immigrant groups was in the Norwegian research 6,9. The differences were significant: Iranians were most secularized, their score was 4,0, meaning that religion is of less significance to them, while the Somali scored 9,6.[2]

2 Kristian Rose Tronstad, 'Levekårsundersøkelsen blant innvandrere', www.ssb.no/emner/02/sa_innvand/sa103/kap8.pdf, 157-158.

On this background one could believe that very few Iranians are converting to Christian faith, but that is not the case. Since the mid-1980s many Iranians have converted, and Iranians are today the immigrant group with the largest number of convertees from Islam to Christianity.

This author grew up in Iran as a Muslim. After studying the Qur'an as an adult, I made the decision to become an atheist. In 1988 I fled to Norway after five years in prison because of my activism against the regime in Iran. At Haraldvangen refugee center I met Christians from Gå Ut Senter Bible School. They showed me true friendship and were motivated by love despite our different stand in questions of faith. To me as an atheist this was fascinating.

This made me curious and motivated me to become more acquainted with Jesus of the Christians. After reading both the New and the Old Testament, things started to connect. I started to form a new picture of who God was. I realized I had believed in God in 28 years without realizing who He was in the way I now read in the Bible! Among other things I found that Jesus did not suffer a natural death, but died on the cross (that death was really dying). He rose again from the dead and was taken up to heaven. He walks with us today while at the same time being in heaven.

I found that God could not be in both books and that only through the Bible one can meet God and find salvation. The different pieces of my life puzzle fitted into place when I chose to become a Christian and was later baptized.

Christian Work Among Iranians – A Short History

I moved to Oslo in 1990 when I was accepted at Norwegian School of Sport Sciences. In the beginning I had no contact with other Iranians until I met with Haik Hovsepian, the pastor and overseer of Protestant churches in Iran. We met in Oslo through friends in the Santal Mission (now Normisjon). Some time later I met another Iranian Christian who had a call to serve Iranians in Oslo. After much conversation and prayer we started work among Iranians in Oslo. I came to learn that some had met for Bible study and other gatherings for Parsi-speakers in various parts of Norway. But the first Iranian Christian service took place at Christian Cross-Cultural Outreach (KIA) in Geitmyrsveien in 1991 after inviting Iranian Christians and spiritual seekers in the greater Oslo region.

I have met many Iranians since 1990 who have received Jesus as their Savior and God after being offered Christian service and love, or through dreams and visions. I experienced that God gave me increasing love for my own people and sorted things out practically so that an exciting work was established. This work has grown larger every year.

From the beginning we had an impression that Iranians in particular were especially open to the gospel. Generally Jesus is greatly respected among Iranians. Evangelism to Iranians has seen good progress up to 2008. Beginning in autumn 2008, however, I as well as Iranians in some other countries, have experienced powerful negative reactions from Muslims when Jesus is presented as God and Savior.

Evangelism

There is a lot of talk these days on how to do Muslim evangelism. According to those who are part of the Iranian Christian community, most of them have been led to Jesus by friends. Real friendship, real concern and the communication of God's love through practical deeds are pulling people to the kingdom of God. If we wish to share our faith with Muslims, the road passes through friendship. That is particularly the case in Norway, which has now become a multicultural community with more than 500,000 immigrants from all over the world. I have seen for myself what practical love can do.

In our work in Oslo I have met many strong seekers and recently converted people who have told me that they started to read the Bible because of the love and concern they had experienced from Christians. As pastor in the Iranian Evangelical Lutheran Church in Oslo, I have had a chance to baptize many Iranians since 1992. This would have without a doubt led to the death penalty if it had happened in Iran. Despite such laws, the church grows in Iran and outside.

In other Scandinavian countries the same is happening as we can see in Oslo. Our congregation has had some summer camps together with Iranians of Denmark, and we have visited and made contacts with Iranians of Sweden. Today we know of more than 300 Christian Iranian congregations and fellowships outside Iran, seven of them are in Scandinavia. These fellowships have weekly services. All this has happened after the revolution of 1979. Today we reckon that there are at least 50,000 registered Christian Iranians outside Iran. In Norway we estimate that more than 400 Iranians have been baptized after being taught extensively and become part of a Christian congregation. This has happened despite the fact that apostasy in Islam is one of the six areas that earns you the death penalty.

Some gather in special Parsi-speaking communities, but many have also found their home in Norwegian churches and fellowships. This we see happening all over the country.

Iran has also a church of secret believers where people gather in small cells or house fellowships.

The Work of God

Other reasons why Iranians with Muslim background approach Christianity may be the special way God seems to be moving among them, namely often through dreams, visions or miracles. Some report to have seen a white figure or an angel who instructs them to read the book of the Christians or to make contact with Christians. Upon reading the Bible or in conversation with Christians the many pieces come together. Traditionally there is an opening for dreams and visions in Persian culture, something which God seems to make use of.

In the background there is also an echo of the old prophecy of Jer 49:38-39, which means a lot for Iranians: "I will set my throne in Elam and destroy her king and officials, declares the LORD. Yet I will restore the fortunes of Elam in days to come, declares the LORD."

Challenges

Can we imagine a multicultural congregation, or are we more than satisfied with our mono-cultural? If the answer is yes, are we then prepared for what we can meet ahead? What do we do when three to five foreigners (recently converted Christians or seekers) come to our congregations? How have we made our preparations, and how do we come to meet them? Do we consider them as our fellow human being, or as objects of our excitement for evangelism? Can we make use of their abilities and resources and thus include them as whole persons? Do we train and disciple them long enough before baptism, or do we baptize them too soon? The challenges are lining up!

Mission can never meet Islam, but humans can meet humans. Real persons must meet real persons where they are.

This task is 90% hands and feet and 10% words – it takes time. Our task is to point to Jesus, but not to show our contempt for Muhammad. Muslims vary from country to country. Iranians are now open to the gospel. More than 300 pastors are now serving churches in Europe and USA, and one figure counts 300,000 in Iran itself. There was not one single Iranian church outside Iran before the revolution in 1979.

How Do We Meet?

There has been and still is a lot of pictures, on both sides, that serve to scare and create fear of the other. Christians can talk of the threat of Islam, and Muslims speak of the threat from Zionism and the West. Such mutual fear and generalized condemnation is an obstacle to open dialogue. It is important that both parties

- come out into an open room
- dare to seek common values
- work towards tolerance and respect for all religions and their value systems
- realize that I am a racist
- meet each other with respect and acknowledge each others right to freedom and practice of religion

What is different and foreign tends to create fear, and many dare not approach people of other religions. Knowledge and common experiences, however, clear away misunderstandings and prejudice.

The Price to Be Paid in Order to Convert to Christianity

The development described in this paper has not passed unnoticed in Iran. The following document shows among other things the reaction of Iranian authorities towards Christian converts. The situation has become increasingly worse since August 2008, as the Iranian parliament is currently considering the death penalty for apostasy besides giving the regime the right to prosecute Iranians all over the world.[3]

> The Iranian Parliament is reviewing a draft penal code that for the first time in Iranian history legislates the death penalty for apostasy. The draft clearly violates Iran's commitments under the International Covenants on Human Rights, to which the State is party. "The draft penal code is gross violation of fundamental and human rights by a regime that has repeatedly abused religious and other minorities," stated Institute on Religion and Public Policy President Joseph K. Grieboski. "This is simply another legislative attempt on the part of the Iranian regime to persecute religious minorities in the country and around the globe, especially Bahá'ís." Article 112 examines the extraterritorial application of the norms of the code, by extending its jurisdiction over actions that take place outside the country. Article 112-3-1 refers to actions "against the government, the independence and the internal and external security of the country." Security as a term is not defined in the law, thereby making any action qualified as such. Consequently, groups considered dangerous to the regime all over the world can be liable for actions taken outside Iran that are considered as contrary to the security of the country. Article 225-7 of the code states, "Punishment for an Innate Apostate is death," while Article 225-8 says, "Punishment for a Parental Apostate is death, but after the final sentencing for three days he/she would be guided to the right path and encouraged to recant his/her belief and if he/she refused, the death penalty would be carried out." "A careful review of the draft clearly shows that it is nothing more than a legislative tool to consolidate power around the regime and extend its religious tyranny globally," Mr. Grieboski commented. "Such legislation will not be accepted by the international community and that message must resoundingly be sent to Tehran."

All Religious Minorities Experience Discrimination

Not only Christians, but all religious minorities experience degrees of discrimination in the Islamic Republic of Iran. Norwegian authorities and human rights activists and Christians themselves have differing opinions on the extent of the discrimination. According to the Norwegian authority handling these questions (The Norwegian Country of Origin Information Centre – Landinfo), Christianity is an allowed minority of religion protected by the constitution of Iran. On their information pages one is told that that the problem with Iranian authorities is linked to active evangelism and baptism of previous Muslims.[4] The internationally acclaimed Christian organization Open Doors, which supports persecuted Christians, ranked Iran in 2010 as the second worst

---

[3] This quote was downloaded from the Institute on Religion and Public Policy website at www.religionandpolicy.org.

[4] www.landinfo.no/id/403.0, compare with US State Department info pages: www.state.gov/g/drl/rls/irf/2009/127347.htm, accessed 25.05.2010.

country to live in as a Christian.[5] On the internet and YouTube one can find articles, pictures and film clips that will document the risk of being a Christian in Iran.[6]

President Ahmadinejad is reported to have said publicly that he has the ambition to stop the advance of Christianity. How he would like to do this is more unclear, but the suggestion referred to above to incorporate the religious sharia laws on death penalty into the civilian law of Iran has passed through the Iranian parliament and is presently considered by the so-called Council of Warders.

Conclusion

If you hide your faith, it is not dangerous to be a Christian in Iran, but active Christians pay a high price, and also if the activities take place outside the home country. There are many examples of how Iranian authorities closely monitor what Iranians are doing abroad, including Norway. I have experienced this both in our own and in another Iranian congregation in Oslo! In the course of my work as pastor I have baptized about 70 Iranians, and since 2008 I have received three anonymous death threats. For every baptism I perform I earn a death sentence according to Iranian law.

---

[5] www.opendoors.no/sider/tekst.asp?side=3911, accessed 25.05.2010.

[6] E.g. www.opendoors.no/opendoors/vedlegg/PU-mai-juni-2010.pdf, accessed 25.05. 2010, www.youtube.com/results?search_query=christians+iran&aq=0.

Global Migration: Mission to Iranians in Scandinavia

A Response to Nasser Fard

Solveig Omland

Iranians coming to Norway is part of a new migration trend. Currently Iranians are the tenth largest immigrant minority in Norway.[1] In a survey done by SSB[2] among Iranians in Norway, numbers show that 30% of the Iranians had not been raised Muslim. Among the same group 50% labelled themselves as *non-religious* or secular.[3] According to SSB official statistics show that in Iran 98% of the population are Muslims.[4] Iranian immigrants in Norway are religious and political refugees, and as a result the Iranian minority in Norway does not reflect the same percentage of Muslims as the SSB's statistics show. Still, it could be argued that Iranian immigrants are familiar with a Muslim tradition.

Then focusing on missions to Iranians in Scandinavia, or in Norway which will be my focus, two trends shed some light on the current situation. First, Norwegians have a long history of Christian ministry and overseas missions. Over the last hundred years Norwegian mission organizations have sent missionaries to various countries all over the world.[5] Second, Norway has traditionally experienced little immigration, and mainly from neighboring countries.[6] Over the last fifty years the percentage of immigrants from the majority world has increased[7] and around 50% of the immigrant population in Norway is currently from the majority world.[8] Iranians in Norway are a fairly

---

[1] Kristina Kvarv Andreassen and Minja Tea Dzamarija, 'Innvandere og norskfødte med innvandrerforeldre', in Gunnlaug Daugstad (ed), *Innvandring og innvandere 2008* (Oslo/Kongsvinger: Statistisk Sentralbyrå, 2008), 15.

[2] SSB (Statistisk Sentralbyrå) *(Statistics Norway)*.

[3] www.ssb.no/samfunnsspeilet/utg/200903/03/index.html, accessed 4.3.2010.

[4] www.ssb.no/samfunnsspeilet/utg/200903/03/index.html, accessed 4.3.2010.

[5] Olav Uglem, *Norsk Misjonshistorie* (Oslo: Lunde Forlag, 1979).

[6] Saphinaz-Amal Naguib, 'The Northern Way: Muslim Communities in Norway', in Yvonne Y. Haddad and Jane I. Smith (eds), *Muslim Minorities in the West* (Walnut Creek, California: Altamire Press, 2002), 162.

[7] Svein Blom, 'Residential Concentration among Immigrants in Oslo', *International Migration Quarterly Review* 37.3 (1999), 617 and Bente P. Puntervold, *Søkelys på den norske innvandringspolitikken – etiske og rettslige dilemmaer* (Kristiansand: Norwegian Academic Press, 2004), 32.

[8] Marianne Gullestad, 'Invisible Fences: Egalitarianism, Nationalism and Racism',

new phenomenon as is present Middle Eastern and Muslim immigration in Europe in general.[9] Concluding on these two trends, one can say the traditional understanding of overseas mission to be witnesses "to the ends of the earth" (Acts 1:8), is changing since we are experiencing that people "from the ends of the earth" are living among us. The result of migration should lead to creative reflection on how to do missions and how to meet new challenges.

In the following I will reflect on some theories that may shed some light on a holistic mission to Iranians in Norway.[10] First, the initial contact and potential challenges in interreligious and intercultural communication, then focus on the church, fellowship and integration of Iranians, and lastly, I will mention Iranian converts as a potential resource for the Norwegian church. Due to my knowledge and background my focus is on the Norwegian context, but the reflection may be applicable to Denmark and Sweden also.

Intercultural Communication – A Semiotic Challenge

When talking to a person from a Muslim tradition one has to be aware that the concepts and words mentioned can be interpreted differently than intended. Cragg states that the Qur'an does not present Jesus as the Son of God, but is referred to as servant of God and Messiah.[11] The Qur'an also speaks of Jesus as one of the greatest prophets.[12] Even though there are many similarities between the Muslim and Christian image of Allah/God, Elass states that "Allah is utterly transcendent" which differs from the Christian understanding of a close, personal God.[13] Also, the idea that Allah is one, challenges the Christian, Trinitarian understanding of God.[14]

Turning from these two examples to theory, contextualization has been and is important in Christian intercultural communication. Sanneh states that for Christianity to succeed across cultural boundaries "translatability is the source."[15] Fiske states that in communication the decoding, done by the receiver, "is as active and creative as encoding", done by the sender of the

---

Journal of Royal Anthropological Institute 8 (2002), 47.

[9] Wasif Shadid and Sjoerd van Koningsveld, 'The Negative Image of Islam and Muslims in the West: Causes and Solutions', in Wasif Shadid and Sjoerd van Koningsveld (eds), *Religious Freedom and the Neutrality of the State: The Position of Islam in the European Union* (Sterling, Virginia: Peeters, 2002), 191.

[10] This paper is a response to Nasser Fard's paper on missions to Iranians in Scandinavia. I have chosen to pick up on some of the issues raised by Fard, and in addition I have introduced a couple of issues that may help to shed light on mission to Iranians in Scandinavia.

[11] Kenneth Cragg, *Jesus and the Muslim* (Oxford: Oneworld, 2003), 30-31.

[12] Mateen Elass, *Understanding the Koran* (Grand Rapids, Michigan: Zondervan, 2004), 54.

[13] *Ibid.*, 84.

[14] *Ibid.*, 91.

[15] Lamin Sanneh, *Translating the Message* (Maryknoll, N.Y.: Orbis Books, 1998), 51.

message.[16] Symbols and signs, including words, can give different associations when different people interpret the signs.[17] Peirce points out that in the interpretation of the sign, referring to an object, the 'user's experience of the object' influences the process.[18]

Concluding, a crucial question is who is communicating the gospel to Iranians. If Christian Iranians, they have knowledge about the potential complex associations the Iranian listener may have. If ethnic Norwegians are the communicators, these theories may be of help especially if they have not lived abroad and had first-hand experience of how intended message and interpreted message are not necessarily the same.

Norwegianness and Integration – An Ecclesiological Perspective

How do the Iranian converts want to integrate into the Christian community? Is an Iranian Christian church a desirable choice or would the Iranians prefer to be part of a congregation with an ethnic Norwegian majority? For many the first alternative might seem tempting, and if strengthening ethnicity is desirable, this might be the recommended route. Yang and Ebaugh's findings from ethnographic research at a Chinese Church in Houston concluded that as the church tried to offer something different than the surrounding churches, the result was a Sinification process where the church became more ethnically Chinese (e.g. celebrating Chinese New Year and mandarin speaking services). In the church's evangelistic outreach to encourage church growth, they only reached a small group: Chinese immigrants in the Houston area.[19] Arguing for an effort to establish ethnically diverse congregations, Priest and Priest mention that if an ethnically diverse country, in this case America, "comprises primarily racially homogeneous congregations, this contributes to the racialization of our society."[20] Even though establishing ethnically diverse congregations might be challenging, such churches "will provide a clear witness to the unity found in Christ, while also nurturing intercultural and interracial skills."[21] If the Iranians choose to integrate in congregations with a majority of ethnic Norwegians it can enrich the Iranians, the ethnic Norwegians and the society.

---

[16] John Fiske, *Introduction to Communication Studies* (London/New York: Routledge, 2006), 42.

[17] *Ibid.*, 42.

[18] *Ibid.*, 42.

[19] Fenggang Yang and Helen Rose Ebaugh, 'Religion and Ethnicity among Immigrants: The Impact of Majority/Minority Status in Home and Host Countries', *Journal for the Scientific Study of Religion* 40.3 (2001), 376.

[20] Kersten B. Priest and Robert J. Priest, 'Divergent Worship Practices in the Sunday Morning Hour: Analysis of an "Interracial" Church Merger Attempt', in Robert J. Priest and Alvaro L. Nieves (eds), *This Side of Heaven – Race Ethnicity and Christian Faith* (New York: Oxford University Press 2007), 290.

[21] *Ibid.*mpt', 290.

If Iranian Christians choose the Norwegian church they will meet a church that expresses Christianity, but also *Norwegianness*, e.g. an altarpiece representing Jesus as a white person. Jensen mentions that culture "dissolves when we are members of it, but crystallises when meeting people from different cultures."[22] Christianity and culture tend to mutually influence each other. For ethnic Norwegians the *Norwegianness* is probably not that obvious. In the event of greater ethnic diversity in the church the goal for the Norwegian church should not be to neglect its cultural context, but to acknowledge it. This will help Iranian Christians to realize that it is not necessary to become Norwegian or white to become a Christian or grow as a Christian.[23]

The Iranian Christians – A Resource in Norwegian, Christian Context

On an ending note I would like to emphasize the awareness of the potential positive resource Iranian Christians are in Norwegian society and in the Norwegian church.

First, if Iranian Christians are part of the established churches in Norway, they come with an enriching perspective. Iranians could through a different perspective – esthetically, experientially, devotionally – enrich Christian traditions in Norway.

Second, the Iranians (all Iranians, not only Christian Iranians) can in interaction with Norwegians, contribute towards a more true representation of Iranians than what is presented in the media. Gullestad, inspired by Said's *Orientalism*, states that Westerners are influenced by a post-colonial perspective where *otherness* often creates stereotypical, untrue images of *the other*.[24] Through interaction with Iranians, Norwegians can experience a wider, more representative perspective of Iran and Iranians.

Third, a consequence of technological development makes it possible for Iranians to keep contact with relatives and friends across national boundaries and establish transnational networks.[25] Ideas and beliefs are transported across national borders and ideoscapes[26] are established. This could, bringing it full circle, give Iranian Christians in Norway the possibility to do missions to people at "the ends of the earth" (Acts 1:8).

---

[22] Iben Jensen, *Interkulturel kommunikation i komplekse samfund* (Frederiksberg: Roskilde Universitetsforlag, 2007), 18.

[23] Marla Frederick McGlathery and Traci Griffin, '"Becoming Conservative, Becoming *White?*": Black Evangelicals and the Para-Church Movement', in Robert J. Priest and Alvaro L. Nieves (eds), *This Side of Heaven – Race, Ethnicity, and Christian Faith* (New York: Oxford University Press 2007), 146.

[24] Marianne Gullestad, *Misjonsbilder – Bidrag til Norsk Selvforståelse* (Oslo: Universitetsforlaget, 2007), 25.

[25] Connie Christiansen, 'New Media Consumption among Immigrants in Europe', *Ethnicities* 4.2 (2004), 188.

[26] Cf. Arjan Appadurai, referred to in Iben Jensen, *Interkulturel kommunikation…*, 44-45.

In this essay I have raised some theories and discussions on the topic of holistic missions to Iranians in Norway. I have mentioned communication theory that can be of help in the initial meeting with Iranians, the idea of integration of Iranians in established congregations, and the resource of having Iranians in Norwegian society and in the Norwegian Christian congregations.

In the Midst of Umma on the Internet: Religious Profession and Witness in a Globalized Era

F.O. Thoresen

At the outskirts of one of the main cities of Norway, two young Christians originating from a predominantly Muslim context on the Horn of Africa are logging on to the internet. Others, of the same ethnic origin, dispersed across the globe, are about to do the same. They are getting ready to meet others for Christian fellowship, transcending national borders. This group preparing for worship in their native language constitutes a global, ethnic, Christian fellowship. In a private 'room' on the internet, they share joys and sorrows. They comfort and pray for one another. They share testimonies and scriptural teachings. Having enjoyed the strength of corporate fellowship, they leave their private room and engage in public debates online. Thus, in the midst of the Muslim *umma*, they are sharing a witness of their newfound faith, blessed by the protection of electronic anonymity.

This essay seeks to highlight a limited perspective of globalisation, identified as the complex intersection of migration, *new social media*[1] and religious profession.[2] The emphasis is on a small group of immigrants

---

[1] Social media employs the internet and web-based technologies to provide social dialogues where a number of people are able to participate. Social media is "a group of internet-based applications that build on the ideological and technological foundations of Web 2.0, and that allow the creation and exchange of user generated content" http://en.wikipedia.org/wiki/Social_media with reference to Andreas M. Kaplan and Michael Haenlein, 'Users of the World, Unite! The Challenges and Opportunities of Social Media', *Business Horizons* 53 (2010), 59-68.

[2] As such, the article aspires to contribute towards the discourse on mediatization, religion and the new social media. Stig Hjarvard defines mediatization as the process where, "The media have developed into an independent institution in society and as a consequence, other institutions become increasingly dependant on the media and have to accommodate the logic of the media in order to be able to communicate with other institutions and society as a whole". Stig Hjarvard, 'The Mediatization of Religion: A Theory of the Media as Agents of Religious Change', *Northern Lights* 6 (2008), 11. The debate connected to the mediatization concept has so far been dominated by various theoretical approaches, and more empirical analysis contributes towards further penetration of this field. Stig Hjarvard, 'The Mediatization of Society', *Nordicom Review* 29 (2008), 110.

constituted by Christian converts from Islam, originating from Somalia. Two male individuals, residing in south-western Norway, make up our case study. They have shared their stories through in-depth qualitative interviewing.[3] The article will seek to identify both challenges and opportunities for Christian profession in this context.

Mission in the Era of Globalisation

The concept of *globalisation* was introduced during the 1990s and has since increasingly become a catch-word of social theory. Historians have, however, traced the roots of present days' globalisation centuries into the past. A.G. Hopkins has identified four sequences, or categories, of globalisation, with traits emerging in a pre-modern era.[4] It is of interest to this case study that *migration* and *diaspora groups* are identified as integral constituents of globalisation throughout this wide time span. Post-colonial globalisation from the 1950s has introduced a third trait of interest by the growth of international *media* and *information technology*. At present, "local knowledge has become universal information."[5] Hence, the role of *space* and *locality* has for some time been exposed to a fundamental transformation. The increasing mobility and migration of a considerable part of global inhabitants are also challenging the traditional territorial approach to mission. The colonial era, with a mission movement apparently in wedlock with Christian colonial powers, was seen to represent 'Christendom' over against a heathen world. Such an approach to the missionary task cemented a territorial interpretation of mission, excluding mission within Christendom.[6] For various reasons this traditional one-sided

---

[3] Although the number of confessing Christians from this contextual background is very limited, the article is modest towards claims of a more general representativeness. Nonetheless, by introducing these stories to other studies of more general character, careful attempts at generalizations is made possible (*analytic generalization*). The potential of generalization in this context is accordingly 'what might be', rather than 'what is'. On this, see: Steinar Kvale, *Det Kvalitative Forskningsintervju* (Oslo: Gyldendal Akademisk, 2009), 160-177. As the current number of Somali Christians in Norway probably does not exceed 15-20 individuals, statistical knowledge is not considered relevant. At present, no larger group of Somali Christians exists in any single location in Norway, although some individuals keep contact particularly through the internet. It is nevertheless the conviction of the author that the experiences made by these individuals should be shared. The ethnic Somali population remains one of the people groups least reached by the gospel worldwide, presumably numbering no more than one-two thousand.

[4] A. G. Hopkins, *Globalisation in World History* (London: Pimlico, 2002), 1-9. Hopkins is a prominent British historian in the field of economic history. From 2002 he was the Walter Prescott Webb Professor of History at the University of Texas at Austin.

[5] *Ibid.*, 8. See also McKenzie Wark, *Virtual Geography: Living with Global Media Events* (Bloomington: Indiana University Press, 1994).

[6] Wilbert R. Shenk, 'The Training of Missiologists for Western Culture', in John Dudley Woodberry, Charles Edward van Engen and Edgar J. Elliston (eds), *Missiological*

interpretation of the missionary challenge cannot be maintained. The dual development of arrivals of considerable numbers of immigrants to the West from areas which historically have been on the receiving end of Western mission initiatives, combined with the emergence of a growing mission movement based in the Global South underscores this shortcoming.[7] Nonetheless, mission is still very much considered a responsibility to be faced outside of the traditional sphere of Christendom. Hence, the church in the Western world has, generally speaking, only to a limited extent realized both missionary opportunities and responsibilities with regard to the increasing immigrant population in its midst.[8]

The Somali Case – Setting the Background

Siyaad Barre, the long-standing military dictator of Somalia, was toppled from power in 1991, causing a national power vacuum. For the past nineteen years, despite various interventions by the international community, a central government has been lacking in Somalia. Considerable areas of the country, particularly in the southern part, have been ravaged by turmoil, causing scores of refugees to flee their country of origin. Hence, by 2010, Somalis proportionately constitute one of the largest refugee populations of the world.[9]

Individualism and Holism in the Somali Context

Luis Dumont, identifies two different types of societies, representing either *holism* or *individualism*. The former, according to Dumont, is the case with societies where the paramount value is vested in society rather than the individual. In such societies, the corporate amounts to more than the mere sum of the involved individuals. His definition of individualism represents an opposite situation. The paramount value of the society is here interpreted to be

---

Education for the Twenty-First Century: The Book, the Circle, and the Sandals (Maryknoll, N.Y.: Orbis Books, 1996), 122.

[7] Abandoning the traditional territorial approach to mission does not necessarily entail a dismissal of the Christian church's particular responsibility towards geographical areas or people groups where no relevant witness of Jesus Christ and the Gospel exists. It rather makes mission more composite and complex than the traditional Christendom-Heathendom dichotomy.

[8] Wilbert Shenk establishes that ecclesiology in the western world during past centuries has had a pastoral attention rather than a missional. Wilbert R. Shenk, 'The Training of Missiologists for Western Culture', 120-123. It should be underscored however, that the ecclesiological shift during later years with an increased emphasize on 'missional ecclesiology' is a step in the right direction.

[9] According to Statistics Norway, by January 2009 Somalis constituted the second largest non-European immigrant population to Norway, amounting to more than 23,000. Approximately 75% have arrived within the last ten years. www.ssb.no/english/subjects/02/01/10/innvbef_en/fig-2009-04-30-01-en.gif (accessed 11.01.2010); www.ssb.no/english/subjects/02/01/10/innvbef_en/tab-2009-04-30-14-en.html (accessed 11.01.2010).

found in the individuals.[10] This basic definition of various types of societies is of particular relevance to the Somali case. Somali society is a traditionally kinship based society.[11] The acknowledged Somali scholar, Ioan M. Lewis, has described this trait in the following way:

> 'Our kinsmen, right or wrong' is the basic motto of Somali social life. As the foundation of social co-operation, kinship enters into all transactions between and amongst individuals. There is no significant area of Somali social activity where the influence of kinship is absent.[12]

Hence, in Dumont's definition, Somali society may be claimed to represent holism. Clan, kin and family constitute the contexts of social interaction, and the individual is invariably part of this 'social web'. Traditional Somali society is constructed in such a manner that the individual in every context or life situation remains a representative of his clan, and benefits from kinship protection. Consequently, the individual cannot survive being a maverick, completely detached from his clan. Either to remain within or distance oneself from the corporate is, accordingly, not a real choice. Somali immigrants to Europe are most often 'born and bred' in this context.[13]

Traditional Somali society, however, carries an imbedded tension between the individual and the corporate. Despite meeting the requirements of 'holism'

---

[10] Louis Dumont, *Essays on Individualism: Modern Ideology in Anthropological Perspective* (Chicago: Univ. of Chicago Press, 1986), 25. As such, this classification is interrelated with the classic discussion within social theory regarding structur- or actor-oriented theories. For an introduction, see for instance Martin Hollis, who pursuits this discussion based on the approaches of Karl Marx and John Stuart Mill. Martin Hollis, *The Philosophy of Social Science: An Introduction* (Cambridge: Cambridge University Press, 1994), 1-20.

[11] According to Dunn, "In traditional society, identity is largely pre-given through membership in the group and community, determined externally by systems of kinship and religion," Robert G. Dunn, *Identity Crises: A Social Critique of Postmodernity* (Minneapolis, Minn.: University of Minnesota Press, 1998), 52-53. Although I agree with Dunn's main point, I find it difficult to maintain such a strict delimitation as his statement may seem to indicate with regard to contemporary 'traditional societies'. All societies are to varying degrees exposed to external influence, and a more static interpretation of culture is thus increasingly difficult to retain.

[12] I. M. Lewis, *Blood and Bone: The Call of Kinship in Somali Society* (Lawrenceville, N.J.: Red Sea Press, 1994), vii.

[13] I can follow Gadamer when he points out that social change is itself in continuity. Hans Georg Gadamer, *Truth and Method* (London: Sheed and Ward, 1993), 280-285. With regards to the Somali context, David D. Laitin and Said S. Samatar advocate a similar understanding: "The examples just cited represent a mere fragment of the many ways in which town Somalis have adopted the vocabulary – and by implication the imagery – of their pastoral forebears to deal with urban life. These examples serve to illustrate that although many Somalis no longer lead a pastoral life, they nevertheless continue to draw on their pastoral heritage to meet the challenges and opportunities of a changing, technologically sophisticated world." David D. Laitin and Said S. Samatar, *Somalia: Nation in Search of a State* (Boulder, Colo., London, England: Westview Press; Gower, 1987), 27.

in the terminology of Dumont, Somali society is characteristically known to be highly individualistic. The social structure has historically been egalitarian, lacking a central government, while loyalty to a considerable extent has been situational rather than institutionalized. Hence, the context has provided ample space for the individual's personal choices and manifestations of life.

> In lineage segmentation one, literally, does not have a permanent enemy or a permanent friend – not even a permanent Muslim friend – but only a permanent attention to the availability of self-improving opportunities. Depending on a given context, a man – or a group of men, or a state, for that matter – may be your friend or foe. Everything is fluid and ever-changing.[14]

From an 'etic' perspective, concepts such as *loyalty* and *commitment* accordingly remain particularly challenging in the Somali context. Depending on the actual situation the person is free to shift loyalties and side with potential enemies, in order to obtain short-term objectives.[15] Consequently, the kinship framework does not keep the Somali from being highly individualistic and rather non-conformist. Thus rather than constituting two "mutually irreconcilable ideologies", as claimed by Dumont,[16] individualism is to a certain extent controlled and limited by the kinship structure, particularly as manifested through Somali customary law (*ᶜaado*).[17] Somali society

---

[14] Said S. Samatar, 'Unhappy Masses and the Challenge of Political Islam in the Horn of Africa', *Horn of Africa* 20 (2002), 3. A similar perspective is presented by Notten: "Somalis are indeed outspoken in their opinions and fear no one. In their individual life as well as collectively as a nation, they tend to be extremely independent. Yet every person has a fixed place in Somali society, determined mostly by accident of birth into a close-knit family and by the need for economic survival in a semi-arid natural environment. Thus Somali society shows a remarkable blend of independence and order, of freedom and discipline." Michael van Notten and Spencer Heath MacCallum, *The Law of the Somalis: A Stable Foundation for Economic Development in the Horn of Africa* (Trenton, NJ: Red Sea Press, 2005), 31.

[15] "Still, kin solidarity is not absolute. Every ancestor in a genealogy represents a point of potential fission as well as unity. The lineage system in Somalia is therefore referred to as 'segmentary', and considered well adapted to a mobile way of life. It is characterized by something of a paradox: the very forces – of loyalty, mutual interest – that draw people together can also set them against one another in rivalries between clans or sub-groups within them. There are two reasons for this: loyalties are relative, nested within ever broader and therefore more diffuse kinship segments." Virginia Lee Barnes and Janice Patricia Boddy, *Aman: The Story of a Somali Girl* (New York: Pantheon Books, 1994), 300-301. See also Laitin and Samatar, *Somalia: Nation in Search of a State,* 31.

[16] Dumont, *Essays on Individualism,* 25.

[17] *ᶜaado* is a term used for Somali culture in a wide sense. It relates to cultural features such as dress, food and customs in general. Within *ᶜaado,* the narrower concept of *xeer,* constitutes "customary procedure founded upon contractual agreement", and regulates relationships between groups. "The majority of *xeer* agreements binding groups relate principally to collective defence and security, and to political cohesion in general," I. M. Lewis and Said S. Samatar, *A Pastoral Democracy: A Study of Pastoralism and Politics Among the Northern Somali of the Horn of Africa* (Hamburg/Oxford: LIT; James Currey

accordingly may be argued to represent a hybrid of these two, where the limitations posed by customary law are rather few, but tend to be definite. It further needs to be acknowledged that Islam in traditional Somali society represents a fundamental and integral constituent of customary law.[18] Religious deviation accordingly constitutes intolerable departure from customary law.[19]

The Stories of Hussein and Ali[20]

Hussein first came in contact with Christianity in an East African country outside of Somalia. Although he was touched by the Christian message, he feared sanctions from his fellow countrymen, and remained a non-religious practitioner in his ethnic environment. He has now spent several years in Norway and at present many people know that he has become a Christian. He still has some limited contact with his family, "but it is not like before. Some believe I am not a normal person." His wife took their children and left him when she found out that he had converted to Christianity. In daily life, he generally stays away from other Somalis.

Some years back, Ali befriended a Christian Somali in a country adjacent to Somalia and used to discuss religion with him. When he later was granted refugee status in Norway, his past interest in Christianity had not ceased. Through a continuous comparative study of the Qur'an and the Bible he opted for Christianity. He has now been a Christian for approximately three years, but still only his close relatives realize that he has left Islam. Nonetheless, they have continuously tried to make him change his ways, both by threats and lure.

---

with the IAI, 1999), 162. The two terms are some times employed interchangeably.

[18] According to Hersi, "Islam as a religion and a system of values so thoroughly permeates all aspects of Somali life that it is difficult to conceive of any meaning in the term Somali itself without at the same time implying Islamic identity". Ali Abdirahman Hersi, 'The Arab Factor in Somali History: the Origins and the Development of Arab Enterprise and Cultural Influences in the Somali Peninsula', PhD-thesis (University of California, Los Angeles, 1977), 109. There are, however, several aspects where Somali customary law has been in conflict with and taken precedence over Islamic law. See e.g. Michael van Notten and Spencer Heath MacCallum, *The Law of the Somalis: A Stable Foundation for Economic Development in the Horn of Africa* (Trenton, NJ: Red Sea Press, 2005), 37.

[19] This often implies severe consequences for converts to Christianity. From personal communication and experience I have several times witnessed a recognisable pattern of community behaviour towards Christian converts: (1) oral threats; (2) gradually intensified corporal punishment; (3) expulsion from the family home; (4) loss of family communion; (5) loss of inheritance. This has constituted a gradual development. In some cases spouse and children have also be removed from the convert by force. During later years (particularly in Southern Somalia) executions of Christian converts have occurred regularly. See www.compassdirect.org/english/country/somalia/14479, accessed 18.02.2010.

[20] To secure the informants' anonymity, names utilized in this essay are fictitious. Specific references regarding the interviewees have also been made general.

Hussein and Ali became acquainted through shared Norwegian friends. Their friendship has since developed. At present they mutually support each other and share Christian community with one another. I asked them if, for Somalis, there were any differences, between converting to Christianity in Europe and in East Africa.

> You can get all you need for your life and you can stay alone. You can be who you want and believe what you want. In Kenya and Africa it is different. People have to live together and help each other. If someone becomes a Christian who lives in Kenya or Ethiopia or Somalia, it is more dangerous. He can be killed. He can lose his family, and maybe no one will help him. In Europe I lost all of the Somali community. I am not one of them now because of my belief. …I used to have many friends, but I have lost all others.[21]

This statement by Hussein actualizes the question of religious mobility against the contextual background of holistic and individualistic hybridism as already presented.

Muslim Somalis and European Individualization

Frank Peter has written an enlightening article on the interrelation between individualization and religious authority in Western European Islam. He asserts that secularization, individualization and privatization lead to a relative loss of influence of both imams and religious institutions among Muslim immigrants to the Western world.[22] A number of studies have established that a similar development is taking place in Muslim communities across Europe.[23] This merger of European individualism and Muslim authoritarianism, furthering a fragmentation of religious authority, represents an interesting perspective also with regards to Christian witness to Muslim Somalis. Since converting to Christianity, Hussein had lost the basic support and fellowship of his Somali friends and relatives. Nonetheless, the context of Norwegian 'individualism', where, as Dumont asserts, the paramount value of society is broadly interpreted to be found in the individuals, made it possible to break with the corporate and follow his private and 'unprecedented' religious convictions. Hence, although religious conversion might inevitably lead to loss of communion, and to considerable disadvantages following from such a loss, Hussein knew that in practical terms he could survive on his own. He did not remain dependent on the help and support vested in belonging to a large community, as had been the case previously.

An issue that repeatedly was brought forward by Ali and Hussein in this regard is the returning challenge of security. Possible community sanctions toward converts, particularly in East Africa, were considered to render religious

---

[21] Hussein, in interview.

[22] Frank Peter, 'Individualization and Religious Authority in Western European Islam', *Islam and Christian-Muslim Relations*, 17 (2006), 107.

[23] See e.g. Peter G. Mandaville, *Transnational Muslim Politics: Reimagining the Umma* (London: Routledge, 2001).

conversion almost impossible. Although the fear of religiously motivated homicides was limited in a Norwegian context, a general insecurity towards possible sanctions remains: "It is good for my security to be among Norwegian Christians. … We don't know who we are going to meet or who we are going to discuss with. Then, anything can happen."[24] This insecurity could however not prevent a divergent religious orientation since the Norwegian society was expected to provide basic protection. Hence, religious conversion continues to be disadvantageous in several aspects, but the converts consider themselves to be in a position to face the consequences.

Individualism and Autonomy

Hussein's statement above, regarding the possibility of a Christian to survive "on his own" in Norway, is intelligible and informed by the context of imbedded tension in traditional Somali culture between the individual and the community (or individualism and holism according to Dumont's definition). An egalitarian and anti-authoritarian trait, so characteristic to Somali society, is traditionally balanced by Somali customary law (*ᶜaado*) and kinship. In the Western world the role traditionally filled by customary law and kin changes. As the individual to a lesser extent remains dependent upon his kin, available sanctions towards deviation from customary law diminish. Accordingly, there is a real possibility of Somalis in the Western world embracing a form of modern individualism. I assert, however, that in the case of Somali converts to Christianity, this does not lead to further individualism, but rather to autonomy. Autonomy, Renaut claims, is not a freedom without rules, but rather 'auto-nomy', accentuating self-rule. The autonomous individual remains in dependency of norms, not an authoritarian and imposed law, but rather norms that are self-established and freely accepted by the individual.[25] Hence autonomy has to be defined differently from a modern, disconnected, individualism.[26] Somali converts thus embrace personally accepted norms, rather than an authoritarian, imposed law. This experience towards stronger religious autonomy is presumably not an experience solely made by Christian converts. Olivier Roy has argued that the encounter with European individualism leads to a democratization of Islam where the individual Muslim to a greater extent is forced to reflect on his religious beliefs.[27] Such a development has contributed towards increased religious differentiation within Muslim communities across Europe. Presumably, it also provides new opportunities for Christian witness to Muslims and unprecedented possibilities for religious conversion from Islam.

---

[24] Stated by Hussein.

[25] Alain Renaut, *The Era of the Individual: A Contribution to a History of Subjectivity* (Princeton, N.J.: Princeton Univ. Press, 1997), 39.

[26] *Ibid.*, 56.

[27] Olivier Roy, *Globalized Islam: The Search for a New Ummah* (New York: Columbia University Press, 2004).

Religious Space[28] and the Internet

According to Hussein, the challenge with regards to a Christian witness to Somalis is to transcend the boundaries of Somali communities in Europe, and access individuals. Such communities often endeavour to uphold a corporate and homogeneous standard for accepted cultural and religious orientation. The most pressing requirement is accordingly to create necessary space for Christian witness.

> Muslims, even if they may have many questions, they are scared of their fathers and relatives. Now we know that there are many Somalis who live alone. Even those cannot come and ask you about Jesus and Christianity, but they can watch TV or they can understand radio and use the internet.... In Paltalk, you can meet with a hundred people at one time, and you can tell all of them and one or two can believe what you say.[29]

Hence, the *social media* may be of particular relevance for external contact and communication in a context where people characteristically live more individualized lives, with a formal and legal religious freedom, but remain within culturally defined religious limitations.[30] Various groups on Paltalk[31] preserve both national and religious identities, and as such different virtual rooms in Paltalk create new religious space on the internet. These rooms facilitate interreligious witness and dialogue in a potentially anonymous and safe context. Ali explains that Somalis are frequent contributors to Paltalk. "Among people from Africa, Somalis are on the top. They have more than a hundred different rooms where they chat. There are many Muslim leaders who log on and want to discuss with us. We are not afraid of anybody.... We discuss with them." Hussein adds, "When people see someone from Somalia who believes in Jesus, and talk the Somali language, then they are interested to hear what we are saying. Others become very aggressive." Through the process of globalisation with substantial mobility of populations, the traditional understanding of religious space has become more complex and blurred.[32] The

---

[28] On the discussion regarding production of religious space, see e.g. Elizabeth McAlister, 'Globalisation and the Religious Production of Space', *Journal for the Scientific Study of Religion*, 44 (2005), 249-255.

[29] Hussein, in interview.

[30] Hoover, Clark and Rainie argue that the most significant impact of the internet with regards to religion in the US is a development where the individual comes to exercise more autonomy in matters of faith contrasting that of formal authorities. S. M. Hoover, L.S. Clark and L. Rainie, 'Faith Online', in *Report from the Pew Internet & American Life Project* (2004) www.pewinternet.org, 20.

[31] In Hussein's words, "Paltalk is like a chat room. Many Somalis use it. I believe it is the easiest way to get in contact and discuss with Somalis.... We have our own room called 'Somali Christian', and all are welcome. Paltalk can be about many different things. They have music rooms, business, Islamic rooms and they have rooms for Christians. You can find anything. So, we have our own room, and we tell people about Jesus."

[32] Concepts such as 'Christendom' and 'Heathendom', or 'dar-al-Islam' and 'dar-al-

internet, constituting a transnational and inter-religious space, however, provides a new territory for developing religious and ethnic identities. As highlighted by Ali, Somalis are reputed to be active and frequent users of modern media.[33] Hence, the internet may be a particularly important arena providing space for a future Christian witness towards the global Somali population.

Global Space for Unilingual Christian Worship?

> We have our prayer room and pray. Sometimes we do a Bible study with the Somali Christians.... Before we open our room we know that we are going to be attacked. So we pray. Anyone who feels like praying will pray. We pray that the Lord must show these people what He wants, not just us. So, that is what we do, but then we are on the private room with the Christians. Some people, they also sing.[34]

As Hussein points out, Paltalk and similar chat communities apparently carry significant potentials also with regards to Christian worship. Somali Christians across the globe are few and scattered. Residing in the Western world, some have never experienced Christian worship in their native language, and very few have access to regular fellowship with other Christian Somalis.[35] Advantages to Christian witness and communion with people of common language and cultural background, have been thoroughly emphasized through the past missiological debate regarding such approaches to mission as the

harb' may not be as clear-cut and distinct as what used to be the case. As the Western world is becoming increasingly multi-cultural and multi-religious it is also a question to what extent for example the West remains a 'Christian space'. On this, see e.g. Lamin O. Sanneh, *Disciples of All Nations. Pillars of World Christianity* (New York: Oxford University Press, 2008), and Philip Jenkins, *The Next Christendom: The Coming of Global Christianity* (New York: Oxford University Press, 2002).

[33] As an example it can be mentioned that in 2002, despite lacking a central government, telecommunications in Somalia flourished: "In addition to numerous local radio stations (and often associated newspapers and web sites) a VHF and UHF radio system linked most parts of the country. There were six or more private mobile telephone systems and two television networks, one with 22 channels and the other six. Video parlours were popular also, and international telephone calls were amongst the cheapest in the world," I. M. Lewis, *A Modern History of the Somali: Nation and State in the Horn of Africa* (Oxford: James Currey, 2002), 298.

[34] Hussein, in interview.

[35] From a survey regarding the importance of religion among teenagers in Sweden, Lövheim concludes that although the importance of internet on religious formation may have been overestimated, the situation might be different with regards to marginal religious groups. "Religious minorities can find access to alternative sources of information and form supportive networks of likeminded via the internet," Mia Lövheim, 'Rethinking Cyberreligion? Teens, Religion and the Internet in Sweden', *Nordicom Review*, 29 (2008), 215.

'homogeneous unit principle' and the 'people group strategy'.[36] Although objections have been raised regarding a possible lop-sidedness in the theoretical basis of these approaches, the main emphasis on shared ethnic identity remains.[37] Although Christians theologically are 'one in Christ', the unity in Christ does not eliminate all biological or cultural diversity. In Paltalk, the group of Christian Somalis has found a global arena for unilingual and common cultural worship, materializing in *joint Bible study*, *prayer* and *singing*. A more formal framework for the communion is also present as the participants freely enter or leave their room of worship. The Paltalk private chat room accordingly forms a joint religious space for the participants. Hence, the group constituting a cyber community in Paltalk carries some of the most central characteristics of a Christian church. Apparent benefits of this arena, apart from facilitating experience of community and a shared fate, include also the possibility of retaining participant anonymity and hence, increased security.

Despite such benefits, I assert that Paltalk and similar chat communities are curtailed by inevitable limitations, and the substitutive potential of a cyberchurch to a local congregation therefore calls for a certain restraint.[38] A lack of face-to-face fellowship has implications for fundamental aspects of Christian fellowship such as participating in corporate sacramental communion, social interaction and care in neighborhoods, and in-depth friendships. The possibility of retaining anonymity further might have the consequence of counteracting in-depth commitment. As no one can be held accountable to a specific group of defined members, a consumer relationship towards the chat community may easily develop. As such, there may not be a cohesive group with a mutual commitment.[39] I maintain that this argument is of particular relevance when relating to ethnic Somalis, where commitment traditionally has been regulated within the tension of contractual relationships and a situational loyalty. Thus I assert that the Paltalk chat communities, and other similar cyber communities, in the long run mainly represent an important supplementary potential to membership in local congregations.[40]

---

[36] See e.g. Egil Grandhagen, 'De unådde folkeslag', in Jan-Martin Berentsen, Tormod Engelsviken and Knud Jørgensen (eds), *Missiologi i Dag* (Oslo: Universitetsforlaget, 1994), 363-372.

[37] On the wider discussion regarding social and biological identity formation, see Dunn, *Identity Crises.*

[38] The term 'cyberchurch' was coined during the 1990s, embracing a wide variety of Christian spiritual expressions on the internet. During later years it has particularly been linked to the emerging church movement, and has as such often included an element of critique towards the organized and institutional church. The connection between the emerging church movement and the 'cyberchurch' terminology, does however not exclude other church communities from being included in the term.

[39] Advocates of communion ecclesiology have through past decades thoroughly established the New Testament's emphasis on the Christian congregation as a community of believers. Such New Testament images employed to the church as the 'People of God' or 'Body of Christ' underscores a similar perspective.

[40] A similar perspective has materialized from descriptive surveys made on the

Conclusion

The process of globalisation during the last century has dramatically altered the global religious map. Pondering in retrospect the situation a few decades ago, religious space still had a definite territorial character. At present, former heartlands of Christianity such as Europe, embraces a considerable Muslim population. The influx of peoples of various religious orientations constitutes new and unprecedented challenges to European Christianity. This development is evident with regards to Muslim converts to Christianity, settled in Europe. Hussein and Ali have shared stories from their lives as Christian Somalis in Norway. Their witness has highlighted various perspectives:

1. A fundamental tension had become evident between the individual and the expectations of the corporate. This is a pattern recognizable also within traditional Somali culture. This innate tension, however, goes through a transformation when it is forced to interact with European individualism, a development which to some extent is familiar to European Islam in general. As individualism paired with egalitarianism represents a well-established trait of traditional Somali culture, a merger with radical European individualization calls for further attention. From the witness of Hussein and Ali, this cultural merger does not, however, result in 'unchecked' individualism, but rather in a strengthened autonomy.

2. The opportunity provided by the *new media,* of developing new religious space, represents unprecedented possibilities for these Christians belonging to a context where Christianity is under pressure. This is the case both with regard to Christian fellowship and a Christian witness. The new social media carry the inherent advantage of such aspects as anonymity, availability, and cultural unity across global boundaries. As Somalis are among the most ardent users of these media, the arena may prove particularly important to this people group both for establishing and maintaining Christian community and for witnessing to other Somalis about their faith. As such, the growing influence of the new social media may prove to alter future possibilities of religious communion and witness among marginalized religious groups. Christian community on the internet may, however, in the long run turn out to be more significant in a supplementary than a substitutive perspective.

---

interrelation of religious life 'online and offline', see Lövheim, 'Rethinking Cyberreligion?', 214. Regarding Christian Somalis it should also be added that apart from being an arena for Christian witness and fellowship, Paltalk has on several occasions brought people physically together for joint communion and worship.

In the Midst of Umma on the Internet: Religious Profession and Witness in a Globalized Era

A Response to F.O. Thoresen

Tomas Sundnes Drønen

To describe global change is a challenging task. Thoresen's paper on Somali converts in Norway shows that "small facts can speak to large issues"[1] and that rather modest empirical facts can help us interpret global change. The focus of Thoresen's paper is clear in the sense that the case is of general interest to anyone preoccupied with the future of global mission, and the geographical focus is equally interesting for anyone preoccupied with 'reaching the unreached' in a globalized era.

I will use this occasion to comment on two central aspects of the paper and try to show that interpretation of the challenges of global mission is not only a challenging task, it is also a very difficult one. The crystal ball of Christian mission is for the time being very cloudy, but behind the two skies that I have chosen to call globalisation and commitment, my hope is that we can catch small glimpses of the future, which can encourage us to rethink the global Christian commandment.

Mission in a Globalized Era

In one of the first books that we might call a 'globalisation classic', *Jihad vs. McWorld*, Benjamin Barber shows that the g-word is a slippery term. His first scenario of the new global condition leads to "the grim prospect of retribalization",[2] where small societies choose to isolate themselves from the rest of the world, and are ready to pick up arms in order to fight for what they believe in. The second scenario in Barber's prophecies is a uniformed homogenization of world culture, where fast music, fast computers, and fast food play the leading role. Fifteen years after the publication of the book we

---

[1] A slight modification of Clifford Geertz' famous words, "Small facts speak to large issues." Clifford Geertz, *The Interpretation of Cultures* (New York, N.Y.: Basic Books, 1973), 23.

[2] Benjamin R. Barber, *Jihad Vs. Mcworld* (Times Books, 1995), 3.

might say that Barber was right. Globalisation has led to both marginalization and homogenization, the world has become both 'Babel and Disneyland'.

Thoresen points to several important perspectives of globalisation when he claims that migration, new social media, and religious profession are key concepts for anyone interested in studying global mission in a new millennium. He also mentions that we can trace the roots of the term globalisation in a pre-modern era. I do, however, agree with Jan Aart Scholte who claims that in order for the new g-word to make sense as an analytical term, it has to represent something qualitatively new, and not just sum up the terms internationalization, liberalization, universalization, and westernization.[3] Scholte argues that our new social condition is first of all defined by "transplanetary relations and supraterritoriality".[4] Thoresen's focus on space and locality is thus of utmost importance if we are to foresee the future challenges of global mission.

It might be argued that the majority of the future of Christianity, the Global South, still live their lives very much on the soil of their forefathers, attending what Paul Gifford calls "the mainline churches".[5] And this might be so, but anyone interested in the future should look for change within the body of Christian churches, what Gifford calls "the newcomers".[6] The newcomers he refers to are Pentecostal, charismatic, and born-again churches, and together they make up the fastest growing body in global Christianity. If globalisation actually influences religious profession, this is where we should look for transplanetary and supraterritorial changes. In the following I will therefore briefly present some recent changes in the church-landscape in two African countries very much influenced by traditional, mainline churches, namely Nigeria and Cameroon, trying to keep in mind the question of relevance to Thoresen's article, and to the situation of the two Somali immigrants, Hussein and Ali, in Norway.

Globalisation and Religious Change

One of the fastest growing churches in Nigeria today is David Oyedepo's Winners Chapel.[7] The church was started by Oyedepo in 1981, and according to their homepage, the church is now established in more than 300 cities all over Nigeria, it is present in 35 nations, and has large communities in London and New York. The headquarters of the church is Canaanland in Ota, a Lagos suburb, where the Faith Tabernacle (which is said to be the largest church-

---

[3] Jan Aart Scholte, *Globalisation: A Critical Introduction* (Hampshire: Palgrave Macmillan 2nd edition, 2005), 54-59.

[4] Scholte, *Globalisation,* 60-64.

[5] Paul Gifford, *Ghana's New Christianity: Pentecostalism in a Globalising African Economy* (London: Hurst & Company, 2004), 20-23.

[6] Gifford, *Ghana's New Christianity,* 23-27.

[7] The church is also called Living Faith Church, and the mission department is called Living Faith Ministry Worldwide. The homepage of the church is 'David Oyedepo Ministries International Inc.', http://davidoyedepoministries.org/, accessed 9.4.2010.

building in the world) can seat 50,000 persons, and where 250,000 persons are supposed to be able to follow one of the three weekly Sunday sermons outside the church. The most interesting part of Winners' missionary strategy is, from my perspective, not the fact that the church is said to have 400 buses that are used to transport people in the Lagos area to the sermons, neither that they are about to buy their third aircraft.[8] What is interesting is their large focus on the internet, providing a homepage where anyone is invited to participate in the activities of the church, regardless of geographical location. Here you can follow services from the Faith Tabernacle live, you can get in contact with the church, you can download sermons as podcast, you can read other Christian testimonies, you can donate money, and you can take part in several other church activities, everything through your computer.

During my time as a missionary in Cameroon, I considered cyber-mission to be a very bad idea on the world's poorest continent. But David Oyedepo is not a white, well-educated missionary. He is an African visionary evangelist, who foresaw the coming of cheap internet-cafés in most towns and cities in sub-Saharan Africa, and turned this foresight to his advantage. Not least considering the large Nigerian communities in cities like London and New York, where many members are successful businessmen and academics, but still lack a spiritual home.

This is where our thoughts should wander back to Hussein and Ali, and where the crucial question is as obvious as it is painful for us in the western post-Christian world: why do Hussein and Ali need the internet to have a Christian fellowship? Why have we failed as a receiving Christian community? We have sent missionaries to the end of the world, but why have we not been able to receive the Christian brothers and sisters who come to visit us as immigrant workers and refugees?

The question might partly be answered if we make a quick visit no Ngaoundéré, a town in the northern part of Cameroon, not far from the Nigerian border. In order to find *Eglise Biblique de la Vie Profonde* in the Joli Soir quarter, you will have to ask one of the local residents to guide you through narrow paths deep into the residential area. There you will find a concrete building, with no sign or cross indicating that this is a Christian church, but with a large satellite dish on the roof. Every Sunday around fifty believers gather in this modest church, in an area inhabited by both Christians and Muslims. The small congregation deep inside the Joli Soir quarter is, however, part of a larger global network. Deeper Life Bible Church was started as a Bible study group in 1973 by the math professor William F. Kumuyi, and has grown into a global ministry that, according to the church homepage, has 800,000 members in Nigeria alone.[9]

What we have to ask ourselves is why fifty church-members, most of them migrants from the English speaking part of Cameroon, meet in this small

[8] http://en.wikipedia.org/wiki/Winners'_Chapel, accessed 9.4.2010.

[9] www.dclm.org/AboutUs/PastorWFKumuyi/tabid/56/Default.aspx, accessed 9.4. 2010.

church in order to watch Pastor Kumuyi's sermons on television in a town where there are two large cathedrals (one Lutheran and one Catholic), at least ten other mainline congregations and more than twenty smaller Pentecostal or born-again churches. Is this Jihad or is this McWorld, is it Babel or is it Disneyland?

Globalisation and Commitment

Thoresen's main concern about the new social media is the lack of commitment that might be the result if Christians like Hussein and Ali remain anonymous in the cyber chat-rooms. His case study reveals interesting aspects of being a refugee from a Muslim country in the West, but leaves us with little information concerning the actual commitment to a Christian community, be it territorial or virtual. My contention is that a strong focus on traditional Christian communities, which according to Thoresen is defined by "corporate sacramental communion, social interaction and care in neighborhoods, and in-depth friendship,"[10] might be a hinder to further success for the global mission movement. 'The Christian Revolution'[11] in the Global South is not about creating small, well-organised Christian communities. It is about William Oyedepo who manages to gather 100,000 people any given Sunday at Canaanland, and it is about William F. Kumuyi who manages to gather fifty believers in front of a television screen in Ngaoundéré. Thoresen's concern is to what extent these believers are committed to the Christian community to which they belong, and I agree with him that Christian communities are of importance, but I think that we still have to be very careful in trying to define what these communities should look like.

Commitment is closely connected to the question of identity, another topic discussed in Thoresen's paper. The topic is of such importance that it has to be further elaborated in order to help us understand the relationship between globalisation, commitment and Christian communities. If a focus is maintained on Alain Renaut's presentation of individualism as "modern and disconnected,"[12] I fear that important aspects of our new global condition will be neglected. Autonomy might be a good term describing the identical changes which occurs within Hussein and Ali, but avoiding the term individualism in trying to describe social change in a globalized era would be a mistake. Urbanization and migration have obvious implications related to identity-change, and a change in personal relations to territorial and ethnic 'holism' can be observed by anyone studying social relations in urban areas in Africa.

---

[10] Thoresen, 'In the midst of Umma on the Internet: Religious Profession and Witness in a Globalized era.'

[11] Philip Jenkins, *The Next Christendom: The Coming of Global Christianity* (New York, N.Y.: Oxford University Press, 2007), 1-19.

[12] Cited from Thoresen.

Concluding Remarks

The crucial final question is the following: how does globalisation and migration affect future world mission? My contention is that globalisation has serious effects on Christian communities. 'Soul-floating' will be a consequence of the fact that more Christians than ever before in history have become voluntary migrants or refugees due to political oppression and climate change. New Christian churches are created and these communities use new technology in order to reach people looking for a spiritual home. Commitment to the Christian message in a globalized era does not necessarily mean commitment to one particular congregation from the cradle to the grave. And I think that individualism, through a positive interpretation of the term, will increase personal freedom to choose a church that meet personal needs, be it mainline, Pentecostal, or virtual. The main challenge in a global perspective is for us, the traditional western churches, to become relevant to our own social surroundings. And if we manage that, we might also become a relevant alternative to Hussein and Ali's chat-room on the internet.

The Global Youth Culture: Targeting and Involving Youth in Global Mission

Bård-Eirik Hallesby Norheim

All Popular Culture is Youth Culture

> Today, *all* popular culture is youth culture, and vice versa, and *all* age groups participate in it – forcing young people to turn to increasingly marginal and dangerous alternatives in order to distinguish themselves from adults.[1]

These are the words of Professor in Youth, Culture and Church at Princeton Theological Seminary, US, Kenda Creasy Dean, in an article on *The New Rhetoric in Youth Ministry*. Dean therefore claims that the youth ministry of the church plays a crucial, strategic role in the mission of the church, as youth ministry is often the place where processes of re-shaping the church start. Dean points out that future church leaders get their life-shaping experiences in the context of youth ministry, and the faith proclaimed and matured in the context of youth ministry may enable "those also conversant in culture – teenagers, for instance – to baptize culture for Christ."[2]

Youth are often perceived as agents in the on-going change of the world. We are told that the Obama-campaign, 'Change we can believe in', succeeded much because of the way it managed to involve young people. In many ways this campaign serves as an ideal-type for the way we like to perceive Christian youth ministry, as well – involving youth in church and mission is expected to bring about (often numerical) change – here and now and for the future. In this case study I will look at some of the main features of the so-called global youth culture and discuss in which ways it challenges the mission of the church. I will focus in particular on what it takes to target and involve youth in global mission – and whether the concept of 'targeting and involving' is a helpful way to coin the way the church and her mission should relate to the global youth culture.

---

[1] Kenda Creasy Dean, 'The New Rhetoric of Youth Ministry', *Journal of Youth and Theology*, 2:2 (2003), 14.
[2] *Ibid.*, 15.

The Global Youth Culture

In many ways today's youth are the quintessential inhabitants of postmodern and global life – they are the first generation to live integrated with the changing spheres of cyberspace, and hyper reality where media culture, laptops, stem cell research, and other emerging technologies are radically altering all aspects of life.[3] Therefore shared global youth culture trends or subcultures, such as the hip hop culture, are "not individual responses but are constructed intersubjectively."[4] Music (production) plays a special role within this evolving global youth culture. It is not purely a matter of aesthetics. Ultimately it is "a part of a larger capitalist production, something to make money from."[5]

But is there really such a thing as *the* global youth culture? Any attempt to consider youth culture as a global phenomenon is at the same time an attempt to include youth in the current accounts of global change.[6] Obviously, the notion of youth itself has geographic characteristics as the term means different things in different places.[7] That means that young people have different levels of access to the products that exist because of globalisation. But still, globalisation nonetheless has effect on the daily lives of youth in different contexts, although in different ways.[8] Globalisation, understood as the evolving of the global market or consumer culture, makes for very different life conditions for young people. Young people in the so-called developing world are forced into working at an early age and under poor conditions to produce things like shoes or computer hardware, which youth in the so-called developed world wear or use for either their high-paid work or increased periods of leisure.[9]

It seems tempting to conclude that the lives of young people are *determined* largely by the changes caused by the global market – although this plays out in different ways in different contexts. However, youth researchers suggest that the lives of young people are not just *determined* by the effects of globalisation, rather globalisation *over determine* the lives of young people. Therefore,

> When we think about the global youth as over determined – dealing with many different things at once – we realize that young people are not just the puppets of globalisation. Instead, we begin to see that the global youth are able to mix and modify both the products and consequences of corporate globalisation.[10]

---

[3] Bart Vautour, 'Global Youth', in Shirley Steinberg, Priya Parmar and Birgit Richard (eds), *Contemporary Youth Culture: An International Encyclopedia,* vol. 1. (London: Greenwood Press, 2006), 25.

[4] Jennifer Kelly, 'Hip Hop Globalisation and Youth Culture', in Steinberg et.al., *Contemporary Youth Culture*, 34.

[5] *Ibid.*, 36.

[6] Vautour, 'Global Youth', 25.

[7] Robert J. Helfenbein, 'A Critical Geography of Youth Culture', in Steinberg et.al., *Contemporary Youth Culture*, 23.

[8] Vautour, 'Global Youth', 28.

[9] Vautour, 'Global Youth', 28.

[10] Vautour, 'Global Youth', 29.

As agents on the global market, youth are also actively relating to the new progressive spirituality evolving on the global market. This progressive spirituality offers a particular *mythos* focusing on the unfolding universe as the grounding narrative within which human existence makes sense. This differs from a secularist worldview that depicts human life as devoid of meaning and value and other than that created by humans themselves. The universal story, on the other hand, places humanity as one small element in a grander narrative of cosmic unfolding. Similarly, human consciousness is seen not as a site for nihilism or existential despair, but as a symptom of the universe becoming conscious of itself.[11]

Addressing the Global Youth Culture

This way of conceptualizing the larger human narrative makes it harder to promote the gospel as medicine for troubled souls, or the thing that fills the empty hole inside. This is a challenge for the typical culture-pessimistic church response to the global youth culture, which chooses a reluctant or even fundamentally critical approach to the dynamics of the global youth culture. The culture-pessimistic approach is an important reminder that youth may be particularly fragile when it comes to how capitalist globalisation endangers both economic solidarity and trust in relationships.[12] But the culture-pessimistic approach is not the only viable approach. One can easily find more constructive, or culture-optimistic, approaches which have emerged within Christian youth ministry. The way contemporary Christian worship has developed over the last two decades is a typical example of an intentional response to the dynamics of the global youth culture, where Christian youth ministry has sought to adapt to different musical 'taste communities' and youth subcultures. Obviously, the attempt to try to couple the style of Christian youth ministry with contemporary culture has taken different paths throughout the last decades. Post WWII Christian youth ministry pretty soon tried to mime the rebellious character of youth culture, and often Christian youth ministry was constructed as an alternative to the (church) culture of the parental generation, offering more trendy ways to communicate with young people. But how should Christian youth ministry relate to the on-going cultural change, where youth culture is no longer necessarily an alternative subculture of rebellion?

Over the last two decades or so we have seen radical changes in how the parental generation relate to youth and their culture. Today's youth are friends with their parents on Facebook – as their parents also naturally inhabit the world of social media. And maybe even more importantly, the mainstream

---

[11] Gordon Lynch, *The New Spirituality: An Introduction to Progressive Belief in the Twenty-first Century* (London: I.B. Tauris, 2007), 159.

[12] M. J. Joseph, 'Perspectives on Youth in a World of Globalisation', in Adrian Watkins, and Nathaniel, Leslie (eds), *Gospel and Globalisation: Second South Asia Christian Youth Conference* (Delhi: Indian Society for Promoting Christian Knowledge, 2006), 66-68.

youth culture represents the establishment rather than challenging it. Every (youth) subculture has (had) its own idols, or icons, as "the admiration of idols connects young people with international fan communities where they can share their secret wishes and fantasies."[13] But the idols of the contemporary youth culture idols are no longer the rebellious Marlon Brando or James Dean, but more 'flexible' idols, like David Beckham. Where as the idols of the newly 'invented' post-war youth culture of the 1950s depicted youth as rebellious, as a protest generation against parents, "the idols of the 1990s and beyond are multiple coded idols."[14] These idols are idolized simply because of the way they appear or because of their virtuous performance and play with media patterns. David Beckham is a typical example of such a 'flexible' idol. He is definitely an idol – and product – of the global youth culture, but he is not a rebellion idol marking a watershed between youth and their parents. Therefore Kenda Creasy Dean is right in claiming that all popular culture is youth culture, but I am not sure she is right in the way she stresses that this is forcing young people to turn to marginal and dangerous alternatives in order to distinguish themselves from adults. However, more importantly, as popular culture and youth culture merges and subversively forces the end of youth (culture) to a later stage in life, the church can no longer exclusively facilitate her youth ministry as an *alternative* to the church of the parental generation.

Staged Authenticity

But how should the church and her youth ministry relate to the contemporary global youth culture? One of the problems with many of the attempts by the church to address the global youth culture, are that they fail to recognize what is probably the main virtue in the consumer dynamic of the global youth culture – the claim for *authenticity*. *Perceived authenticity* seems to be a key marker within the different global youth (sub-) cultures. This authenticity is often defined or materialized in both external ways – through for instance dress code – and more in internal ways – through music and code language.[15] The point is that authenticity is defined from the perspective of the individual choice – it is real, because it feels real. Much empirical research on youth and young adults also indicates that authenticity is a key factor also when it comes to how young people choose and legitimize even their religious preferences.[16]

Authenticity seems to serve as a kind of 'filter' for young people as they relate to the enormous amount of products offered by the global popular

---

[13] Birgit Richard and Heinz-Hermann Krüger, 'The Importance of Idols in Adolescence', in Shirley Steinberg, Priya Parmar and Birgit Richard (eds), *Contemporary Youth Culture: An International Encyclopedia*, vol. 2. (London: Greenwood Press, 2006), 300.

[14] *Ibid.*, 306.

[15] Kelly,'Hip Hop Globalisation and Youth Culture', 35.

[16] See e.g. Teija Mikkola, Kati Niemelä and Juha Petterson, *The Questioning Mind: Faith and Values of the New Generation* (Tampere: Church Research Institute, 2007).

culture/youth culture. One may feel tempted to critique the rather narrow and individualistic claim on authenticity. The other alternative, of course, is for Christian youth ministry to try to 'play along with it' – in other words, it is tempting to 'stage authenticity' in order to reach out to young people. But this is not a good strategy with lasting effects. UK youth ministry researcher, Nick Sheperd, analyzed *Soul in the City*, a mission project involving 9,000 young people coming to London for two weeks of the summer of 2004. The 'mission' was organized by the well-known youth congregation Soul Survivor, Watford. Sheperd claims that such 'mission projects' often tend to stage authenticity in the way that authenticity of a culture is staged for tourists.[17] Sheperd is worried that such extraordinary mission trips force the local practitioners in youth ministry to fit their work into the life-cycle of the tourist paradigm of the youth mission event.[18]

For me personally the concept of 'staged authenticity' is a recognizable concept. When my wife and I were working as youth ministry missionaries in Estonia, we often had youth groups from Norway and other countries to visit. It was sometimes tempting to 'stage authenticity' in order to satisfy the expectations of the visiting group. One of our local co-workers jokingly said that the churches in Estonia should join in building a 'mission tourism museum', showing off the different cultural 'products' and assets asked for: an active church board member (preferably female), a poor street child, and some *authentic* Estonian young people eager to interact and to be inspired.

The point is that the claim on authenticity challenges the way we 'do' mission with young people. It is always tempting to make it more 'juicy' than it really is – in stead of just praying, we offer 'prayer while rafting'. This is missing the point. The problem is that our individualistic culture often reduces faith to something vague, lacking in real content. Therefore we need to foster discipleship which is not cut off from real life, rather embodied in the whole of life. Or else faith easily becomes the choice of the consumer, not the commitment of a follower.[19] To be even more concrete: we need to seek and develop particular communities, empowered by God's Spirit, who "not only lives out the gospel internally, but opens up the gospel externally by the way it lives, so that others may see and respond."[20]

[17] Nick Sheperd, 'Soul in the City – Mission as Package Holiday: The potential implications of a "tourist" paradigm in youth ministry', *Journal of Youth and Theology* 5:2 (2006), 70-75.

[18] Sheperd, 'Soul in the City – Mission as Package Holiday', 80.

[19] Glen H. Stassen, D. M. Yeager, and John Howard Yoder, *Authentic Transformation: A New Vision of Christ and Culture* (Nashville, Tennessee: Abingdon Press, 1996), 192.

[20] Darell L. Guder (ed), *Missional Church: A Vision for the Sending of the Church in North America* (Grand Rapids: Eerdmans, 1998), 247.

The Practice of Discernment

But how do we do this in the context of the global youth culture? Should we just embrace every aspect of the global youth culture and try to embody it in the context of the different local faith communities? US youth ministry theologian, David. F. White, is critical to much of global youth culture and what he refers to as "illusions of postmodern youth ministry". White claims that the problem is that "style has become the new substance",[21] Christian youth ministry has not sufficiently addressed the powers involved in the global youth (consumer) culture, and the powers involved in the "practice" of the gospel and faith. White therefore argues that youth ministry needs to re-discover the reformed doctrine of vocation and the practice of *discernment*. White writes:

> Teaching youth to discern 'power and principalities' involves a range of skills, including learning to exegete their culture – how it holds them and others in caring or exploitative ways, learning to grasp God's work amidst the culture – including Biblical/theological reflection and prayer, and learning to mobilize or join in collaborative action with other youth and adults in responding to God's call.[22]

White makes use of insights from liberation theology's proposal as he aims to involve young people in the practice of discernment. White, as a radical consumer culture critic, finds that the global youth culture needs to be de-mythologized by young people themselves. But they need tools to do so. This is where the church has to rediscover her ancient toolbox of spiritual practices, which may help youth to understand the world through the lenses of the gospel. White further explains that, "the practice of discernment has historically been viewed as a means of resolving particular dilemmas that arise – whom to join in marriage, which career to pursue, whether or not to relocate to another city."[23]

White in many ways states the obvious, that there is no such thing as discipleship in general, and that Christian faith and practice require incarnation in particular times and places. But I think it is crucial to admit that, if the church and her mission aim at 'targeting and involving' youth in global mission, she needs to understand the nature of the global youth culture as fundamentally pop culture. Consumer culture, that is. And if we do admit this, we also have to critically examine the whole concept of 'targeting and involving'. Using the practice of discernment, 'targeting' is in many ways a highly problematic concept. It reveals a consumer approach to young people, a kind of 'management by objectives' attitude to mission, where we run the risk of objectivising young people. And if it is one thing that youth in the age of *authenticity* do resent, it is being objectivised.

---

[21] David F. White, 'Illusions of postmodern youth ministry', *Journal of Youth Ministry* 6:1 (2007), 24.

[22] White, 'Illusions of postmodern youth ministry', 22.

[23] David F. White, *Practicing Discernment With Youth: A Transformative Youth Ministry Approach* (Cleveland, Ohio: The Pilgrim Press, 2005), 7.

Relational youth ministry has often been pictured in rather objectivising, instrumentalist terms, e.g.: "If you pass your faith on to two people, and if they pass it on to two more, the whole world will be saved in 20 years – and Jesus will come back." This kind of reductionist mathematical rhetoric on eschatology and the mission of the church becomes a fallacy in the light of a contemporary youth culture where many young people already feel they have conquered the world – by the art of travelling. The eschatological end of the world may not be the same if you have already travelled to the geographical end of the world. US youth ministry theologian Andrew Root has recently critiqued this instrumentalist tendency in youth ministry, where relations become means to achieve a higher end. Root, drawing on Dietrich Bonheoffer's radical Incarnation theology and Bonhoeffer's concept of *Stellvertretung*, which Root translates "place-sharing", claims that in youth ministry relations are a goal in and for themselves. It is in the dynamic of a loving relation that the presence of Christ in this world may be revealed.[24] Although Root may in part be overemphasizing relations over against the more 'external' practices which characterize and constitute the church – such as the Word, baptism, the Lord's Supper, the practice of forgiveness, service, prayer, worship and discipleship – I think Root is right in his fundamental critique of how the church often has approached youth in an instrumental way. By involving young people in mission, you never know in an instrumental way who and what they might target next. Therefore to target youth in an instrumental way, as if the outcome of this was known in advance, is to miss the point, as the point of the *missio Dei* is that we are all 'targeted' by the work of the triune God.

Targeted and Involved – *The God-Bearing Life*

Having said all this, there is definitely a strong *missional* aspect of all relational (youth) ministry. Likewise; there is a strong *relational* aspect of the mission of the church: We are all *sent*, participating in the relational mission of the triune God – "as the Father has sent me, so I send you" (Jn 20:21). Therefore, there is a relationship of interdependency between young people and the church when it comes to mission in the global youth culture in this time of change. Young people instinctively know the marks of youth culture, and the church needs this knowledge to proclaim, perform and recognize the marks of the church within the different contexts of the global youth culture.[25] Therefore youth should also be seen as *the agents of global mission*, who even may 'target and involve' adults.

---

[24] Cf. Andrew Root, *Revisiting Relational Youth Ministry: From a Strategy of Influence to a Theology of Incarnation* (Downers Grove: InterVarsity Press, 2007); Andrew Root, *Relationships Unfiltered: Help for Youth Workers, Volunteers, and Parents on Creating Authentic Relationships* (Grand Rapids: Zondervan, 2009).

[25] Cf. Norheim, Bård Eirik Hallesby, "From ghetto to communitas: Post-Soviet youth ministry and leadership on a pilgrimage to Emmaus", *Journal of Youth and Theology*, 5:1 (2006), 78.

The starting point for mission is that all of God's creation is targeted and involved by the sustaining and redemptive work of the triune God. But more than that, God involves *us* in his redemptive action for the world, much as Mary was involved. She was blessed and called to become a God-bearer, a *theotokos*. When we are involved in global mission, God empowers us in similar ways to become God-bearers, bringing Christ to the world – and to ourselves.

And in this God-bearing global mission God may call us to be *midwives* – assisting and welcoming, young and old are born to new life in Christ.[26]

---

[26] Cf. Dean, Kenda Creasy and Ron Foster, *The Godbearing Life: The Art of Soultending ministry* (Nashville: UpperRoom Books, 1998).

THE GLOBAL YOUTH CULTURE: TARGETING AND INVOLVING YOUTH IN GLOBAL MISSION A RESPONSE TO BÅRD EIRIK HALLESBY NORHEIM

Tor Erling Fagermoen

Commenting on what we have just heard, and also the corresponding article which I have had the opportunity to read in advance, I will start by saying that I find Norheim's analysis of the global youth culture in the broader perspective to be well worth listening to. He obviously has insights on what this culture is all about, and also offers perspectives on what this new knowledge of the situation we are all in means in a local church context.

Norheim has himself been a missionary to Estonia. It would have been interesting to hear a bit more of how he himself was originally involved in global mission, why he was going abroad as a missionary, and what strategies he used there when it came to involving and even targeting young people in Estonia to join him in his work. As we have heard in this conference, the church is really 'glocal' – everything is understood from below.

Authenticity is no doubt one of the key concepts we have to get a grip on, if we are to deal with youth and youth culture. Norheim reminds us that we run the risk of 'staging' an authenticity in large youth festivals and in our churches, really not being authentic at all, but just pretending to be so – trying to communicate but being authentic in an artificial way. This is also a problem when it comes to involving young people in global mission, e.g. offering mission-trips during the summer. Norheim mentions this as well, as does Eckhard Schnabel in his paper, arguing that he does not consider short-term mission trips to be real mission, but rather "sanctification tourist tours." Mission is indeed hard work. But I really value short-term mission as well, and I want to take the opportunity to comment on it, since it has relevance for the topic.

Mission is first and foremost a long-term commitment: learning a language, learning a culture, trying to give the Gospel flesh and blood where it is not yet heard or understood. I really believe that without long-term commitments mission is dead and gone. Short time involvements can have a value, though. As Schnabel points out, it can be of value for the young person himself and herself. Sanctification can happen. Being exposed to the needs and the differences in the world is a good thing. For some it is a start of a long-term commitment, either as senders or as missionaries themselves. And if the short-term engagement is well planned in cooperation with the long-term workers, it can even have an impact and be a strategic tool on the mission field.

However, returning to Norheim's paper, I have some critical remarks and some questions.

No one likes to be targeted, objectivised. That is true. You pose, and I quote, "'Targeting' is in many ways a highly problematic concept." Maybe it is. One of the main characteristics of youth culture is its market-orientation. We certainly run the risk of devaluating young people and ourselves into mere consumers, and church/mission agencies to mere shops, if we are not aware of what we are doing and how we do it. Even so, from my point of view, I want to emphasise the concept of mission as a sending activity.

It is of course true that all mission is 'Missio Dei', as much as the Father did send his Son. He is still working, and now in a triune way, but as the Lord put it in Jn 20.21, "Just as the Father has sent me I also send you." The concept of mission as a sending activity needs somehow to 'target' both locally and globally. The question is more *how* to target, than *if* we should target. We need to be sensitive. We need to be listeners more than shouters. We need to be servants, not bulldozers.

So Norheim seems slightly too reluctant when it comes to involving young people in mission as such. The interesting discussion here is again on *how* to involve, and I would have liked to hear more from him on that matter. He mentions as a crude example: if we all win two friends for Christ every year, the whole world would be reached in 20 years, and Jesus will return. Norheim criticises this, but falls short of giving us an alternative to peer evangelism. To be precise, I would like to hear from Norheim what role he thinks young people could play in the on-going mission activity God is doing in the world.

I would suggest prayer as an example of something every young person can take part in. In our Bible School we hold prayer walks, both here in Oslo, and on trips to mission fields. It is a 'soft' way of evangelism that cannot do any harm. Even in areas restricted for Christian mission these can take place.

Norheim asks as he argues, "Is the global youth culture something good or bad?" Well, is any culture good or bad? Isn't that what we have learned, that both sending cultures and receiving cultures are not good or bad, but both good and bad? There will be elements that need to be challenged or rejected, but there will also be elements to approve of and learn from. This goes both ways, as Norheim says, "Youth are the agents of global mission, sometimes even targeting and involving us – adults."

The point is that transformation by the Spirit is needed in any culture, and that every person individually needs that same transformation to happen. I would have liked to hear Norheim discuss that a bit more. As the global youth culture, as Norheim states correctly, is equivalent to popular culture, this is our culture. It is global, and it is opening up new perspectives and exciting opportunities for global mission. What we need to discuss is how people in our global, popular culture can be reached. What are the obstacles, what are the possible bridges, and how can we make ourselves – including our young people

– aware that we are all agents, not only cultural agents, but missionaries. I would suggest that we view not only individual Christians, but also every local church, to be missionaries sent to the present culture with its variety of subcultures by the living and triune God.

Norheim states, “We need to radically reflect on what global mission is in the context of global youth culture.” Yes, we need to do that, and in the last paragraph of the paper we are likened to being a midwife watching a new birth to life in Christ. Isn’t that exactly what mission is about, besides loving our neighbor unconditionally in a serving way, irrespective of its countable results – even if the context on both the sending and receiving part is something as difficult to grasp as the global youth culture?

The young generation is not only the future, it is the present generation. It is the generation impacting, and in many ways, leading the world at the moment. I agree that authenticity is a key, and it is comforting to know that no one is as authentic as God. He wants us to take part in His mission, and as much as he says, “You shall be holy, because I am holy,” I can sense him saying, “Be authentic like I am authentic.”

Can We – and Dare We – Present a Global Truth in a Pluralistic Age?

Stefan Gustavsson

The Christian faith has a global perspective, from beginning to end.

Genesis begins with God creating the whole universe and defining humanities place within it. The story of salvation, particular in its inception with God choosing *one* specific individual and gradually building *one* specific community, had a global intent from start. The blessing given to Abraham and subsequently to Israel was "for all peoples on earth".[1] Similarly, the good news about the unique individual Jesus Christ has drastic implications for everyone. To quote Paul, when he challenged the pluralistic culture in Athens, God "commands all people everywhere to repent. For he has set a day when he will judge the world with justice by the man he has appointed. He has given proof of this to all men by raising him from the dead."[2]

The Christian church is called to be a witness for this truth. But can we – and should we – also *argue* for the Christian faith and present it as a global truth?

Christianity has been under heavy attack in the west during the last 200 years and much of the church today lacks confidence in the truth of its own message. Both the modern and the postmodern era have radically challenged the Christian faith, in regard to the *content of truth* and in regard to the *concept of truth.*

Modern Thinking and the Content of Truth

Emphasis on global truth did not emerge with Enlightenment thinking. It has been part and parcel of Western thought all the way back to the ancient Greek philosophers. Take Aristotle, in his famous definition of truth: "To say of what is that it is not, or of what is not that it is, is false, while to say of what is that it is, and of what is not that it is not, is true; so that he who says of anything that it is, or that it is not, will say either what is true or what is false."[3] This definition presupposes that truth is related to a reality shared by all human beings.

What did, then, emerge with Enlightenment thinking?

---

[1] Gen 12:3.

[2] Acts 17:30-31.

[3] Aristotle, *Metaphysics,* book 4, chapter 7.

First there was a new emphasis on reason and science as the only tools for reliable knowledge. Other ways – like intuition or revelation – were either ignored or downplayed. All knowledge was expected to conform to science and the scientific method. Secondly there was a new worldview with nature as the only real factor. The supernatural – God and a spiritual realm – was either ignored or downplayed.

The twofold result was a naïve view of knowledge and a reductionist view of reality. Enlightenment thinking changed the way we attain truth and limited the scope of truth only to nature.

The Christian faith was challenged in these two areas. The response should have been arguments for a broader view of knowledge (there are more to be known than science can tell us) and arguments for a broader view of reality (there is a supernatural reality beyond nature). Unfortunately, too much of the church in different ways either succumbed to the modern way of thinking (liberal theology) or withdrew from the intellectual debate (conservative theology). Generally speaking, the apologetic response to Enlightenment thinking, at least from the Protestant part of the church, was weak.

Postmodern Thinking and the Concept of Truth

Long before the word *postmodern* became popular Jean-Paul Sartre said, "There can be no eternal truth if there is no eternal and perfect consciousness to think it."[4] It is this perspective that undergirds much of the postmodern thinking, with its assault on global truth. In the words of Jean-François Lyotard, "Simplifying to the extreme, I define postmodern as incredulity toward meta narratives." [5] In a similar way, Michel Foucault encourages us to, "reject all theory and all forms of general discourse. This need for theory is still part of the system we reject."[6] Here the challenge is not the content of truth, but the denial of global truth as a valid concept.

Has this change from modern to postmodern thinking made claims about global truth impossible and therefore finally made Christian apologetics obsolete? My answer is no. Why?

First, the postmodern denial of global truth is theoretically incoherent. The denial itself becomes a new global truth. But it is impossible to deny truth, since every denial will be a new claim to truth. Why succumb to an incoherent idea?

Second, western culture is, in many areas, far from postmodern. Take science as an example. It operates on the assumption that there is an external reality that we can have knowledge about. And that reality is the same for everybody on the whole globe. The debate about global warming, to take just

---

[4] Quoted in Os Guinness, *Time for Truth* (Leicester: IVP, 2000), 84.

[5] Jean-Francois Lyotard, *The Postmodern Condition: A Report on Knowledge* (Manchester University Press 1984), xxiv-xxv.

[6] Michel Foucault, *Power/Knowledge: Selected Interviews and Other Writings* (New York: Pantheon, 1980), 231.

one recent example, presupposes from all sides in the debate that there are global truths. Or take ethics. The new view on homosexuality, that it should be affirmed and embraced, which is now the dominant view in much of Western society, is not seen as relative or context-dependent. It is seen as the right and true view and therefore something that we should convince other cultures about. It is seen as a global truth. Or take the recent discussion about religion, launched by the so-called new atheists. The whole discussion is built on the concept of global truth, the accusation being that all claims about a metaphysical reality are false.

These examples show that the concept of global truth is still very much with us, in scientific, ethical and religious discussions. The fact of globalisation itself proves that we can, despite all our differences, communicate with each other all over the globe.

Claims about global truths are not only possible, they are unavoidable. There is no reason at all for the Christian church, even in a supposedly postmodern culture, to downplay the absolute and universal claim of the gospel.

Third, postmodern philosophy is not so much a philosophy in its own right, as it is a critique of other perspectives. This means that when everything has been deconstructed, there is not much on offer for the questioning mind. But philosophy is love for wisdom, and philosophy cannot, in the long run only deconstruct. Inevitable, it must also give answers. For example, a young group of philosophers in Sweden a few years ago published a book with the telling title, *You Can't Be a Sceptic Towards Truth,*[7] critiquing postmodern scepticism for undermining the philosophical enterprise.

There are, to be sure, a lot of valuable insights within the postmodern thinking, showing the inevitable subjective and personal dimension in all searches for knowledge and the power play that often goes on beneath the surface.

But in its rejection of truth as a concept, it is a dead-end street. As Os Guinness reminds us, "...truth is far from dead. It is alive and well, and in an important sense, undeniable."[8]

Of course we need not only relate to postmodern thinking on a theoretical level. A pragmatic response to postmodern attitudes to life, where we are trying to find bridges for the gospel, is much needed. Christian communicators need to go a long way to find ways to connect to the postmodern culture – in order to "become all things to all people so that by all possible means I might save some", as Paul says.[9] But at the same time the philosophical and theological perspectives must inform and shape the pragmatic. Principles must come before pragmatics, as they did for Paul. His pragmatic approach was for the "sake of

[7] Michael Nyhaga (ed), *Man kan inte vara skeptiker när det gäller sanning: Fem svenska filosofer* (Symposium, 2004).

[8] Guinness, *Time for Truth,* 14.

[9] 1 Cor 9:22.

the gospel" and "under Christ's law."[10] In the long run, the only thing that really works is truth.

My conclusion is that the advent of postmodern thinking has not diminished the need for apologetics – rather, it has doubled it. Now the Christian church has two major challenges to deal with: the concept of truth (that there is such a thing as attainable truth) and the content of truth (that it is the Christian message that is the truth).

Lesslie Newbigin has said, "No belief system can be faulted by the fact that it rests upon unproved assumptions. What can and must be faulted is blindness to the assumptions one is relying upon."[11] Both modern and the postmodern perspectives are loaded with assumptions (for example, naturalism often as the guiding worldview). Many of these assumptions contradict foundational assumptions within the Christian faith. It is therefore crucial that assumptions on all sides are brought out into the light.

A Recovery of Christian Apologetics

We live in a time shaped by the modern and the postmodern perspective. In light of these challenges there is an urgent need for a recovery of Christian apologetics. We are called not only to dialogue about truth and be witnesses for truth; we are also called to proclaim and argue for the truth.

Christian apologetics is built on a number of convictions, grounded in the biblical texts.

First, every human being is created in the image of God. That means, among other things, that we have been given a mind and with it the possibility to think and understand. Even though the postmodern culture often favors feelings and experiences, reason is a tool that everybody uses.

Second, this world is created by God and belongs to him. Through it he reveals something of the beauty and glory of his own being. Everyone therefore already has been in some kind of contact with Him, even before the gospel message is communicated.

It is foundational in the Christian faith that knowledge about the world and about its Creator is available for us. God has created us with faculties that are relevant for gaining knowledge, and he has revealed himself and made himself knowable. This connection between general and special revelation, to use the theological terms, is of crucial importance for the apologetic task. The created reality fits with the biblical message. The created world and the revealed Word have the same source and belong together.

Third, both Christ and the first Christians faced a pluralistic culture. They were aware of alternative perspectives and yet they argued for the truth of the gospel.

---

[10] 1 Cor 9:21.

[11] *Lesslie Newbigin – Missionary Theologian: A Reader* (Grand Rapids: Eerdmans, 2006), 217.

Jesus' public ministry took place in a Jewish context, were the majority shared a number of beliefs. Still, it was not a monolithic culture. Jesus was constantly in conversations with people who begged to differ. We read of his dialogues and debates with Pharisees and Sadducees, with Samaritans, Greek pilgrims and Roman authorities. And he argued for his message. People noticed that Jesus gave "a good answer"[12] and that he "silenced the Sadducees."[13] According to Luke, his critics "were unable to trap him in what he had said there in public. And astonished by his answer, they became silent."[14]

The first Christians were active in an even more pluralistic context. The gods Zeus and Hermes are mentioned in Acts 14 and the philosophies of Epicurus and Zenon are mentioned in Acts 17, as well as all the idols in the city of Athens.

The apostles knew well that not everyone would be convinced by their message and that much more is at stake than just good arguments. But still they in their witness for Christ argued coherently for their truth claims.

A bird's eye view over the Acts of the Apostles shows this very clearly. Following Paul to different cities around the Mediterranean, Luke says this about Paul's ministry:

- In Damascus: "proving that Jesus is the Christ"[15]
- In Jerusalem: "talked and debated"[16]
- In Thessalonica: "reasoned with them... explaining and proving"[17]
- In Corinth: "reasoned in the synagogue, trying to persuade"[18]
- In Ephesus: "reasoned... arguing persuasively...[19]
- In Rome: "explained ... declared to them ... and tried to convince"[20]

My conclusion is that we, living in an increasingly pluralistic culture, have a similar task as Paul had. We must give a response to the challenges of modern and postmodern criticism of the gospel and present a positive and convincing case for the truth.

In his article *The Rebirth of Apologetics*, Avery Dulles writes about a revival we need to see in many more places around the globe:

> All over the United States there are signs of a revival [of apologetics]. Evangelical Protestants are taking the lead. Apologists of the stature of Norman L. Geisler, William Lane Craig, and J. P. Moreland are publishing scholarly works on natural theology and Christian evidences. Unlike the liberal Protestants of an earlier vintage, these evangelicals insist on orthodoxy; they uncompromisingly maintain the fundamental Christian doctrines of the Trinity, the Incarnation, the

[12] Mk 12:28.
[13] Mt 22:34.
[14] Luke 22:26.
[15] Acts 9:22.
[16] Acts 9:29.
[17] Acts 17:2-4.
[18] Acts 18:4.
[19] Acts 19:8-9.
[20] Acts 28:23-24.

Atonement, and the bodily resurrection of Jesus. And their method succeeds. The churches that combine a concern for orthodoxy with vigorous apologetics are growing. Their seminaries attract large numbers of enthusiastic students. A similar revival is occurring, albeit more slowly, in Catholic circles.[21]

[21] Avery Dulles, 'The Rebirth of Apologetics', *First Things,* 143 (May 2004), 18-23.

Can We – and Dare We – Present a Global Truth in a Pluralistic Age? A Response to Stefan Gustavsson

Ingrid Eskilt

To present global truth in a pluralistic age is legitimate and possible, but challenging! It requires boldness as well as humility! It calls upon reflections concerning our church history as well as our contemporary epistemology, theology and missiological methods.

Today's society seems to have no common "plausibility structure", no pattern of belief and practice which is accepted within a given society.1 The British mission leader Lesslie Newbigin holds that the church and every bearer of the gospel inhabit a "plausibility structure" which in many ways runs contrary to the governors of all cultures in this world, and certainly it runs contrary to today's Western pluralistic culture. A reference to the authority of the Bible seems irrelevant for most contemporary European citizens. Despite this, from a Christian perspective, pluralistic society also has elements that need to be positively evaluated.

The era of Christendom, the heritage from Constantine which gave the Christian church political power to persecute all heretics, is brought to an end. As a non-Lutheran citizen in a Lutheran cultural context I certainly appreciate that. Today everybody is allowed to and has to make their own decisions concerning worldview and religion. Our situation of pluralism is pretty much similar to that of the early church. In their pluralistic situation they were boldly bearing witness to their crucified and risen Lord before their fellow citizens.

Our challenge, however, differs from theirs, through our post-Christendom situation. Many Europeans seem spiritually open, except for impulses from the Christian church, where the phrase *believing without belonging* seems to be a good description.[2] In the ordinary Europeans' mind, the church today is easily linked to the Constantine tradition with narrow-mindedness and insensitivity towards people with other beliefs. Our presentation of a global truth will easily be rejected as arrogant and considered as an outdated legacy from the time of

---

[1] This concept is formulated by the sociologist Peter Berger, cf. Leslie Newbigin, *The Gospel in a Pluralistic Society* (Grand Rapids: Eerdmans, 1989), 8.

[2] Grace Davie, 'Religion in Europe in the 21th century', in Inger Furseth and Paul Leer-Salvesen (eds), *Religion in Late Modernity: Essays in Honor of Pål Repstad* (Trondheim: Tapir Academic Press, 2007), 39.

colonialism and imperialism. We as Christian European missionary movements have over the last generations asked for forgiveness for what can be perceived as the arrogant parts of our mission history. Our greatest challenge today is perhaps to reclaim a new boldness in our presentation of the global truth, but we need a humble boldness in our presentation.[3]

At the same time as we positively acknowledge the descriptive fact of plurality in our world, we must reject pluralism as a normative ideology. This ideology tells us that every truth claim is just subjective and relative.[4] There is a strong cultural push towards undisciplined tolerance in today's Western pluralistic society. Multiculturalism is the political correct attitude – the major religions and a variety of differing lifestyles are all to be accepted as more or less equally legitimate and valid. A deep suspicion towards any attempt to privilege any tradition or lifestyle is the reigning principle.[5]

We can freely present a global truth in our pluralistic age. It is ethically legitimate if our presentation is done in humility and with respect towards people with other faiths.[6] This presentation is a democratic and civil right. 'The Oslo Coalition on Freedom of Religion or Belief' confirms the civil right of religious people to freely propagate their faith: "Making truth claims is inherent in missionary activities, but the presentation of these should take into consideration the feelings of others. Hostility and ridicule are unacceptable, but well-reasoned, persuasive critique should never be so."[7]

We do, however, have an epistemological challenge in order to find a road in the middle between our modern/colonial past and our postmodern/relativistic contemporary situation. In the modern era most European missionaries had a positivistic epistemology, believing we had a photographic view of the global truth. The postmodern reaction, however, is to have a subjective instrumental position, where any picture of a global truth whatsoever is rejected. Whatever we perceive is just a subjective mental picture which is true for me. I will be regarded as intolerant if I present it as global truth for you or anybody else in the world.

---

[3] David Bosch, *Transforming Mission: Paradigm Shifts in Theology of Mission* (New York: Orbis Books, 1991), 489.

[4] Newbigin, *The Gospel in a Pluralistic Society,* 243-244.

[5] Harold Netland, 'Religious Pluralism and the Quest for Truth', in David W. Baker (ed), *Biblical Faith and other Religions: An Evangelical Assessment* (Grand Rapids: Kregel Academic Books, 2004), 25.

[6] da Silva argues for the legitimacy of missionary work in a pluralistic society from an ethical and epistemological perspective. See Antonio Barbosa da Silva, 'Mission eller dialog? – en kritisk analys av kontroversen mission eller dialog ur kunskapsteoretisk och etisk synvinkel', in Agne Nordlander (ed), *En värld – En Religion? Religionsteologisk Refleksjon* (Uppsala: Ingång. Johannelund teologiska skriftserie no.3-4, 2002), 55-59.

[7] *Missionary Activities and Human Rights: Recommended Ground Rules for Missionary Activities (A Basis for Creating Individual Codes of Conduct).* The Oslo Coalition on Freedom of Religion or Belief, Oslo (2009), §2.1.1.3, 5.

The American Christian anthropologist Paul G. Hiebert calls the way in the middle, critical realism.[8] To him, that means the global Truth with capital 'T' is real, and we can bear witness to that Truth. But we should do so in humility, because each individual sees this truth in bits and pieces and from their tradition and perspective. It is not a photographic view, but a model or a map of real Truth. Christian sisters and brothers from other parts of the world also have their perspectives, models and maps of the same Truth, and together we have a broader picture of global Truth, even if it still is not a photographic picture of the total.

The goal of knowledge in the modern positivistic epistemological position is an absolute and objective truth, the Great Unifying Theory. In the postmodern, instrumentalistic position, however, knowledge is seen as subjective, pragmatic, dependent on perspective and relative. In the globalist, critical realist position, truth is both Truth with capital 'T' and truth with small 't', both absolute and perspectival both objective and subjective.

The global point of view says that I have come to know the absolute Truth, but my way of perceiving that Truth is limited by my human nature. I do not see the whole picture, but what I have seen I have to tell publicly and freely. Even if I have found the answer, I am still a searcher because I see only as a poor reflection as St. Paul says in I. Cor 13:12. It is tainted by my culture, my age, my historical position and who I am as a person, but one day I shall see the Truth face to face.

This is in correspondence with the incarnation. The incarnate God laid upon himself human limitations (Phil 2.7). We are sent like He was sent, in humility and weakness (Jn 20.21). There have been times when we as European missionaries have presented the global truth in triumphant ways. That era is definitely put to an end. In a post-Christendom situation we have to present the global truth from a marginalized position without the privileges which belonged to the Constantine era. The global truth must be presented in a humble incarnate manner, mostly in the form of a witness, and most of all through transformed Christ-like disciples. This makes our task personally challenging.

Globalisation not only changes how we view missions but also how we do it. In the modern era when we knew the objective truth, evangelism was often the proclamation of theological verities and attacks on other religions.

This rarely works today – attacks and arguments seldom win people. It is seen as proud and not sensitive. The missionary attitude has changed – we are not God's lawyers, but his witnesses.

Different epistemological positions can be seen in discussions among evangelical Christians today. A main discussion is whether truth is an abstract propositional truth which can be found through reason and logic and is

---

[8] Paul G. Hiebert, *Missiological Implications of Epistemological Shifts: Affirming Truth in a Modern/Postmodern World* (Pennsylvania: Trinity Press, 1999), 68-116.

objective and context-independent, or whether truth in this world will always be embedded in contexts, more like what we in the West call existential truth.[9]

We can talk about global truth in a pluralistic world, but we must present it in an incarnated humble but brave manner, and from a marginalized place compared to our privileged position in the days of Christendom. A voice from the margins can be heard in a pluralistic society if the global truth simultaneously is demonstrating its power to transform lives in holistic ministries.[10] "Many people of the world will not believe what strangers say until they see how strangers live."[11] Christianity has in its core an intrinsic humility and started its career in this world from the margin.

So we *can* present a universal global truth, but *dare* we do so in a pluralistic age where such truths are regarded as inhuman, narrow-minded and intolerant, at least in the West?

There has been a change in the understanding of *tolerance* during the last decades in our society. The legacy from Voltaire and Mills explains tolerance as acknowledging, without necessarily actively supporting, other people's right to claim opinions different from mine and the majority of the population, and acknowledging their right to live their lives in accordance with that opinion.[12]

Today a person who holds another opinion in some ethical question is easily branded as being full of condemnation, intolerance and discrimination. This shift in the understanding of tolerance seems therefore now to imply a demand for approval, active support and legitimization of other people's opinions, truths and lifestyles.

This is dogmatic relativism, far removed from the classical understanding of tolerance. It is not logic that all life styles, truth claims and opinions in a society are equally valid. In a pluralistic society, different criteria, opinions and lifestyles have to be brought into open debate and held up for scrutiny.[13]

In the pluralistic cultural context in which the contemporary Western church exists, the church should, in the words of Harold Netland,

> seize the opportunity and lead the way, demonstrating how to be both deeply committed to our Christian convictions and also appropriately accepting of

---

[9] A discussion between the British mission leader Lesslie Newbigin and the Professor in Philosophy of Religion at Trinity International University in Illinois, Harold Netland, can be seen in Philip S. Sampson, Vinay Samuel and Chris Sugden (eds), *Faith and Modernity* (Oxford: Regnum, 1994), 60-115. A commentary to this discussion is found in Vinoth Ramachandra, *The Recovery of Mission: Beyond the Pluralist Paradigm* (Grand Rapids: Eerdmans, 1996), 167-170. To the use of truth as existential truth, see Robert J. Schreiter, *The New Catholicity: Theology between the Global and the Local* (New York: Orbis, 1998), 41-42.

[10] Kenneth Ross, 'Old Church and New Evangelism. A Scottish Perspective on Christian Mission in Today's Europe', in *Missiology,* vol. XXXVII, no.4 (2009), 511-525.

[11] Schreiter, *The New Catholicity,* 42.

[12] *Store Norske Leksikon,* vol. 14 (Oslo: Kunnskapsforlaget, 2nd edition, 2006), 410 (my translation).

[13] Bjørn Øyvind Fjeld, 'Toleranse og pluralisme – nødvendige, men krevende idealer', unpublished paper, Kristiansand, 2010.

> diversity… we should demonstrate through our actions and attitudes as well as words that we do accept ethnic and cultural diversity and we will support the right of other religious communities to live and practice in our midst. But at the same time we cannot abandon our commitment to Jesus Christ as the one Lord and Savior for all humankind.[14]

[14] Netland, *Religious Pluralism,* 42.

Part C
Future Vision and Summary

PRIORITIES IN GLOBAL MISSION FOR THE NEXT DECADE: NORWEGIAN MISSIONARY SOCIETY

Kjetil Aano

As head of a Western based mission organisation, perhaps I should limit my point of view to that perspective. However, as a mission leader based in the West, I constantly relate to both Southern and Eastern churches and missions. These relations influence both my perspectives and my work. One of the main priorities for the coming decade(s) is to my mind, to enhance global relations, the interchange between nations and continents, and global Christian co-operation in order to support and inspire in a way that is mutually beneficial.

Before trying to be a bit more specific in relation to what are our main challenges, allow me to share with you a short reflection on where we come from as Western missions.

While 'mission' has always been part of the identity of the Christian church, 'missions' as organised undertakings, separate structures in the way that we know them, are a fairly recent phenomenon or historical novelties.

But through their brief history, missions changed the face of the global Christian church. Without these movements, the spread of Christianity had not taken place; and the global church as we know it today, would not have happened.

Missions had a strong position, and were (are?) effective instruments in God's hand. However, like all tools, they may become less effective when the material to be worked, changes.

After the Second World War, the notion of Western based mission became gradually more problematic, and we were increasingly accused of running errands of Western political, economic and cultural interests. These accusations are not totally unwarranted.

The accusations have had far-reaching consequences – particularly in Europe, where also other societal changes decreased the role and influence of organised religion drastically. Take Norway and the Norwegian Missionary Society (NMS) as an example. From 1947 to 1949 NMS organised an exhibition, where we presented our work on a two-year tour all over the country. This exhibition was officially opened by Prince Harald (now King) and had more than one million visitors during its two year run. The total population of our country was less than 3.5 million at the time.

Missions and missionaries were – together with explorers and other dare-devils – the grand heroes of the nation. They were considered the conquerors of darkness and suppressors of ignorance, and pioneers of civilization and development.

Forty years later all that has changed. In popular opinion missions were removed from the pedestals of heroism and became the worst villains of the Western world. Of all that was wrong with the West, the missions were the worst. They/we were presented as bigoted, intolerant expressions of narrow-minded religion, often not fit for the modern world. Therefore, it is only natural that missions die from within, as recently expressed in one of the (smaller) newspapers here in Norway.[1] But perhaps more serious for the missions, is that we become basically invisible, both in media and society at large – we are not interesting enough even to generate opposition. This makes it very difficult to gather the kind of popular support for our work that is necessary for any expanding and dynamic movements.

I'm not here trying to offer a profound analysis of our predicament. But I would like to point to a couple of consequences that I see for missions based in Western Europe.

1. As movements and structures we were weakened, both as far as popular support and financial support are concerned. On the other hand, this allowed us to develop as counter-cultures, and some of us have survived rather well as that.
2. However, our role as counter-cultures may often lead to a certain isolation from necessary challenges both from the general society of which we are a part, but also from discussions, reflections and discourses that take place within the global church. In our case, I believe it has had two very practical consequences:
    - It seriously impeded our role in helping the historical Western churches to rediscover that mission is a basic dimension of being church. Western churches had for roughly one thousand years controlled religious life in their respective societies. This changed rather swiftly during the former century (it started earlier, but reached its peak toward the end of the twentieth century). The critique of missions made it difficult for the churches to rediscover that mission is the mode in which the church is called to live.
    - Secondly, we here in the Nordic countries left the arena of ecumenism to liberal forces, and it is only recently that we as missions of conservative and orthodox attitudes have rediscovered the necessity of being ecumenical in our approach to the global Christian challenges.

During the former two to three decades, much has changed again.

[1] *Dag og Tid*, March 2010.

1. Missions have discovered that we can not only survive, but thrive; but we need to be able to adjust the tools we use to the material to be worked.
2. Mission as a dimension of being church, is back. And there is a very interesting convergence of understanding and points of view between evangelical traditions traditionally not related to the conciliar ecumenical bodies, and the ecumenical traditions of the historical churches. This is pointed out by Tormod Engelsviken,2 and it coincides with my own experience.

With this as a back-drop, allow me to highlight some issues that I see as priorities in global mission for the coming decade:

1. Interaction: expressing an intent of interaction between Western missions and churches and missions from the two-thirds world; and finding ways of doing it.

2. Mission and missions: holding together *mission* and *missions.*

a. The church needs to be constantly reminded that mission is a dimension of being church, and that to be truly church implies being shaped by its mission.

b. But any church that is preoccupied merely – or even primarily – with how it functions locally, will eventually lose its soul and its touch.

3. Working ecumenically: this is of increasing importance, and has several important implications, of which I mention three:

a. Many emerging churches receive inputs from different church traditions. We need to learn to encourage and accept the emergence of new church profiles.

b. Missions of different theological traditions need to learn to co-operate more closely. In the Middle East the media works this way. The Church Mission Society is Anglican based, but ecumenical. In Mali NMS is part of a church-planting network that is widely ecumenical.

c. We need to support co-operation and integration of immigrant churches/congregations into our churches and organisations, even if they challenge our confessional profiles.

4. Empowering sister churches. Western missions come out of a tradition where we have partly thought and even partly acted as if God's commission was given exclusively to us. Off course we don't think that any more. Nonetheless, we need to be reminded again and again that God's call to mission is given to his entire church, his global church. In my experience as a mission leader from the West, we may play an important role whereby we empower our Christian sisters and brothers to boldly take part in God's mission in spite of very different circumstances. But it is equally important that we as Western

[2] See Engelsviken's article elsewhere in this volume.

actors see ourselves at the receiving end – we need to work hard on that; to learn that mutuality is a reality and not merely a play on words.

5. Theological challenge 1: The relationship of preaching and good works/diakonia. We need to see both as genuine expressions of God's will and to avoid making one an instrument of the other. (Good works as a means to opening hearts for the gospel, or preaching the gospel as a means of efficient social climbing – these things happen, but that is not why we do them.) And we need to avoid separating these two aspects of our calling from one another. This is particularly challenging for those of us who receive public funding for development projects, where the conditions for the funding is that it is not used for specifically religious purposes. We need to listen to our sister churches where the spiritual and the physical are more tightly knitted together, and also more boldly express our Christian understanding of this relationship to our funding bodies.

And finally, we need to work hard bridging the gap in our Western churches between those who see the mission of God primarily expressed through good works, and those who see the mission we are called to undertake first and foremost as the preaching of the gospel. The one cannot exclude or replace the other!

6. Theological challenge 2: The question of theology of religion. We no longer live in a world where we aim at religious domination through the suppression of other faiths. They are here, and as Christians we need to relate to people of other faiths. The question of dialogue is therefore not merely a theoretical issue. It is a matter of how we interact with people around us, and this takes place on several levels:

a. In the world of practical co-operation, in school, local community and society.
b. Learning how to understand and respect one another's convictions, and to learn more about the other, while still wishing to be faithful to one's own faith and convictions.
c. Entering into genuine exchanges, knowing that through this I will both influence my counterpart, and be influenced myself.

To me, it is vital, particularly in a Western setting, to combine an open dialogical attitude with a clear conviction that dialogue does not render unnecessary, exclude or replace the need of sharing the gospel through preaching or witnessing.

Perhaps the many challenges may be summed up a bit simpler. In a way it is all about what the former president of Zambia, Kenneth Kaunda, said in a political meeting political in Oslo a few years back: "It is about following Jesus - and being clear about it."

Secondly it's also about letting go of control. In the Western tradition we have used some time and energy trying to let go of our hegemonistic tradition. We need to learn to be humble in our mission, and to accept that God might choose to act differently.

Recently I visited a sister church in Hong Kong. The Chinese pastor asked me to share a word. I did. I think it was appreciated. Then he came forward, put his arm around my shoulder, looked at the congregation, and said:

> Dear friends: here you have an unsuccessful mission leader! What he said was true on many levels.

Then he added:

> And here I stand as an unsuccessful Chinese pastor. But friends, remember that it is that which seems unsuccessful in the eyes of the world that God can use!

I think he hinted at something really vital, and perhaps one of the greatest priorities of mission leaders and missions from the West: to accept that God may choose to work otherwise.

So therefore, in our humiliated state and in our lack of success, we can share boldly God's good works and graceful words with the world.

Priorities in Global Mission for the Next Decade: Norwegian Lutheran Mission

Ola Tulluan

As three General Secretaries have been asked to reflect on the same theme, I think it will be understood if our contributions reflect the thinking of our respective organizations. Last year the Norwegian Lutheran Mission adopted a new mission strategy document for the next decade. Much can be said, but the time allotted to me, does not allow for extensive elaboration of our priorities. I will just direct our attention to some concerns that will be high on the agenda in the coming decade.

Firstly, we confirm that our primary task is to win souls for Jesus.

That is our joy and God-given calling. So it has been since the very beginning of the mission. NLM intends to prioritize the least reached people groups. By 'least reached' we mean people groups where there is still no Christian congregation, or where the Christians need help from the outside to bring the gospel to others. However it may be, for us mission entails crossing boundaries.

We believe that focusing primarily on the least reached is in accordance with Paul's mission strategy: "It has always been my ambition to preach the gospel where Christ was not known, so that I would not be building on someone else's foundation" (Rom 15:20). He said so, without neglecting the churches he had established.

It is a matter of fact that the number of missionaries among those who have already heard about Jesus is still greatly disproportionate to the number working among those who have never heard the gospel. According to statistics from the Joshua Project, only 2.5-4% of missionaries work among the least reached one-fourth of the world's population. The majority of these people groups are Muslims. For every million unreached Muslims there are less than three missionaries.

Secondly, to meet this need we intend to challenge people to live dedicated missionary lives, prepare them for missionary service, and send them out to serve God among the nations.

Jesus said to his disciples: "Peace be with you! As the Father has sent me, I am sending you" (Jn 20:21). Mission and sending is a biblical concern. There was enough to do in the church in Antioch. Nevertheless, the Holy Spirit worked so that Paul and Barnabas were chosen and sent as missionaries to new areas (Acts 13:1-13; 15:25; 26:17). The Great Commission calls us to go out.

NLM intends in the coming decade to carry on the call to be a sending agency. Mission is not primarily to send money and provide financial support. Biblical mission entails sending missionaries that use the word of God as a means of grace in preaching and teaching.

Many of the least reached ethnic groups and people groups live in areas where it is impossible to work with missionary visas. These areas are often developing and in search of skilled labor. Most of these countries will be open to giving work and work permits to Christian professionals, or 'tentmakers' if you prefer that phrase. These professionals are not always able to evangelize openly, but they are permitted to be Christians who live out their faith, build relationships, are part of the community, live among the people, love them and learn their language. To effectively achieve that, you need long-term commitments. NLM intends to support Christian professionals who wish to work among the least reached people groups.

Thirdly, it is a priority for us to demonstrate love and care for all human beings.

Every individual person is created by God and loved by God – regardless of religious affiliation. This gives infinite value to human beings. Jesus cared for all people. He saw their plight and their needs. In our work, we wish to follow in Jesus' footsteps also in this way (Mk 12:31). As Christians, we have a special responsibility for the poor, the sick, and the infirm. Many people live in conditions that are unacceptable, especially women and children. We intend to plan and operate programs ourselves as well as cooperate with like-minded churches that accept the responsibility to do acts of mercy with the view of helping human beings that suffer.

Acts of mercy are love for one's neighbor put into practice. We must emphasize the individual Christian's responsibility to care for their neighbors on an everyday basis. But the church also has a responsibility to perform acts of mercy. In our priority both health services and educational projects are important, and increasingly clean water projects. Women, mothers and children are among the groups that will be given priority. Likewise, the Christian value of human beings compels us to advocate fundamental human rights and combat all sorts of injustice. In many parts of the world the church is an able agent for peace and reconciliation. They need our help.

The goal of this type of work is that people may be enabled to improve life conditions for themselves and their community. In our strategy such work is primarily directed towards poor and marginalized groups. Development aid is directed to all human beings, regardless of religious and ethnic identity.

Fourthly, we will focus on cooperation and partnership.

From the outset of any mission work, it is important to develop local leadership. Capacity building is a prioritized task.

We want to establish sustainable structures in independent churches. The goal is to avoid long term dependency. But even in a situation where the mission has 'phased out' its activities, we will normally maintain a close relationship with the partnering church. In some places, missionaries may be given particular assignments upon request from the local church. In other areas, the contact may take a different shape.

Mission work should take place in close cooperation with other churches and mission agencies that share our purpose and the biblical basis for our faith. In reaching out to the least reached people groups, it is profitable to cooperate through international networks. This ensures better use of our resources as well as continuity. NLM intends to have good contact with evangelical movements that work on a biblical basis.

Fifthly, media work is an important part of our mission strategy.

Radio is a wide-reaching medium, both in so-called 'open' and 'closed' countries. The internet opens new opportunities. Good Christian literature should be made available, especially for educational purposes. When we are reaching a new people group with the gospel, it is important that the Bible, or parts of the Bible, is available in their language. Where this is lacking, Bible translation work should be prioritized. In this respect, we welcome possible cooperation with Wycliffe Bible Translators International.

Sixthly, focus on immigrants in Norway.

It is also important to reach new immigrants in Norway. We will focus especially on people groups that belong to areas of special focus in our work outside the country. Here we will work in understanding and cooperation with NLM's Home Office and various units that have a special focus on these target groups, such as IKF (International Christian Fellowship) and KIA (Christian Cross-Cultural Outreach).

Today NLM works in several countries in South America, Africa, and Asia. We want to take responsibility for the work we have begun, but not in such a way that we create dependency or so that we in actual fact run local churches.

Looking toward the year 2020, NLM will prioritize reaching Muslim people groups and other groups that belong to the category 'least reached'. So far, work in East and West Africa, Indonesia, Turkish-speaking people groups in Central Asia and China has been identified.

As a mission agency we will always be on the move and open to be called to new areas and people groups. In the period until 2020, we will be open to researching and possibly beginning work in new areas/groups if opportunities should open up.

The goal is that by the year 2020 60% of our resources – both human and financial – will be spent in new areas of special focus.

Priorities in Global Mission for the Next Decade: Normisjon

Rolf Kjøde

Mission agencies in Norway have worked closely together for decades and with good relations also on leadership level. In the midst of our specifics we participate in the same divine calling understood as people sent to witness to Christ in word and deed - also cross-culturally. From the side of Normisjon we do appreciate these close ties within the mission movement in Norway, and we also do admire the significant role that our national sister movements have played over the years in world mission. As more traditional organisations today we face the same challenges in a changing world, and, thanks to God, in a world-wide changing mission pattern.

Theological Convictions

Priorities in global mission for a limited period of time could be considered a mere strategic question about utilising our recourses of money and personnel. In my opinion this is a technical angle which is not useful enough when planning the mission of the church for the kingdom. All our strategies must be based upon and directed by our theological convictions. This implies that we must break away from a narrow marketing model and perhaps even hold on to strategies that don't pay off in a short time span like ten years. Strategy in the realm of the Spirit should always be aware of its limited horizon, as our mission primarily is accomplished in obedience to a higher calling where the gospel itself pays off when time is reap. Thus I want to start with emphasising some very important theological convictions for the coming decade before turning to the strategic reflections.

Uniqueness of Christ

The mission of the church has at all times been rooted in the conviction of the uniqueness of Christ. So why bother mentioning it here – among friends and faith mates, I mean? As for us living in pluralistic Europe, I believe this must be emphasised over and over again. Our culture is not only plural in a descriptive way. Plurality has turned to a sort of hard pluralism which must be considered the credo of our time. If we get familiar enough with this credo, it not only impacts liberal majority churches with their sometimes-indistinct dialogue programmes replacing the proclamation of the gospel. In the end it also impacts us severely as we so easily either withdraw from the public scene to our own ghettos, or we present a gospel customised such as not to offend people of good will. In either ways our mission will fail. Thus we need, over and over again, to re-establish the Biblical truth that the risen Jesus Christ is the only way of salvation for every people and for every single human being of the earth. If we fail to teach our children and youth this uniqueness, we will continue to loose grips in the coming decade.

Reaching the Least Reached

The uniqueness of Christ is the foundation of all that we do in Christian mission. He's the only way of salvation, and in his incarnation, death and resurrection there is full reconciliation and hope, abundantly available for all peoples of the earth. There is enough for all, and it is meant to be for all. Repeatedly, thus, Jesus challenges his disciples to break the ethnic and national boundaries by bringing the Gospel to all peoples. This is the decisive sign of the return of Jesus and the final breakthrough of the kingdom (Mt 24.14). We soon can agree that we don't know the exact ethnic definition used by Jesus while talking about the peoples to be reached, but it's enough to understand that the power of the Gospel should be made known in places where it has been unknown (Rom 15.20). In my opinion we need to re-establish this vast commission as the leading mission of the church – giving everyone the same opportunity of salvation by reaching the least reached people groups. It's somehow my concern that we are loosing touch with this, even within the evangelical wing of the church. That would be a betrayal of our divine calling to mission.

Biblical Holism

We do experience in our own country that even among evangelical Christians we tend to play down the role of a Biblical holism in mission, as we're adopting a narrow understanding that doing social work is doing holistic mission. There has been a necessary debate, especially among our American friends, aiming to raise the conscience among evangelicals about our Christian obligation to social responsibility. As for Norwegian mission, though, this has to some extent been an integral part from day one – for my organisation all the time since Lars Olsen Skrefsrud entered the country of India, starting up his work among the marginalised *adivasis*. As I see it, the fight for a Biblical holism of words and deeds, of proclamation and social work, of evangelisation and diaconal work, is not threatened these days by playing down the role of social involvement or even development work. Even deeply committed Christians in our own organisations respond more easily to images of crying or laughing children than to the fact that the world is loved by God but condemned without Christ. We do appreciate the opportunity of being supported by public Norwegian development money to civil society and NGOs in our cooperating countries, but we should be very much aware about how these monies impact our attitudes. Our calling is not to end up as Red Cross or Save the Children. Bless their most important ministries on God's created earth, but as for our mission, it has an even higher calling: to lead the nations to obedience to the gospel. That implies that the Christian church takes responsibility for preaching and doing justice, but we cannot accept a use of 'holistic mission' tied to a narrow understanding as social work. Proclamation of the gospel and discipling people are not options but defines the cutting edge of what we understand as Biblical holistic mission.

Strategic Reflections

As for strategic priorities for the next decade, I want to reflect both upon how and with whom we can reach further, what the prioritized programmes should be and whether we should look towards certain geographical areas. This is primarily a reflection upon strategies to be chosen by my own organisation, Normisjon, but I guess some of it might even have a general address.

How and With Whom?

Global mission has changed radically – and to the better – by the vast involvement from the churches in the global South. The changed situation also has challenged the mindset of the Western Christians, from understanding ourselves as the geographical and spiritual centre of mission, to being a partner with a whole lot to learn from the church in the global South. As far as the situation leads us to humility, we have taken this development as a divine lesson. As far as it leads us to discouragement, we still have eyes to be opened for God's own capability to lead his mission as he in such amazing ways is mobilizing his church in the global South these years.

Partnership in mission

The pattern of Christian mission has changed permanently from our way of thinking of it as one-way traffic, to being a global partnership in mission including the whole church taking the whole gospel to the whole world. This slogan from Lausanne 1974 was then considered more like a vision. In our days we can see it happen before our eyes. What a privilege, then, to live exactly these days, to see the global church working shoulder to shoulder to fulfil the commission that our Lord and Savior passed on to us. For my organisation this implies that the time of establishing traditional Norwegian mission stations in foreign countries, is more or less history. All our new missionary efforts in the future will, while still sending Norwegian full-time missionaries, be in partnering with other churches and organisations, often dominated by the Southern church and with ourselves as junior partners.

Tent making strategies

The vast majority of unreached people groups today live in countries that are not very accessible for traditional missionary sending. In addition to emphasising partnership building in mission, this implies that Christian mission also needs to emphasise tent making strategies to a much bigger extent for the years ahead. Knowledge and professional skills are important commodities in the world as we see it today. Students are expected to an increased degree to spend study time abroad, professionals are very much in demand in big companies in many countries, and entrepreneurs are welcome in many countries as they establish industry or other jobs. The Spirit might find its ways behind closed borders. We even 'support him' by sending Christian radio and television programmes, and we do hear testimonies about how this changes people's lives. Even so, we know that most people can't get to know Jesus on a deeper level without encountering living disciples that give the gospel plausibility. Thus we are in desperate need of cross-cultural tentmakers for the years ahead, professionals who are dedicated to be witnesses and mentors in deeds and work.

What?

Establishing an increased partnership building in mission and extending tent making strategies for closed countries is decisive for the mission of the church today and tomorrow. But what are our contributions within these models? While being established as partner or as tentmaker, where should we put our emphasis to be strategically on target? Among all that could be mentioned, I will in short underline two aspects of this.

Formation of disciples and leaders

What we primarily need in strategic mission is formation of disciples and disciple-based leadership. In Normisjon we have taken this as a main focus, being the red thread to be recognised in all countries where we are established – Norway included. Starting off early is of utmost importance. Thus we primarily try to reach the youth to help them implement what it means to be a lifelong believer and follower of Jesus Christ. Only by moulding lifelong discipleships we will be able to fulfil the worldwide mission. Only by discipling young people, we can raise tomorrow's leadership in mission. And tomorrow is very close.

Bible translation

The second aspect I will mention is Bible translation. Even though it might be said that the New Testament is translated to languages covering the mother tongue of 80% of the world's population, reaching the unreached people groups still demands a huge translation job. The gospel can hardly be rooted in the hearts of people without being presented in the language of the heart. Translating the Bible, or at least the New Testament, is therefore a condition for fulfilling the mission of Jesus to 'panta ta ethne' and should be given priority in our mission strategies.

Where?

Christian mission is not entirely a matter of geography, but geography is a concern. It is important that we can complement each other so as to reach out in many new areas. I want to finish this short presentation by mentioning one area of high priority in Normisjon and one area where I want to challenge all of us.

South Asia

Normisjon started up in India. During the last years we have seen a revitalised effort for mission within our partnering church and even on a broader scale of the whole Lutheran church body of India. Indian churches today send some ten thousand missionaries cross-culturally – in their own country. They are probably the country today, perhaps after the USA, sending most missionaries cross-culturally. At the same time there are more than 2,000 language groups in India who have not been brought in touch with the gospel. India is by far the country with most unreached language groups, followed by China, Pakistan, Bangladesh and Nepal. North East India, Bangladesh and Nepal constitute Normisjon's core area for international mission, and these figures tell me very clearly that we are not finished in the area. Norwegian missionaries will to a very little extent accomplish the mission for the coming years, but we do see partnerships developing with the churches in all these countries.

Europe?

So what about Europe? Mission leaders around the globe are very concerned for the status of the gospel on this very continent, and understandably so. I don't think Norwegian mission should withdraw from the larger international arena to concentrate on Europe alone, even though I understand and share the very deep concern about our own spiritual status. I guess that we must think it the other way round. As we build up partnership mission on all other continents, this should also be the case for our own Europe – and even for Norway? In the European cities and capitals the ethnic churches from the South are today the fastest growing faith communities. London and Paris have for some years faced a revitalisation of church life through immigrants, and we tend to see some of the same here in Oslo – by this we can close the strategic circle. For a while I believed that each people mainly should be evangelised by its own kin, but I am now pretty much convinced that we need to open up for the inspiration that is made available to us by the presence of the vibrant churches from Ethiopia, Philippines, Ghana, China or other nations.

Conclusion

A few years ago I secured an agreement between the Norwegian and Kenyan evangelical student movements. While asking Dr. Wachira, who was General Secretary of FOCUS Kenya at the time, if it was possible for him to release some of his best student leaders to come and stay for a period each year in Norway, he replied, "We are not interested in any ethnic exhibition!", being aware that that is the way we at times have presented our African friends to the Norwegian mission scene. "On the contrary," I said, "what we want to accomplish is to receive from you what has overwhelmed me while encountering your student movement. You are rich where we are poor, with your powerful prayer life and your bold testimony. We want you to come and share it with us, as this is where we have failed."

Elisha asked for a double portion of Elijah's Spirit. European Christians seem to be in need of the same prayer – and for the deep and long lasting partnership with the churches of Asia, Africa and Latin-America.

Mission and Globalisation: Some Lessons to be Learned – A Brief Summary

Hans Aage Gravaas

The presentations and discussions at the Fjellhaug Symposium 2010 focused on various matters related to Christian mission in a globalized world. Some issues discussed were:

The Outcomes of Modernity

We must learn to understand the outcomes of modernity, summarized by the term globalisation, and their impact on:

- The nature of specific human cultures, the modes of interaction between different cultures, and between individuals within a given culture;
- Belief systems, worldviews and on how people express and practice their faith;
- The theoretical reflection and the practical ministry of the Christian church.

Emic and Etic Descriptions

We must learn to distinguish between emic and etic descriptions of and responses to the changes that take place in a certain society. We must learn to see the positive and negative dimensions of globalisation and at the same time be aware of the fact that we evaluate the various dimensions differently.

Positive Elements of Globalisation

Some positive elements of globalisation are:

- Increased mobility, flexibility and proximity;
- Possible exchange of ideas, insights and resources;
- Sharing of benefits and a better life;
- Increased opportunities for making religiosity a matter of individual choice;
- Increased opportunities for mission and evangelization.

Negative Elements of Globalisation

Some negative elements of globalisation are:

- The secularization processes and anti-religious attitudes that seem to accompany modernity and globalisation. Are phenomena such as atheism or split-level Christianity/Islam/Buddhism etc. automatic consequences of modernity?
- Intensification of certain religious convictions. Is rigorous religious fundamentalism in the non-Western world a counter reaction – not to Christianity, but to imposed modernity?
- The unfair distribution of power between the beneficiaries and benefactors of globalisation. Is the wealthy West setting the agenda in every corner of the world and "telling the poor how to be happy"? Is cultural imposition more likely to happen than freedom to change from within or from below?
- Exposure to increased plurality. We are exposed to a well-decorated and extremely confusing religious market place.

Local – Global – Glocal

We must learn to see the interconnection of the local and global dimensions of church and mission. Both dimensions are to be considered equally important. Our world is glocal.

Theological Continuity and Translatability

A local church that loses sight of theological continuity and the international horizon of the global church becomes a tribal church or a tribal religion. On the other hand, a church that neglects local interpretations of Christianity contradicts the incarnational dimension and the translatability of Christian faith. Solid and biblically based contextual theologies do not exclude themselves from international input. In fact, intercultural readings of theology are necessary to keep local theologies on a sound and healthy track.

An Internationally Relevant Message

The God of the Bible is my God, our God, and the God of all creation. The saving intervention of Jesus Christ, the Messiah, is therefore an internationally relevant message. The communication of the Christian message and the current state of world Christianity is the responsibility of the local church and the totality of all local churches, the global church.

Evangelism and Contextualization Not Modern Phenomena

Oftentimes the history of mission has been portrayed as West-East or North-South traffic. Such interpretations of history are at best imbalanced or at worst wrong. We have several examples of enthusiastic worldwide commitment to Christian evangelization from the first chapters of church history up to know. This history also tells us that contextualization or similar expressions are not modern phenomena, although the terminology as such is of recent origin.

Theology of Mission and Missionary Models in Scripture

We must learn to appreciate the theology of mission and modes of missionary endeavor portrayed in Scripture itself. The interaction between personal motivation, situational challenges, divine intervention and strategic planning is fascinating. The ministry and the substitutionary death and resurrection of Jesus Christ and the achievements of Peter, Paul and their contemporaries are breathtaking. We should take time to read Eckhart Schnabel's paper several times, and his books on this topic.

The History of Missions: Lessons to Be Learned

As we celebrate Edinburgh 1910 we must acknowledge the bright and dark sides of a multifaceted history and legacy. We honor the courageous efforts to bring the gospel to areas where the name of Christ was not yet known. Simultaneously we regret the triumphalistic and colonialistic attitudes that sometimes accompanied Christian witness and mission. However, we must learn from our mistakes. The mistakes of the past must not encourage the Christian church to keep quiet or to become inactive, but to correct the errors of the past.

Continuous Focus on the 'Unengaged Unreached People Groups' (UUPG)

In light of the legacy of Edinburgh 1910 we need a revitalized focus on peoples of the world that are yet to be reached with the gospel. Church history has revealed a serious temptation or inclination among local churches to be self-possessed and self-occupied. This temptation or inward focus might very well also affect mission organizations that considered international mission to be their special responsibility.

New Maps – New Models?

In the time to come we must adapt to a current shift in world Christianity. The task of world mission rests on shoulders of the global church and certainly not on Western churches and mission agencies alone. A revised mapping of world

Christianity and mission is necessary as well as new modes of cooperation between local churches and organizations within the global church. In my opinion, Ralph Winter's distinction between sodality and modality structures of church and mission is still valid and worthwhile to consider as we prepare for the future. The evangelistic mission movements help to revitalize the existing churches as well as being on the cutting edge of world evangelization. Mission is still the task of 'the burning hearts'.

Interreligious Conflicts and Missiological Implications

In a time of increased international political turbulence and conflicts we need to address the roots of interreligious conflicts between Islam and Christianity and the intercultural interaction between different groups within the global world. Dr. Chawkat Moucarry presented an extremely helpful paper with political, religious, theological and missiological implications that encourage careful consideration and reflection. It is hard to spell out a detailed program, but I would recommend us to scrutinize his paper and publications and reflect on the missiological implications discussed by Moucarry in dialogue with his respondent, Professor Jan Opsal.

Migration and Youth Culture

We were exposed to issues such as relating to migration and targeting youth culture. An understanding of reasons behind migration and the processes of migration is extremely helpful and necessary as we aim at understanding the world, dealing with the challenges of the world, and as we prepare for communicating the gospel to all nations. In the same way, understanding youth culture is of utmost importance. Youth culture finds itself, as culture in general, in a challenging intersection between the local and the global. On a global level the local responses to youth culture encompass premodernity, modernity, postmodernity and post-post modernity at the same time. Let us not call this a problem, but a challenge. We are encouraged to understand and respond simultaneously.

Universal Truth in a Pluralistic Age

Stefan Gustavsson presented thought-provoking and extremely important and relevant perspectives on communicating universal truth in a pluralistic age. We must not ignore the fact that we live in a pluralistic age or isolate ourselves from the truth claims of dissonant voices of pluralism. We must listen to these voices, try to understand them and respond to them. Representatives of other worldviews or religions must not be reduced to being perceived of as pure targets of mission, but people that are created in the image of God and subjects to his caring love; a love that was expressed in the fullest sense in the substitutionary death and resurrection of Jesus Christ.

No Christian Cultures – The Gospel to All Cultures

There is no such thing called Christian culture. No cultures are purer or cleaner than others. Cultures are human constructions that develop and change, but people of all cultures can become Christians. Culture consists of both good and evil. Despite the existence of contextual theologies it is important to distinguish between the continuity and discontinuity of theology. Scripture does communicate truth claims that are universally true and that are to be obeyed by all people that call themselves Christians. The apostle Paul says: "I am obligated both to Greeks and non-Greeks, both to the wise and the foolish. That is why I am so eager to preach the gospel also to you who are in Rome. I am not ashamed of the gospel, because it is the power of God for the salvation of everyone who believes, first for the Jew, then for the Gentile" (Rom 1:14-16).

Three Lutheran Responses

We were listening to the priorities of the General Secretaries of two Lutheran mission organizations in Norway (one was unable to attend in person because of volcanic ashes from Iceland!). I appreciated their thoughts and reflections on the future and am very happy that they shared their thoughts in a place where international partners were gathered. I believe that international arenas of discussion are important. As far as church-mission or church-church relationships are concerned, we have to move from dependency towards independence and interdependence. This is how it should be. Mission is a joint endeavor of the global church, based on God's message, commandment, support and blessing.

May God bless us all!

Selected Bibliography

Allen, Roland. 2001

Missionary Methods: St. Paul's or Ours? Reprint. Grand Rapids: Eerdmans.

Alon, Gedalyahu. 1977

Jews, Judaism and the Classical World: Studies in Jewish History in the Times of the Second Temple and Talmud. Jerusalem: Magnes.

Anderson, Sir Norman. 1984 [1970]

Christianity and World Religions. The challenge of pluralism. Leicester UK/Downers Grove IL: Inter-Varsity Press.

Andrade, Susana. 2004

Protestantismo indígena: Procesos de conversión religiosa en la provinica de Chimborazo, Ecuador. Quito: Abya Yala.

Andreassen, Kristina Kvarv and Minja Tea Dzamarija. 2008

'Innvandere og norskfødte med innvandrerforeldre.' In *Innvandring og innvandrere 2008*. Ed. Gunnlaug Daugstad. Oslo/Kongsvinger: Statistisk Sentralbyrå, 13-54.

Annis, Sheldon. 1987

God and Production in a Guatemalan Town. Austin: University of Texas Press.

Arav, Rami, and Richard A. Freund, Ed. 1995-2009

Bethsaida: A City by the North Shore or the Sea of Galilee. 4 vols. Bethsaida Excavations Project. Kirksville: Thomas Jefferson University Press/Truman State University Press.

Arnold, Denise Y. 2008

Entre los muertos y los diablos y el desarrollo en los Andes. La Paz: ISEAT.

Asad, Talal. 1986

The Idea of an Anthropology of Islam. Washington, D. C: Center for Contemporary Arab Studies, Georgetown University.

Ådna, Jostein. 2000

Jesu Stellung zum Tempel. Die Tempelaktion und das Tempelwort als Ausdruck seiner messianischen Sendung. WUNT 2/119. Tübingen: Mohr Siebeck.

Balia, Daryl and Kirsteen Kim, Ed. 2010

Edinburgh 2010 Witnessing to Christ Today. Oxford: Regnum.

Barber, Benjamin R. 1995

Jihad vs. Mcworld. Times Books.

Barbosa da Silva, Antonio. 2002

'Mission eller dialog? – en kritisk analys av kontroversen mission eller dialog ur kunskapsteoretisk och etisk synvinkel.' In *En värld – en religion? Religionsteologisk refleksjon.* Ed. Agne Nordlander.

Uppsala: Ingång, Johannelund teologiska skriftserie no.3-4, 43- 67.

Barclay, John M. G. 1996
Jews in the Mediterranean Diaspora: From Alexander to Trajan (323 BCE – 117 CE). Edinburgh: T & T Clark.

Barnes, Virginia Lee and Janice Patricia Boddy. 1994
Aman: the Story of a Somali Girl. New York: Pantheon Books.

Barrett, C.K. 1994-98
The Acts of the Apostles. 2 vols. ICC. Edinburgh: T & T Clark.

Basetti-Sani, Guilio. 1981
The Koran in the light of Christ. Bombay: St. Paul Publications.

Bauckham, Richard J. 2005
'James, Peter, and the Gentiles'. In *The Missions of James, Peter, and Paul: Tensions in Early Christianity.* Ed. B.D. Chilton and C.A. Evans. NTSup 115. Leiden: Brill, 91–142.

Bauman, Zygmunt. 1998
Globalization: The human consequences. Cambridge: Polity Press.

Beckford, James A. and Sophie Gilliat. 1998
Religion in Prison. Equal Rites in a Multi-Faith Society. Cambridge: Cambridge University Press.

Berentsen, Jan-Martin, Tormod Engelsviken and Knud Jørgensen, Ed. 2004
Missiologi i dag. Oslo: Universitetsforlaget, 2. ed.

Berger, Peter L., Brigitte Berger and Hansfried Kellner. 1973
The homeless mind: modernization and consciousness. Middlesex: Penguin Books.

Berger, Peter L. 1999
'The Desecularization of the World: A Global Overview.' In *The Desecularization of the World: Resurgent Religion and World Politics.* Ed. Peter L. Berger. Washington D.C.: Ethics and Public Policy Center.

Berger, Peter L., Ed. 1999
The Desecularization of the World. Resurgent Religion and World Politics. Grand Rapids, MI: The Ethics and Polity Center and Eerdmans Publishing Co.

Best, Ernest. 1981
Following Jesus: Discipleship in the Gospel of Mark. JSNTSup 4. Sheffield: JSOT Press.

Bevans, Stephen. 2003 [1992]
Models of Contextual Theology. Maryknoll: Orbis.

Beyerhaus, Peter. 1996
Er sandte sein Wort. Theologie der christlichen Mission. Band 1: Die Bibel in der Mission. TVG/Heilsgeschichtliche Missionstheologie 1. Wuppertal/Bad Liebenzell: Brockhaus / VLM.

Bird, Michael F. 2006
Jesus and the Origins of the Gentile Mission. Library of New Testament Studies. London / New York: T& T Clark.

Blom, Svein. 1999
'Residential Concentration among Immigrants in Oslo.' *International Migration Quarterly Review* 37:3, 617-642.

Bockmuehl, Markus. 2003
Jewish Law in Gentile Churches: Halakhah and the Beginning of Christian Public Ethics. Grand Rapids: Baker.

Bonk, Jonathan. 2009
'Finance'. In *Atlas of Global Christianity 1910-2010.* Ed. Johnson and Ross. Edinburgh: Edinburgh University Press.

Bosch, David J. 1991
Transforming Mission. Paradigm Shifts in Theology of Mission. Maryknoll: Orbis.

Botermann, Helga. 1996
Das Judenedikt des Kaisers Claudius. Römischer Staat und Christiani im 1. Jahrhundert. Hermes Einzelschriften 71. Stuttgart: Steiner.

Breytenbach, Cilliers. 1996
Paulus und Barnabas in der Provinz Galatien. Studien zu Apostelgeschichte 13f.; 16,6; 18,23 und den Adressaten des Galaterbriefes. AGAJU 38. Leiden: Brill.

Bruce, F.F. 1982
Commentary on Galatians. NIGTC. Grand Rapids: Eerdmans.

Bruce, F.F. 1988
The Book of the Acts. Rev. ed. NICNT. Grand Rapids: Eerdmans.

Brusco, Elizabeth. 1995
The Reformation of Machismo, Evangelical Conversion and Gender in Colombia. Austin: University of Texas Press.

Bø, Bente Puntervold. 2004
Søkelys på den norske innvandringspolitikken – etiske og rettslige dilemmaer. Kristiansand: Norwegian Academic Press.

Caragounis, Chrys C. 1990
Peter and the Rock. BZNW 58. Berlin: De Gruyter.

Casanova, José. 1994
Public Religions in the Modern World. Chicago and London: University of Chicago Press.

Chambésy Dialogue Consultation. 1982
Christian Mission and Islamic Da'wah. Proceedings of the Chambésy Dialogue Consultation. Leicester: Islamic Foundation.

Chandler, Paul-Gordon. 2007
Pilgrims of Christ on the Muslim road. Exploring a new path between two faiths. Lanham MD/Plymouth UK: Cowley Publications.

Chestnut, Andrew. 1995
Born Again in Brazil: The Pentecostal Boom and the Pathogens of Poverty. New Brunswick: Rutgers University Press.

Christiansen, Connie. 2004
'New Media Consumption among Immigrants in Europe.' *Ethnicities*

4:2, 185-207.
Christol, Michel, and Thomas Drew-Bear. 2002
'Les Sergii Paulli et Antioche'. In *Actes du Ier congres international sur Antioche de Pisidie*. Ed. T. Drew-Bear, M. Tashalan, and C.J. Thomas. Collection archéologie et histoire de l'antiquité 5. Lyon / Paris: Université Lumière-Lyon / Boccard, 177–191.
Corrie, John (ed). 2007
Dictionary of Mission Theology. Evangelical Foundations. Nottingham: InterVarsity Press.
Cragg, Kenneth. 1977
The Christian and Other Religion. London: Mowbrays.
Cragg, Kenneth. 2003
Jesus and the Muslim. Oxford: Oneworld.
Cullmann, Oscar. 1962 [1953]
Peter: Disciple – Apostle – Martyr. Second ed. London: SCM.
Cumming, Joseph. 2010
'Muslim Followers Of Jesus?' Published at http://conversation.lausanne.org/en/conversations/detail/10004
Dahl, Øyvind. 2001
Møter mellom mennesker: interkulturell kommunikasjon. Oslo: Gyldendal akademisk.
Daniel, Norman. 1993
Islam and the West. The making of an image. Second Edition. Oxford: Oneworld.
Davie, Grace. 2007
'Religion in Europe in the 21th century.' In *Religion in Late Modernity: Essays in Honor of Pål Repstad.* Ed. Inger Furseth and Paul Leer-Salvesen. Trondheim: Tapir Academic Press.
Davies, Graham. 1989
'The Destiny of the Nations in the Book of Isaiah'. In *The Book of Isaiah/Le Livre d'Isaïe: Les oracles et leurs reflectures unitè complexitè de l'ouvrage*. Ed. J. Vermeylen. BETL 81. Leuven: Leuven University Press, 93–120.
Davies, William D., and Dale C. Allison. 1988-97
The Gospel According to Saint Matthew. ICC. Edinburgh: T & T Clark.
Dean, Kenda Creasy. 2003
'The New Rhetoric of Youth Ministry.' *Journal of Youth and Theology* 2:2, 8-18.
Dean, Kenda Creasy and Ron Foster. 1998
The Godbearing Life. The art of soultending ministry. Nashville: UpperRoomBooks.
Dehqani-Tafti, H.B. 1982
The hard awakening. London:Triangle/SPCK.
Denova, Rebecca I. 1997

The Things Accomplished Among Us: Prophetic Tradition in the Structural Pattern of Luke-Acts. JSNTSup 141. Sheffield: Sheffield Academic Press.

Dihle, Albrecht. 1984
'Indische Philosophen bei Clemens Alexandrinus [1964]'. In *Antike und Orient. Gesammelte Aufsätze*. Ed. V.Pöschl and H. Petersmann. Heidelberg: Winter, 78–88.

Dretke, James P. 1979
A Christian Approach to Muslims. Reflections from West Africa. Pasadena, CA:William Carey Library.

Dschulnigg, Peter. 1996
Petrus im Neuen Testament. Stuttgart: Katholisches Bibelwerk.

Dulles, Avery. 2004
'The Rebirth of Apologetics.' *First Things*, 143, 18-23.

Dumont, Louis. 1986
Essays on Individualism: Modern Ideology in Anthropological Perspective. Chicago: Univ. of Chicago Press.

Dunn, James D. G. 1996
The Acts of the Apostles. EpComm. London: Epworth.

Dunn, James D. G. 2009
Beginning from Jerusalem. Christianity in the Making II. Grand Rapids: Eerdmans.

Dunn, Robert G. 1998
Identity Crises. A Social Critique of Postmodernity. Minneapolis, Minn.: University of Minnesota Press.

Durkheim, Émile. 1982 [1912]
The elementary forms of religious life. London: George Allen and Unwin.

Elass, Mateen. 2004
Understanding the Koran. Grand Rapids, Michigan: Zondervan.

Ellis, Earle E. 1991
'"The End of the Earth" (Acts 1:8)'. *BBR* 1, 123–132.

Engelsviken, Tormod. 2004
‚Den misjonale kirke og utfordringen fra kirken i sør.' In *Hva vil det si å være kirke? Kirkens vesen og oppdrag*. Ed. Tormod Engelsviken og Kjell Olav Sannes. Trondheim: Tapir Akademisk Forlag, 69-92.

Engelsviken, Tormod og Kjell Olav Sannes, Ed. 2004
Hva vil det si å være kirke? Kirkens vesen og oppdrag. Trondheim: Tapir Akademisk Forlag.

Engelsviken, Tormod. 2007
'Church/ecclesiology'. In *Dictionary of Mission Theology. Evangelical Foundations*. Ed. John Corrie. Nottingham: InterVarsity Press, 51-55.

Engelsviken, Tormod. 2010
'Kontekstualisering av den lutherske bekjennelse.' In *Kirkens*

bekjennelse i historisk og aktuelt perspektiv. Festskrift til Kjell Olav Sannes. Ed. Torleiv Austad, Tormod Engelsviken og Lars Østnor. Trondheim: Tapir Akademisk Forlag, 173-186.

Eriksen, Thomas Hylland. 1993
Kulturterrorismen: et oppgjør med tanken om kulturell renhet. Oslo: Spartacus.

Eriksen, Thomas Hylland. 1994
Kulturelle veikryss: essays om kreolisering. Oslo: Universitetsforlaget.

Eriksen, Thomas Hylland. 2003
'Introduction'. In *Globalization: Studies in Anthropology.* Ed. Thomas Hylland Eriksen. London: Pluto Press.

Eriksen, Thomas Hylland. 2008
Globalisering. Åtte nøkkelbegreper. Oslo: Universitetsforlaget.

Escobar, Samuel. 1995
A Time for Mission. Leicester: Intervarsity Press.

Esler, Philip F. 1987
Community and Gospel in Luke-Acts: The Social and Political Motivations of Lucan Theology. SNTSMS 57. Cambridge: Cambridge University Press.

Forum on Religion and Public Life. 2009
Mapping the Global Population: A Report on the Size and Distribution of the World's Muslim Population (pewforum.org/docs/?DocID=450). Pew Research Center, October.

Fernando, Ajith. 1987
The Christian's attitude towards world religions. Wheaton IL:Tyndale House.

Fiske, John. 1990
Introduction to Communication Studies. 2nd edition. London: Routledge.

Fjeld, Bjørn Øyvind. 2010
'Toleranse og pluralisme – nødvendige, men krevende idealer.' Unpublished paper, Kristiansand.

Friedman, Jonathan. 1997
'Global Crisis, the Struggle for Cultural Identity, and the Intellectual Porkbarrelling: Cosmopolitans versus Locals, Ethnics, and Nationals in an Era of De-homogenization.' In *Debating Cultural Hybridity.* Ed. Pnina Werbner and Tariq Mohood. London: Zed Books.

Friedman, Thomas. 2005
The World is Flat: A Brief History of the Twenty-first Century. New York: Farrar, Straus & Giroux.

Foucault, Michel. 1980
Power/Knowledge: Selected Interviews and Other Writings. New York: Pantheon.

Gadamer, Hans-Georg. 1993
Truth and Method. London: Sheed and Ward Limited.

Gaventa, Beverly R. 2003
The Acts of the Apostles. Abingdon New Testament Commentaries. Nashville: Abingdon Press.

Geertz, Clifford. 1973
The Interpretation of Cultures. New York, NY: Basic Books.

Geisler, Norman L. and Abdul Saleeb. 1993
Answering Islam. The Crescent in light of the Cross. Michigan:Baker Books

Gempf, Conrad. 1995
'Mission and Misunderstanding: Paul and Barnabas in Lystra (Acts 14:8–20)'. In *Mission and Meaning. FS P. Cotterell*. Ed. A. Billington. Carlisle: Paternoster, 56–69.

Gibbs, Eddie and Ryan K. Bolger. 2006
Emerging Churches. Creating Christian Community in Postmodern Culture. Grand Rapids: Baker Academic.

Gifford, Paul. 2004
Ghana's New Christianity: Pentecostalism in a Globalising African Economy. London: Hurst & Company.

Goodman, Martin. 2007
Rome and Jerusalem: The Clash of Ancient Civilizations. New York: Vintage.

Gort, Jerald, Hendrik Vroom, Rein Fernhout and Anton Wessels, Ed. 1989
Dialogue and syncretism. An interdisciplinary approach. Grand Rapids, MI: Eerdmans.

Grandhagen, Egil. 1994
'De unådde folkeslag.' In *Missiologi i dag*. Ed. Jan-Martin Berentsen, Tormod Engelsviken and Knud Jørgensen. Oslo: Universitetsforlaget.

Groß, Walter. 1993
'Israel und die Völker: Die Krise des YHWH-Volk-Konzepts im Jesajabuch'. In *Der Neue Bund im Alten. Studien zur Bundestheologie der beiden Testamente*. Ed. E. Zenger. QD 146. Freiburg: Herder, 149–167.

Guder, Darell L., Ed. 1998
Missional Church: A Vision for the Sending of the Church in North America. Grand Rapids, Michigan: Eerdmans Publishing Company.

Guder, Darrell L. 2000
The Continuing Conversion of the Church. Grand Rapids: Eerdmans.

Guiness, Os. 2000
Time for truth. Leicester: IVP.

Gullestad, Marianne. 2002
'Invisible Fences: Egalitarianism, Nationalism and Racism.' *Journal of Royal Anthropological Institute* 8, 45-64.

Gullestad, Marianne. 2007
Misjonsbilder. Oslo: Universitetsforlaget.

Habermas, Jürgen. 2006

'Religion in the Public Sphere.' *European Journal of Philosophy* 14(1), 1-25.

Haddad, Yvonne Yazbek and Wadi Zaidan Haddad, Ed. 1995
Christian-Muslim Encounters. Gainesville FL: University Press of Florida.

Haenchen, Ernst. 1971
The Acts of the Apostles. Philadelphia: Westminster.

Hanciles, Jehu J. 2008
Beyond Christendom: Globalization, African Migration and the Transformation of the West. Maryknoll: Orbis.

Hatlehol, Oddvar. 2009
'Iranians in Norway.' Unpublished manuscript.

Heckel, Theo K. 1999
Vom Evangelium des Markus zum viergestaltigen Evangelium. WUNT 120. Tübingen: Mohr-Siebeck.

Hegstad, Harald. 2009
Den virkelige kirke. Bidrag til ekklesiologien. Trondheim: Tapir Akademisk Forlag.

Hengel, Martin, and Anna Maria Schwemer. 1997
Paul Between Damascus and Antioch: The Unknown Years. London/Louisville: SCM/Westminster John Knox.

Henriksen, Kristin. 2007
'Innvandrerbefolkningen med bakgrunn fra Iran.' http://www.ssb.no/emner/02/rapp_200729/rapp_200729.pdf, 95-105.

Herbert, David. 2003
Religion and civil society. Rethinking public religion in the contemporary world. Aldershot, Hampshire: Ashgate Publishing Limited.

Hersi, Ali Abdirahman. 1977
'The Arab Factor in Somali History: the Origins and the Development of Arab Enterprise and Cultural Influences in the Somali Peninsula.' Thesis presented for degree of Doctor of Philosophy, University of California, Los Angeles.

Hick, John. 1982 [1980]
God Has Many Names. Philadelphia: The Westminster Press.

Hiebert, Paul G. 1989
'Power encounter and folk Islam.' In *Muslims and Christians on the Emmaus road*. Ed. J. Dudley Woodberry. Monrovia, CA: MARC.

Hiebert, Paul G. 1999
Missiological Implications of Epistemological Shifts. Affirming Truth in a Modern/Postmodern World. Pennsylvania: Trinity Press.

Hjarvard, Stig. 2008a
'The Mediatization of Religion. A Theory of the Media as Agents of Religious Change.' *Northern Lights* 6, 9-26.

Hjarvard, Stig. 2008b

'The Mediatization of Society.' *Nordicom Review* 29, 105-134.

Hollis, Martin. 1994
The Philosophy of Social Science: an Introduction. Cambridge: Cambridge Univ. Press.

Hoover, S.M., L.S. Clark, and L. Rainie. 2004
'Faith Online.' In *Report from the Pew Internet & American Life Project*. www.pewinternet.org.

Hopkins, A. G. 2002
Globalization in World History. London: Pimlico.

Huber, Friedrich. 1976
Jahwe, Juda und die anderen Völker beim Propheten Jesaja. BZAW 137. Berlin: De Gruyter.

Huntington, Samuel P. 1993
'The Clash of Civilizations?' *Foreign Affairs*, 72 (3), 22-49.

Huntington, Samuel. 1996
The Clash of Civilizations and the Remaking of World Order. New York: Simon and Schuster.

Jenkins, Philip. 2002
The Next Christendom. The Coming of Global Christianity. New York: Oxford University Press.

Jenkins, Philip. 2008
The Lost History of Christianity. New York: HarperOne.

Jensen, Iben. 2007
Interkulturel kommunikation i komplekse samfund. 4th edition. Frederiksberg: Roskilde Universitetsforlag.

Jervell, Jacob. 1998
Die Apostelgeschichte. KEK 3. Göttingen: Vandenhoeck & Ruprecht.

Jewett, Robert. 2007
Romans. Hermeneia. Minneapolis: Fortress.

Johnson, Todd M. and Kenneth R. Ross, Ed. 2009
Atlas of Global Christianity 1910-2010. Edinburgh: Edinburgh University Press.

Jøssang, Asle. 2009
'In Search of a More Powerful Christ: An Anthropology of Religious Conversion.' Submitted PhD-thesis. Oslo: University of Oslo.

Kaplan, Andreas M. and Michael Haenlein. 2010
'Users of the World, Unite! The Challenges and Opportunities of Social Media.' *Business Horizons* 53, 59-68.

Kateregga, Badru and David W. Shenk. 1980
Islam and Christianity. A Muslim and a Christian in dialogue. Dodoma, Tanzania: Central Tanganyika Press.

Kärkkäinen, Veli-Matti. 2002
An Introduction to Ecclesiology. Ecumenical, Historical and Global Perspectives. Downers Grove, IL.: IVP Press.

Kärkkäinen, Veli-Matti. 2003

An Introduction to the Theology of Religions. Downers Grove: Intervarsity Press.

Kerr, David. 2008
'Missiological Developments from Edinburgh 1910 to Today.' *Swedish Missiological Themes*, 96, 1, 9-26.

Kessler, William Thomas. 1998
Peter as the First Witness of the Risen Lord: An Historical and Theological Investigation. Tesi Gregoriana, Serie Teologia 37. Rom: Gregorian University Press.

Kim, Sebastian and Kirsteen Kim. 2008
Christianity as a World Religion. London: Continuum.

Knitter, Paul F. 1985
No other Name? Maryknoll, NY: Orbis Books.

Kolb, Robert and Timothy J. Wengert, Ed. 2000
The Book of Concord. The Confessions of the Evangelical Lutheran Church. Minneapolis, MN.: Fortress Press.

Kraemer, Hendrik. 1938
The Christian Message in a Non-Christian World. London: International Missionary Council.

Kurtz, Lester. 2007
Gods in the global village. The world's religions in sociological perspective. Thousand Oaks CA: Pine Forge Press.

Kuschel, Karl-Josef and Hans Küng, Ed. 1993
A Global ethic: the Declaration of the Parliament of the World's Religions. London : SCM Press.

Küng, Hans, Josef van Ess, Heinrich von Stietencron and Heinz Bechert. 1986
Christianity and World Religions. Paths to dialogue with Islam, Hinduism and Buddhism. New York: Doubleday.

Kvale, Steinar. 2009
Det kvalitative forskningsintervju. Oslo: Gyldendal akademisk.

Laitin, David D. and Said S. Samatar. 1987
Somalia: Nation in Search of a State. Boulder, Colo., London, England: Westview Press; Gower.

Lakoff, George and Mark Johnson. 1999
Philosophies in the Flesh: The Embodied Mind and the Challenge to Western Thought. New York: Basic Books.

Lambek, Michael. 1990
'Certain Knowledge, Contestable Authority: Power and Practice on the Islamic Periphery.' *American Ethnologist* 17: 1, 23-40.

Landmesser, Christof. 2001
Jüngerberufung und Zuwendung zu Gott. Ein exegetischer Beitrag zum Konzept der matthäischen Soteriologie im Anschluß an Mt 9,9–13. WUNT 133. Tübingen: Mohr Siebeck.

Latourette, Kenneth Scott. 1970 [1945]
A history of the expansion of Christianity. Volume 7: Advance through

storm. A.D. 1914 and after, with concluding generalizations. Grand Rapids, MI: Zondervan.

Latourette, Kenneth Scott. 1993
'Ecumenical Bearings of the Missionary Movement and the International Missionary Council.' In *A History of the Ecumenical Movement, 1517-1948*. Ed. Ruth Spouse and Stephen C. Neill. Geneva: World Council of Churches.

Lausanne Covenant. 1974
'Lausanne Covenant.' http://www.lausanne.org/covenant

Lausanne Committee for World Evangelization. 2004
The Local Church in Mission: Becoming a Missional Congregation in the Twenty-First century Global Context. Lausanne Committee for World Evangelization.

Leirvik, Oddbjørn. 2008
'Islam i Norge.' http://folk.uio.no/leirvik/tekster/IslamiNorge.html

Levine, Lee I. 2005
The Ancient Synagogue: The First Thousand Years. Second ed. New Haven: Yale University Press.

Levinskaya, Irina A. 1996
The Book of Acts in its Diaspora Setting. The Book of Acts in Its First-Century Setting, Volume 5. Grand Rapids: Eerdmans.

Lewellen, Ted. C. 2002
Anthropology of Globalization: Cultural Anthropology Enters the 21st Century. Westport: Bergin & Garvey.

Lewis, I. M. 1994
Blood and Bone: the Call of Kinship in Somali Society. Lawrenceville, N.J.: Red Sea Press.

Lewis, I. M. 2002
A Modern History of the Somali: Nation and State in the Horn of Africa. Oxford: James Currey.

Lewis, I. M., and Said S. Samatar. 1999
A Pastoral Democracy: a Study of Pastoralism and Politics among the Northern Somali of the Horn of Africa. Hamburg - Oxford: LIT ; James Currey with the IAI.

Liua'na, Featuna'I Ben. 2009
'Christianity in Melanesia, Micronesia and Polynesia, 1910-2010.' In *Atlas of Global Christianity 1910-2010*. Ed. Johnson and Ross. Edinburgh: Edinburgh University Press.

Luckmann, Thomas. 1991
'The New and the Old in Religion.' In *Social Theory for a Changing Society*. Ed. P. Bourdieu and J.S. Coleman. New York: Russel Sage Foundation.

Lygunda, Fohle 2009
'Christianity in Middle Africa, 1910-2010.' In *Atlas of Global Christianity 1910-2010*. Ed. Johnson and Ross. Edinburgh: Edinburgh

University Press.
Lynch, Gordon. 2007
The New Spirituality: An Introduction to Progressive Belief in the Twenty-first Century. London: I.B. Tauris.
Lyotard, Jean-Francois. 1984
The Postmodern Condition: A Report on Knowledge. Manchester: Manchester University Press.
Lövheim, Mia. 2008
'Rethinking Cyberreligion? Teens, Religion and the Internet in Sweden.' *Nordicom Review* 29, 205-217.
Maalouf, Amin. 2001
The Crusades Through Arab Eyes. London: Saqi Books.
Macfie, A.L. 2000
Orientalism. A reader. Cairo: Cairo University Press.
Mandani, Mahmood. 2004
Good Muslim, Bad Muslim: America, the Cold War, and the Roots of Terror. New York: Pantheon.
Mandaville, Peter G. 2001
Transnational Muslim Politics: Reimagining the Umma. London: Routledge.
Manila Manifesto. 1989
'Manila Manifesto.' http://www.lausanne.org/manila-1989/manila-manifesto.html
Marsh, Charles. 1980
Share your faith with a Muslim. Kent: STK Books.
Marshall, I. Howard. 1980
The Acts of the Apostles. An Introduction and Commentary. TNTC. Leicester: InterVarsity Press.
Marshall, I. Howard. 2007
'Acts'. In *Commentary on the New Testament Use of the Old Testament*. Ed. G. K. Beale and D. A. Carson. Grand Rapids: Baker, 513–606.
Martin, Bernice. 1998
'From pre- to postmodernism in Latin America: the case of Pentecostalism.' In *Religion, Modernity and Postmodernity.* Ed. Paul Heeles. Oxford: Blackwell Publishers.
Maurer, Andreas. 1999
'In search of a new life: Conversion motives of Christians and Muslims.' Th.D. diss.: Pretoria (abstract available on March 30th, 2010 from: http://www.versoehnung.net/wp-content/uploads/Abstract-Maurer.pdf).
McAlister, Elizabeth. 2005
'Globalization and the Religious Production of Space.' *Journal for the Scientific Study of Religion* 44, 249-255.
McCane, Byron R. 2008

'Simply Irresistible: Augustus, Herod, and the Empire'. *JBL* 127, 725–735.

McCurry, Don, Ed. 1979
The Gospel and Islam. A 1978 Compendium. Monrovia, CA: MARC.

McGlathery, Marla Frederick and Traci Griffin. 2007
'"Becoming Conservative, Becoming White?": Black Evangelicals and the Para-Church Movement.' In *This Side of Heaven – Race, Ethnicity, and Christian Faith*. Ed. Robert J. Priest and Alvaro L. Nieves. New York: Oxford University Press, 145-161.

McGrath, Alister E. 1995
'A Particularist View: A Post-Enlightenment Approach.' In *More than One Way? Four Views on Salvation in a Pluralistic World.* Ed. Dennis L. Okholm and Timothy R. Philips. Grand Rapids: Zondervan.

McGuire, Meredith. 2008
Religion: The Social Context. Belmont: Wadsworth Publishing Co., 3rd ed.

McLuhan, Marshall. 1964
Understanding Media: The Extension of Man. Toronto: McGraw Hill.

Meier, John P. 1991-2008
A Marginal Jew: Rethinking the Historical Jesus. New York: Doubleday.

Micklethwait, John and Adrian Wooldridge. 2009
God is Back: How the Global Revival of Faith is Changing the World. New York: The Penguin Press.

Mikkola, Teija, Kati Niemelä and Juha Petterson. 2007
The Questioning Mind. Faith and Values of the New Generation. Tampere: Church Research Institute.

Mingana, A. 1925
'The Early Spread of Christianity in Central Asia and the Far East.' Bulletin of the John Rylands Library, *9, no. 2, 297-371.*

Mission-Shaped Church. 2004
Mission-Shaped Church: Church planting and fresh expressions of the church in a changing context. London: Church House Publishing.

Mitchell, Stephen. 1995
Anatolia: Land, Men, and Gods in Asia Minor. Oxford: Oxford University Press.

Moffett, S. H. 1998
A History of Christianity in Asia, bd. I. *Maryknoll: Orbis.*

Mogensen, Mogens S. 2001
Contextual communication of the gospel to pastoral Fulbe in Northern Nigeria. Ann Arbor: UMI.

Morey, Robert. 2001
The Islamic invasion. Confronting the world's fastest growing religion. Eugene, OR: Harvest House Publishers.

Moucarry, Chawkat. 2010

'A Plea for Dialogue Between Christians and Muslims.' The Lausanne Global Conversation. http://conversation.lausanne.org/en/conversations/detail/10023.

Murray, Oswyn, and Simon Price. 1991
The Greek City: From Homer to Alexander. Oxford: Clarendon.

Musk, Bill. 1979
'The hunger of the heart.' In *The Gospel and Islam. A 1978 Compendium.* Ed. Don McCurry. Monrovia, CA: MARC.

Musk, Bill. 1984
Popular Islam: An investigation into the phenomenology and ethnotheological bases of popular Islamic belief and practice. Pretoria: UNISA.

Musk, Bill. 1989
The unseen face of Islam. Sharing the Gospel with ordinary Muslims. Eastbourne: MARC.

Myklebust, Olav Guttorm. 1988
Det store oppdrag. Artikler i utvalg 1938-1988. Oslo: Privat trykk.

Naguib, Saphinaz-Amal. 2002
'The Northern Way: Muslim Communities in Norway.' In *Muslim Minorities in the West.* Ed. Yvonne Y. Haddad and Jane I. Smith. Walnut Creek, California: Altamire Press, 161-174.

Nazir-Ali, Michael. 1983
Islam. A Christian perspective. Exeter: Paternoster.

Nazir-Ali, Michael. 1987
Frontiers in Christian-Muslim Encounter. Oxford: Regnum.

Netland, Harold. 2004
'Religious Pluralism and the Quest for Truth.' In *Biblical Faith and other Religions. An Evangelical Assessment.* Ed. David W. Baker. Grand Rapids: Kregel Academic Books.

Netzer, Ehud. 2008
The Architecture of Herod, the Great Builder. Grand Rapids: Baker.

Newbigin, Lesslie. 1989
The Gospel in a Pluralist Society. Grand Rapids: Eerdmans.

Newbigin, Lesslie. 2006
Missionary Theologian: a Reader. Grand Rapids: Eerdmans.

Norheim, Bård Eirik Hallesby. 2006
'From ghetto to communitas: Post-Soviet youth ministry and leadership on a pilgrimage to Emmaus.' *Journal of Youth and Theology* 5:1, 67-84.

Notten, Michael van and Spencer Heath MacCallum. 2005
The Law of the Somalis: a Stable Foundation for Economic Development in the Horn of Africa. Trenton, NJ: Red Sea Press.

Noy, David, Alexander Panayotov, and Hanswulf Bloedhorn. 2004
Inscriptiones Judaicae Orientis. Vol. I: Eastern Europe. TSAJ 101. Tübingen: Mohr Siebeck.

Nyhaga, Michael, Ed. 2004
Man kan inte vara skeptiker när det gäller sanning: Fem svenska filosofer. Stehag: Symposion.

Oftestad, Bernt T. og Nils Aksel Røsæg, Ed. 2008
Mellom kirke og akademia. Det teologiske Menighetsfakultet 100 år, 1908-2008. Trondheim: Tapir Akademisk Forlag.

Onn, Alexander. 2002
'Khirbet Umm el-'Umdan'. *Ḥadashot Arkheologiyot* 114, 64–68.

The Oslo Coalition on Freedom of Religion or Belief. 2009
Missionary Activities and Human Rights: Recommended Ground Rules for Missionary Activities (A Basis for Creating Individual Codes of Conduct). Oslo.

Oswalt, John N. 1991
'The Mission of Israel to the Nations'. In *Through No Fault of Their Own? The Fate of Those Who Have Never Heard.* Ed. W. V. Crockett and J. G. Sigountos. Grand Rapids: Baker, 85–95.

Oswalt, John N. 2006
'The Nations in Isaiah: Friend or Foe; Servant or Partner'. *BBR* 16, 41–51.

Ott, Craig and Harold A. Netland, Ed. 2006
Globalizing Theology. Belief and Practice in an Era of World Christianity. Grand Rapids, MI: Baker Academic.

Pachuau, Lalsingkima. 2009
'Missionaries Sent and Received, Asia, 1910-2010.' In *Atlas of Global Christianity 1910-2010.* Ed. Johnson and Ross. Edinburgh: Edinburgh University Press.

Packer, James I. 1961
Evangelism and the Sovereignty of God. Downers Grove: InterVarsity Press.

Pajuelo, Ramón and Pablo Sandoval. 2004
Globalización y Diversidad Cultural: Una Mirada Desde America Latina. Lima: Instituto de Estudios Peruanos.

Pao, David W. 2000
Acts and the Isaianic New Exodus. WUNT 2/130. Tübingen: Mohr Siebeck.

Pappé, Ilan. 2006
The Ethnic Cleansing of Palestine. Oxford: Oneworld.

Parshall, Phil. 1980
New Paths in Muslim evangelism. Grand Rapids, MI: Baker.

Perry, Alex. 2010
Falling off the Edge: Globalization, World Peace and Other Lies. London: Pan Books.

Pesch, Rudolf. 1976-77
Das Markusevangelium. HThK 2. Freiburg: Herder.

Peter, Frank. 2006

'Individualization and Religious Authority in Western European Islam.' *Islam and Christian - Muslim Relations* 17, 105-118.

Pfander, C.G. 1910
The Mizan ul-Haqq (Balance of Truth). London: The Religious Tracts Society.

Pohl, Christine D. 1999
Making Room. Recovering Hospitality as a Christian Tradition. Grand Rapids: Eerdmans.

Priest, Kersten B. and Robert J. Priest. 2007
'Divergent Worship Practices in the Sunday Morning Hour: Analysis of an "Interracial" Church Merger Attempt.' In *This Side of Heaven – Race Ethnicity and Christian Faith.* Ed. Robert J. Priest and Alvaro L. Nieves. New York: Oxford University Press, 275-292.

Prior, Michael. 1999
Zionism and the State of Israel. A Moral Inquiry. London: Routledge.

Purcell, Nicholas. 1996
'Urbanism II. Roman'. In *Oxford Classical Dictionary, Third ed.* Ed. S. Hornblower and A. J. S. Spawforth. Oxford: Oxford University Press, 1573.

Race, Alan. 1983
Christians and religious pluralism. Patterns in the Christian theology of religion. London: SCM Press.

Ramachandra,Vinoth. 1996
The Recovery of Mission. Beyond the Pluralist Paradigm. Grand Rapids: Eerdmans.

Ramsay, William M. 1896
St. Paul the Traveller and the Roman Citizen. London: Hodder & Stoughton.

Renaut, Alain. 1997
The Era of the Individual: a Contribution to a History of Subjectivity. Princeton, N.J.: Princeton Univ. Press.

Rhodes, Peter J. 2007
'Polis II'. In *Brill's New Pauly.* Ed. H. Cancik and H. Schneider. Leiden: Brill, vol. 11, 470–473.

Riesner, Rainer. 1998
Paul's Early Period: Chronology, Mission Strategy, Theology. Grand Rapids: Eerdmans.

Robertson, Roland. 1992
Globalization: Social Theory and Global Theory. London: Sage Publications.

Roloff, Jürgen. 1988
Die Apostelgeschichte. NTD 5. Göttingen: Vandenhoeck & Ruprecht.

Romm, James S. 1992
The Edges of the Earth in Ancient Thought. Geography, Exploration, and Fiction. Princeton: Princeton University Press.

Root, Andrew. 2007
Revisiting Relational Youth Ministry: From a Strategy of Influence to a Theology of Incarnation. Downers Grove: InterVarsity Press.

Root, Andrew. 2009
Relationships Unfiltered: Help for Youth Workers, Volunteers, and Parents on Creating Authentic Relationships. Grand Rapids: Zondervan.

Ross, Kenneth R. 2006
'The Centenary of Edinburgh 1910: Its Possibilities.' *International Bulletin of Missionary Research*, vol. 30, no. 4, 177-179.

Ross, Kenneth R. 2009a
'From Edinburgh 1910 to Edinburgh 2010.' In *Edinburgh 1910 – 100 år efter.* Ed. Mogens Mogensen. København: Dansk Missionsråd.

Ross, Kenneth R. 2009b
'Old Church and New Evangelism. A Scottish Perspective on Christian Mission in Today's Europe.' *Missiology,* vol. XXXVII, no. 4, 511-525.

Rouse, Ruth and Stephen C. Neill, Ed. 1993
A History of the Ecumenical Movement, 1517-1948. Geneva: World Council of Churches.

Roy, Olivier. 2004
Globalized Islam: The Search for a New Ummah. New York: Columbia University Press.

Said, Edward. 1985 [1978]
Orientalism. London:Penguin Books.

Said, Edward. 1981
Covering Islam. How the media and the experts determine how we see the rest of the world. London: Routledge & Kegan Paul.

Samatar, Said S. 2002
'Unhappy Masses and the Challenge of Political Islam in the Horn of Africa.' *Horn of Africa* 20, 1-10.

Sampson, Philip S., Vinay Samuel and Chris Sugden, Ed. 1994
Faith and Modernity. Oxford: Regnum Books.

Sanneh, Lamin. 1989
Translating the Message – The Missionary Impact on Culture. American Society of Missiology Series, No. 13., Maryknoll, NY: Orbis Books.

Sanneh, Lamin O. 2008
Disciples of All Nations. Pillars of World Christianity. New York: Oxford University Press.

Schirato, Tony and Jen Webb. 2003
Understanding globalization. London: Sage Publications.

Schnabel, Eckhard J. 2004a
Early Mission, Volume 1: Jesus and the Twelve. Downers Grove: InterVarsity Press.

Schnabel, Eckhard J. 2004b
Early Christian Mission, Volume 2: Paul and the Early Church. Downers Grove: InterVarsity Press.
Schnabel, Eckhard J. 2006
Der erste Brief des Paulus an die Korinther. Historisch-Theologische Auslegung. Wuppertal: R. Brockhaus.
Schnabel, Eckhard J. 2008
Paul the Missionary: Realities, Strategies, and Methods. Downers Grove: InterVarsity Press.
Scholte, Jan Aart. 2005
Globalization: a critical introduction. Basingstoke: Palgrave Macmillian.
Schreiter, Robert J. 1997
The New Catholicity. Theology Between the Global and the Local. Maryknoll. N.Y.: Orbis Books.
Scott, James M. 2002
Paul and the Nations: The Old Testament and Early Jewish Background of Paul's Mission to the Nations with Special Reference to the Destination of Galatians. Orig. 1995. Repr.. WUNT 84. Tübingen: Mohr-Siebeck.
Shadid, Wasif and Sjoerd van Koningsveld, Ed. 2002
'The Negative Image of Islam and Muslims in the West: Causes and Solutions.' In *Religious Freedom and the Neutrality of the State: The Position of Islam in the European Union.* Ed. Shadid, Wasif and Sjoerd van Koningsveld. Sterling, Virginia: Peeters, 174-194.
Sheikh, Bilquis. 1982
I dared to call Him Father. Virginia: Kingsway Publications.
Shenk, Wilbert R. 1996
'The Training of Missiologists for Western Culture.' In *Missiological Education for the Twenty-First Century: The Book, the Circle, and the Sandals.* Ed. John Dudley Woodberry, Charles Edward van Engen and Edgar J. Elliston. Maryknoll, N.Y.: Orbis Books.
Shenk, Wilbert R. 2006
'Foreword'. In *Globalizing Theology. Belief and Practice in an Era of World Christianity.* Ed. Craig Ott and Harold A. Netland. Grand Rapids, MI: Baker Academic, 9-11.
Sheperd, Nick. 2006
'Soul in the city – Mission as Package Holiday: The potential implications of a "tourist" paradigm in youth ministry.' *Journal of Youth and Theology* 5:2, 63-83.
Shultz, Jim. 2009
'The Cochabamba Water War.' In *Dignity and Defiance: Stories from Bolivia's Challenge to Globalization*. Ed. Jim Shultz and Melissa Crane Draper. Berkeley: University of California Press.
Siddiqui, Ataullah. 1997

Christian-Muslim dialogue in the Twentieth Century. Basingstoke, Hampshire/New York: Palgrave, Macmillan.

Sizer, Stephen. 2007
Zion's Christian Soldiers. The Bible, Israel and the Church. Nottingham: IVP.

Skarsaune, O. 2001
'Korset i lotusblomsten. Den glemte kristendomshistorien i Asia.' Årbok 1997. Det Norske Videnskaps-akademi, *276-294.*

Skarsaune, Oskar. 2004
'Misjonstenkningen i oldtiden og middelalderen.' In *Missiologi i dag.* Ed. Jan-Martin Berentsen, Tormod Engelsviken og Knud Jørgensen. Oslo: Universitetsforlaget, 2nd ed., 85-105.

Sleeman, Matthew. 2009
Geography and the Ascension Narrative in Acts. SNTSMS 146. Cambridge: Cambridge University Press.

Sordi, Marta. 1986
The Christians and the Roman Empire. Norman: University of Oklahoma Press.

Spedding, Alison. 2004
Gracias a Dios y a los achachilas. Ensayos de sociología de la religión en los Andes. La Paz: Plural Editores.

Spencer, Nick. 2004
Asylum and Immigration. A Christian Perspective on a Polarised Debate. Milton Keynes: Authentic Media.

Sperber, Jutta. 2000
Christians and Muslims. The dialogue activities of the World Council of Churches and their theological foundation. Berlin/NewYork: Walter de Gruyter.

Stackhouse, John G., Jr., Ed. 2003
Evangelical Ecclesiology. Reality or Illusion? Grand Rapids, MI.: Baker Academic.

Stambaugh, John E. 1988
The Ancient Roman City. Baltimore: Johns Hopkins University Press.

Stanley, Brian. 2009
The World Missionary Conference, Edinburgh 1910. Grand Rapids/Cambridge: Eerdmans.

Stassen, Glen H., D. M. Yeager and John Howard Yoder. 1996
Authentic Transformation: A New Vision of Christ and Culture. Nashville: Abingdon Press.

Steigenga, Timothy J. and Edward L. Cleary. 2007
Conversion of a Continent: Contemporary Religious Change in Latin America. New Brunswick: Rutgers University Press.

Steinberg, Shirley, Priya Parmar and Birgit Richard, Ed. 2006a
Contemporary Youth Culture: An International Encyclopedia, vol. 1. London: Greenwood Press.

Steinberg, Shirley, Priya Parmar and Birgit Richard, Ed. 2006b
Contemporary Youth Culture: An International Encyclopedia, vol 2. London: Greenwood Press.

Stern, Ephraim (ed). 1993
The New Encyclopedia of Archaeological Excavations in the Holy Land. Jerusalem/New York: Israel Exploration Society/Carta.

Store Norske Leksikon. 2006
'Toleranse'. In *Store Norske Leksikon, vol. 14*, 2nd ed. Oslo: Kunnskapsforlaget.

Stott, John R. W. 1975
Christian Mission in the Modern World. Downers Grove: InterVarsity Press.

Stroumsa, Guy G. 1996
'Philosophy of the Barbarians: On Early Christian Ethnological Representations'. In *Geschichte, Tradition, Reflexion. Band II: Griechische und Römische Religion. FS Martin Hengel*. Ed. H. Cancik. Tübingen: Mohr Siebeck, 339–368.

Svane, Marita. 2004
Interkulturel dynamik i kulturmødet: en fænomenologisk, individorienteret analyse og forståelse. Aalborg Universitet.

Syrjänen, Seppo. 1987
In search of meaning and identity. Conversion to Christianity in Pakistani Muslim culture. Vammala: The Finnish Society for Missiology and Ecumenics.

Tennent, Timothy C. 2002
Christianity at the Religious Roundtable: Evangelicalism in Conversation with Hinduism, Buddhism, and Islam. Grand Rapids: Baker Academic.

Thelle, N. N. 1949
Kristendommen i China under T'ang, Yuan, Ming og Ch'in. Studier i Chinas misjonshistories tre første perioder. *København: Gads Forlag.*

Towner, Philip H. 1998
'Mission Practice and Theology under Construction (Acts 18–20)'. In *Witness to the Gospel. The Theology of Acts.* Ed. I.H. Marshall and D. Peterson. Grand Rapids: Eerdmans, 417–436.

Tronstad, Kristian Rose. 2007
'Levekårsundersøkelsen blant innvandrere.' http://www.ssb.no/emner/02/sa_innvand/sa103/kap8.pdf, 157-158.

Turner, Bryan S. 1974
'Islam, Capitalism and the Weber Theses.' *The British Journal of Sociology* 25: 2, 230-43.

Turner, Max M. B. 1996
Power from on High: The Spirit in Israel's Restoration and Witness in Luke-Acts. JPTSup 9. Sheffield: Sheffield Academic Press.

Uglem, Olav. 1979

Norsk misjonshistorie. Oslo: Lunde Forlag.

Vadakkekara, Benedict. 1995
Origin of India's St Thomas Christians: A Historiographical Critique. Delhi: Media House.

Vander Werff, Lyle L. 1977
Christian missions to the Muslims, the Record. South Pasadena CA: William Carey Library.

Van Engen, Charles E. 2006
'The Glocal Church: Locality and Catholicity in a Globalizing World.' In *Globalizing Theology. Belief and Practice in an Era of World Christianity.* Ed. Craig Ott and Harold A. Netland. Grand Rapids, MI: Baker Academic, 157-179.

Van Gelder, Craig. 2000
The Essence of the Church. Grand Rapids, MI.: Baker Books.

Vásquez, Manuel A. 1999
'Religious Pluralism, Identity, and Globalization in Latin America.' *Religious Studies Review* 26, 333-341.

Vásquez, Manuel A. and Marie Friedmann Marqueardt. 2003
Globalizing the Sacred: Religion Across the Americas. New Brunswick: Rutgers University Press.

Viviano, Benedict T. 2000
'Peter as Jesus' Mouth: Matthew 16:13–20 in the Light of Exodus 4:10–17 and other Models'. In *The Interpretation of Scripture in Early Judaism and Christianity: Studies in Language and Tradition.* Ed. C. A. Evans. JSPSup 33. Sheffield: Sheffield Academic Press, 312–341.

Volf, Miroslav, Ghazi bin Muhammad and Melissa Yarrington, Ed. 2010
A common word. Muslims and Christians on loving God and neighbour. Grand Rapids MI/Cambridge UK: William B. Eerdmans Publishing Company.

Wagner, C. Peter and F. Douglas Pennoyer, Ed. 1990
Wrestling with dark angels. Toward a deeper understanding of the supernatural forces in spiritual warfare. Ventura, CA: Regal Books.

Walls, Andrew F. 2002
The Cross-Cultural Process in Christian History: Studies in the Transmission and Appropriation of Faith. Maryknoll and Edinburgh: Orbis and T. & T. Clark.

Walls, Andrew F. 2006
'Globalization and the Study of Christian History.' In *Globalizing Theology. Belief and Practice in an Era of World Christianity.* Ed. Craig Ott and Harold A. Netland. Grand Rapids, MI: Baker Academic, 70-84.

Walls, Andrew F. 2009
'Christianity across twenty centuries.' In *Atlas of Global Christianity*

1910-2010. Ed. Todd M. Johnson and Kenneth R. Ross. Edinburgh: Edinburgh University Press, 48-49.

Walls, Andrew F. 2010
'Commission One and the Church's Transforming Century.' In *Edinburgh 2010. Mission then and now.* Ed. David Kerr and Kenneth Ross. Oxford: Regnum 2010.

Ward, H., and J. Wild, Comp. 1997
The Lion Christian Quotation Collection. Oxford: Lion.

Wark, McKenzie. 1994
Virtual Geography: Living with Global Media Events. Bloomington: Indiana University Press.

Watkins, Adrian and Leslie Nathaniel, Ed. 2006
Gospel and Globalisation: 2nd South Asia Christian Youth Conference. Delhi: Indian Society for Promoting Christian Knowledge.

Watt, William Montgomery. 1972
The Influence of Islam on Medieval Europe. Islamic Surveys 9. Edinburgh: Edinburgh University Press.

Weber, Max. 1958
The Protestant Ethic and the Spirit of Capitalism. New York: Scribner.

Wenham, John W. 1972
'Did Peter go to Rome in A.D. 42?' *TynBul* 23, 94–102.

Westerlund, David. 2003
'Ahmed Deedat's Theology of Religion: Apologetics through Polemics.' *Journal of Religion in Africa* 33: 3, 263-78.

White, David F. 2005
Practicing Discernment with Youth: A Transformative Youth Ministry Approach. Cleveland, Ohio: The Pilgrim Press.

White, David F. 2007
'Illusions of postmodern youth ministry.' *Journal of Youth Ministry* 6:1, 7-26.

Wigram, W. A. 2004 [1910]
An Introduction to the History of the Assyrian Church. Or the Church of the Sassanid Persian Empire. Whitefish: Kessinger Publishing.

Wilk, Florian. 2001
Jesus und die Völker in der Sicht der Synoptiker. BZNW 109. Berlin: De Gruyter.

Williams, Trevor. 2009
The Ultimacy of Jesus: The Language and Logic of Christian Commitment. Aureus Studies in Post-Foundational Theology. St Bride's Major, Glamorgan: Aureus.

Williamson, Paul R. 2000
Abraham, Israel and the Nations: The Patriarchal Promise and its Covenantal Development in Genesis. JSOTSup 315. Sheffield: Sheffield Academic Press.

Willis, Avery T. Jr. 1977
Indonesian revival. Why two million came to Christ. South Pasadena, CA: William Carey Library.
The Willowbank Report. 1978
The Willowbank Report. Wheaton, Ill: The Lausanne Committee for World Evangelization.
Wingate, Andrew. 1988
Encounter in the Spirit. Muslim-Christian Dialogue in Practice. Geneve: WCC Publications.
Witherington, Ben. 1998
The Acts of the Apostles: A Socio-Rhetorical Commentary. Grand Rapids: Eerdmans.
Woodberry, J. Dudley. 1989
'Contextualization among Muslims: Reusing common pillars.' In *The Word among us*. Ed. Dean S. Gilliland. Dallas, TX: Word.
Woodberry, J. Dudley, Ed. 1989
Muslims and Christians on the Emmaus road. Monrovia CA: MARC.
Woodberry, J. Dudley, Ed. 2008
From seed to fruit. Global trends, fruitful practices, and emerging issues among Muslims. Pasadena CA: William Carey Library.
Wootton, R. W. F. 1982
Jesus – more than a Prophet. Bromley: Inter-Varsity Press.
World Council of Churches. 1977
Christians meeting Muslims. WCC papers on ten years of Christian-Muslim dialogue. Geneva: World Council of Churches.
World Council of Churches. 1990
The San Antonio Report. Ed. F. R. Wilson. Geneva: World Council of Churches.
World Missionary Conference. 1910
Report of Commission IV: The Missionary Message in Relation to Non-Christian Religions. Edinburgh and London: Oliphant, Anderson & Ferrier; New York, Chicago and Toronto: Fleming H. Revell Company.
World Missionary Conference Edinburgh. 1910
Report of Commission I-VIII / published for the World Missionary Conference. Edinburgh: Oliphant, Anderson & Ferrier.
Yang, Fenggang and Helen Rose Ebaugh. 2001
'Religion and Ethnicity among Immigrants: The Impact of Majority/Minority Status in Home and Host Countries.' *Journal for the Scientific Study of Religion* 40.3, 367-378.
Yoder, John Howard. 1998
The Royal Priesthood. Essays Ecclesiological and Ecumenical. Ed. Michael G. Cartwright. Scottdale, PA.: Herald Press.
Yung, Hwa. 1997
Mangoes or Bananas? The Quest for an Authentic Asian Christian

Theology. Oxford: Regnum.

Zebiri, Kate. 2003 [1997]
Muslims and Christians face to face. Oxford: Oneworld Publications.

Zetterholm, Magnus. 2009
Approaches to Paul: A Student's Guide to Recent Scholarship. Minneapolis: Fortress.

Zwemer, Samuel M. 1909
Islam: a challenge to faith. Studies on the Mohammedan religion and the needs and opportunities of the Mohammedan world from the standpoint of Christian mission. Second Revised Edition. New York: Laymen's Missionary Movement.

Østebø, Terje. 2009
'Une économie salafi de la prière dans la région du Balé en Éthiopie.' *Afrique Contemporaine*, 231, 45-60.

Index

Manila, 117, 127

Contributors

Kjetil Aano, b. 1949. Cand. theol. MF Norwegian School of Theology, Oslo, 1975. General Secretary of the Norwegian Missionary Society (NMS) 2000-. Assistant bishop, Diocese of Stavanger, 1998 – 2000, editor Misjonstidende, 1990-1996. Director of Atsimoniavoko Theological Seminary, Madagascar, 1985-88, evangelist and church planter in the Lutheran Church of Madagascar, 1979-1982. Publications: *Renninga i Guds vev*, Luther forlag, 1979; *Mellom kors og fedregrav*, Luther forlag, 1983; *Blomster på bar kvist*, Luther forlag, 1997; *Å bryte tidsaksen*, Mosaic, 2000.

Jan-Martin Berentsen, b. 1939. Cand. theol. MF Norwegian School of Theology, Oslo, 1964, dr. theol. University of Oslo, 1982. Missionary to Japan, Norwegian Missionary Society, 1966-1974. From 1974 research fellow, later professor of missiology at the MHS School of Mission and Theology, Stavanger. Published books and articles in the field of theology of mission. Professor emeritus in 2006.

Øyvind Dahl, b. 1940. M.Sc. University of Oslo 1968, and dr. phil. in 1993. Lecturer and principal Lutheran Teacher's Training College, Madagascar, 1970-75, director Church Information Office on Developing Countries, Oslo, 1977-81, professor of anthropology and communication, MHS School of Mission and Theology, Stavanger 1982-2007, general secretary, Norwegian Missions in Development, 2001-03. Professor emeritus from 2008. Publications: *Møter mellom mennesker*, Oslo: Gyldendal, 2001; *Signes et significations à Madagascar*, Paris: Présence Africaine, 2006; *Bridges of Understanding* (ed.), Oslo: Oslo Academic Press, 2006.

Tomas Sundnes Drønen, b. 1968. Cand. Phil. MF Norwegian School of Theology, Oslo, 1995. Ph.D., MHS School of Mission and Theology, Stavanger, 2007. Lecturer Institut Luthérien de Theologie de Meiganga, Cameroon, 1998-2003, 2007-2008. Assoc. prof. of intercultural studies, MHS School of Mission and Theology, Stavanger, 2008-. Publications: *La voie de l'islam et la voie de Christ,* ILTM, 2002 ; *Communication and Conversion in Northern*

Cameroon, Brill, 2009; *Med hjertet på flere steder. Om barn, misjon og flerkulturell oppvekst* (ed), Tapir, 2010.

Tormod Engelsviken, b. 1943. Cand. theol. 1969, MF Norwegian School of Theology, Ph.D. Aquinas Institute of Theology, Dubuque, 1981. Lecturer Mekane Yesus Theological Seminary, Ethiopia, 1971-73, lecturer Fjellhaug International University College, Oslo, 1976-78, research fellow MF Norwegian School of Theology, 1978-1983, assoc. prof. missiology, 1984-98, professor 1998-. Editor of Norwegian Journal of Missiology 2006-, moderator of the Church of Norway Council for Ecumenical and Foreign relations, 1999-2003, member of Commission on World Mission and Evangelism, WCC, 1999-2005, member of the Lausanne Theology Working Group, 1985-2000. Published several books and articles on mission, the Pentecostal/Charismatic movement and spiritual conflict.

Ingrid Eskilt, b.1949. Cand. phil, MF Norwegian School of Theology, Oslo, 1986. Ph.D. Trinity International University, Illinois, 2005. Teacher of missionary children, Congo Brazzaville, 1979-82, lecturer Ansgar Theological Seminary since 1986, and assoc. prof. 2005-. Publications: 'Kimbanguistkirken – Nguzabevegelser', *Norwegian Journal of Missiology,* no. 4, 1986; 'Misjon og misjonærtjeneste.' *Missiology i dag.* J-M. Berentsen et.al. (eds), Oslo: Universitetsforlaget, 2004; *An analysis of changing perspectives on the understanding of the missionary call in the Mission Covenant Church of Norway.* Ph.D. dissertation.

Tor Erling Fagermoen, b. 1972. M. Div. Fjellhaug International University College, Oslo, 1995, cand.mag. University of Bergen, 1997. Director of youth ministry, Norwegian Lutheran Mission, 1998–2004, teacher Fjellhaug Bible School, 2004–2008, principal 2008-. General secretary-elect of Norwegian InterVarsity Fellowship. Publications: *Får dere fisk – disipler som vinner disipler*, Lunde, 2003.

Nasser Fard, b. 1959. Secondary school teacher, Oslo, Norway. Sports pedagogue with exams in physical education from Iran and Norwegian School of Sport Sciences, Oslo. Studies in theology in London and at the Free Church Study Center, Oslo. Part-time pastor in the Iranian Lutheran Church in Oslo.

Egil Grandhagen, b. 1947. Cand. theol. MF Norwegian School of Theology, 1972, itinerant preacher and teacher Norwegian Lutheran Mission, 1972-76, consultant Head Office NLM, 1976-79, deputy general secretary NLM, 1979-82, general secretary NLM, 1982-2001. Assoc. prof. in missiology, Fjellhaug International University College and NLM consultant-at-large 2001-. Has published books and articles on missiological issues, particularly on the early growth of the church in Asia.

Hans-Aage Gravaas, b.1961. Cand. theol. MF Norwegian School of Theology, 1987, studies in Missions and Ecumenism, Selly Oak Colleges, Birmingham, 1989, diploma in Amharic, Joint Language School, Addis Abeba, Etiopia 1990, PhD in Intercultural studies, Trinity International University, Deerfield, IL, 1997. Missionary to Etiopia 1990–93, pastor Norwegian Lutheran Memorial Church in Chicago 1993–97, lecturer Fjellhaug International University College, Oslo, 1997–98, mission secretary Norwegian Lutheran Mission, 1998–2001, president and assoc. prof. Gimlekollen School of Journalism and Communication, Kristiansand 2001–2008, president and assoc. prof. Fjellhaug International University College, 2008-. Publications: *Penetrating the Territory of D`amma: Emic Perspectives on the Intercultural Encounters and the Emergence of an Indigenous Church among the D`Irasha (Gidole) of southwestern Ethiopia.* (PhD-thesis).

Stefan Gustavsson, b. 1960. M.Div. University of Lund, 1988. Teacher Nordic L´Abri, 1988-1990, general secretary Credo - Swedish Evangelical Student Movement, 1990-2001, director CredoAkademin 2001-, general secretary Swedish Evangelical Alliance 2001-. Asst. prof. Gimlekollen School of Journalism and Communication, Kristiansand, 2008-. Publications: *Kristen på goda grunder – Om sanning i en tid av tvivel,* Cordia, 1996; *Gör som Gud – bli människa,* Cordia, 2006; *Om Jesus och Jonas,* SEA, 2009.

Knud Jørgensen, b. 1942. MTh from University of Copenhagen, 1970, Ph.D. in Missiology, Fuller Theological Seminary, 1985. Journalist and theologian, served with Radio Voice of the Gospel, Addis Ababa, Ethiopia, Lutheran World Federation, Geneva, International Mass Media Institute, Kristiansand, Go Out Centre, Hurdal, Norwegian Church Aid, Mekane Yesus Seminary, Addis Ababa, and Areopagos Foundation. Dean of Tao Fong Shan, Hong Kong, 2008-2010. Adjunct professor, MF Norwegian School of

Theology, and Lutheran Theological Seminary, Hong Kong. Published several books and articles on journalism, communication, leadership and mission. One of the editors of the Regnum Edinburgh 2010 Series.

Asle F. Jøssang, b. 1956. M.Div. Fjellhaug International University College, 1983, cand. polit. University of Oslo, 1998, PhD. social anthropology 2010. Missionary to Peru 1985-1990, 1992-1997, to Bolivia 1999-2002. Ass. prof. Gimlekollen School of Journalism and Communication, Kristiansand, 2002-. Publications: 'Pachamama tillater det ikke: om forholdet mellom bistand og kulturell bærekraftighet,' *Norwegian Journal of Missiology,* no. 1-2, 2010; *Searching for a More Powerful Christ: An Anthropology of Religious Conversion in Bolivia*, Ph.D. dissertation in Social Anthropology, Oslo, 2009.

Rolf Kjøde, b. 1959. Cand. theol. MF Norwegian School of Theology, Oslo, 1985. Sociology of Religion, Birkbeck College/University of London, 1994. Teacher at Bildøy Bible School 1988-96, student chaplain in Bergen, 1996-98, principal Centre for Bible and Evangelism, Mandal, 1998-2001. Director Norwegian Council for Mission and Evangelisation, 2001-02, International Director, Normisjon, 2002-03. General secretary Normisjon, 2003-. Publications: *Jesus overalt!* Sambåndet, 1995.

Hans Kvalbein, b. 1942. Cand. theol. MF Norwegian School of Theology, Oslo, 1966, dr. theol. University of Oslo, 1981. Ass. prof. MF Norwegian School of Theology, Oslo, 1972-83. Full professor 1983-. Missionary and guest professor Lutheran Theological Seminary, Hong Kong, 1985-86. Publications: *Jesus og de fattige,* Oslo: Luther, 1981; *Matteusevangeliet,* vol. I, 1989, vol. II, 1990. Oslo: Nye Luther/Lunde; *Jesus – hva ville han? Hvem var han?* Oslo: Luther, 2008.

Erling Lundeby, b. 1952. Fjellhaug International University College 1977, cand. theol. MF Norwegian School of Theology, Oslo, 1982, Th.M. in Missiology, Fuller School of World Missions, Pasadena, 1993. Assoc. prof. Fjellhaug International University College 1997-. Served in Kenya with Norwegian Lutheran Mission and Evangelical Lutheran Church in Kenya, 1977-1995, 2003-2005. Published several articles on church and history in Kenya, e.g. 'Structural Tensions and New Strategies: Trends in Evangelical Lutheran Church of Kenya in the period 1990-2005.' *Norwegian Journal of Missiology*, 1/2008.

Chawkat Moucarry, b. 1954 Aleppo, Syria. Ph.D. Islamic Studies, Sorbonne University. Lecturer in Islamic and Middle-Eastern Studies at All Nations Christian College, Ware, 1994-2006. Director of inter-faith relations, World Vision International, 2006-. Publications: *The Prophet & the Messiah.* IVP, 2001; *The Search for Forgiveness. Pardon and Punishment in Islam and Christianity.* IVP, 2004; *Two Prayers for Today. The Lord's Prayer and The Fatiha*. Tiruvalla, 2007.

Bård Eirik Hallesby Norheim, b. 1973. Cand. theol, MF Norwegian School of Theology, Oslo, 1999, cand. mag. University of Oslo, 1999. Children and youth minister, Nordstrand congregation, Oslo, 2000-2003. Missionary pastor Estonian Evangelical Lutheran Church, 2003-2006, research fellow MF Norwegian School of Theology, 2006-. Publications: 'From Ghetto to Communitas: Post-Soviet youth ministry... ', *Journal of Youth and Theology,* vol 5 (2006):1; *Kan tru praktiserast?Teologi for kristent ungdomsarbeid.* Trondheim: Tapir, 2008; 'Tre messer for Milleniumsgenerasjonen', *Prismet,* 3 (2009).

Solveig Omland, b. 1978. MA in Religion, Trinity International University, Deerfield, 2005. Currently enrolled as a PhD-student in Intercultural Studies, Trinity International University. Lecturer Ansgar School of Theology and Mission, Kristiansand, 2007-2009, lecturer Gimlekollen School of Journalism and Communication, Kristiansand, 2009-.

Jan Opsal, b. 1953. Cand. Theol. MF Norwegian School of Theology, Oslo, 1980, lecturer and consultant on Islam, Norwegian Missionary Society, 1986-1995, asst. professor, MHS School of Mission and Theology, Stavanger, 1996-2005, professor, 2005-. Publications: *Mellom kors og halvmåne. Kristne perspektiver på møtet med islam* (ed), Credo, 1994, 'Islam as a Missional Religion.' *Swedish Missional Themes* 92 (2004); *Islam, lydighetens vei*, Oslo: Universitetsforlaget, 2005; 'Islam and Human rights: African voices for reformation.' *Missionalia* 34(1), 2006.

Eckhard J. Schnabel, b.1955. Ph.D. in New Testament Studies, Aberdeen University. Professor of New Testament at Asian Theological Seminary, Manila, Philippines, 1985-1988, Wiedenest Bible College and Freie Theologische Akademie, Giessen, Germany, 1988-1989. Professor Trinity Evangelical Divinity School, Deerfield, 1989-. Publications: *Early Christian Mission. Vol.1: Jesus and the Twelve, Vol. 2: Paul and the Early Church.* Downers Grove: IVP, 2004; *Paul the Missionary: Realities, Strategies, and Methods.* Downers Grove: IV P, 2008.

Dagfinn Solheim, b. 1944. Cand. theol. MF Norwegian School of Theology, Oslo, 1971, D.Miss. Fuller School of World Mission, Pasadena, 1978. Director Kansai Mission Research Center, asst. prof Kobe Lutheran Theological Seminary, Japan. Director China Institute, Fjellhaug, Oslo, 1987-1990. Academic Dean Fjellhaug International University College, 1989-1996, assoc. prof. 1996-. Publications: *The Missionary Movement within the Lutheran Church.* D.Miss-thesis Fuller SWM, 1978; *Innføring i missiology* (with O. Sæverås). Oslo, 1992.

F.O. Thoresen, teacher and researcher specializing on the Horn of Africa. Details withheld on request.

Ola Tulluan, b. 1947. Fjellhaug International University College, MF Norwegian School of Theology, Ph.D. Clayton University. Worked with Indonesian Missionary Fellowship 1977-1989 as director of Batu Bible Seminary. Dean of Studies Singapore Bible College, 1989-1995, assoc. prof. Fjellhaug International University College, 1995-1999, director 1999-2001. General Secretary, Norwegian Lutheran Mission, 2001-2010.

Terje Østebø, b. 1968. Ph.D. History of Religions, Stockholm University, assoc. prof. NLA University College, Bergen, 2008-2010, affiliated researcher, Christian Michelsen Institute, 2008. Asst. prof. Center for African Studies/Dept of Religion, University of Florida, 2010-. Recent publications: 'Ethiopia: on the Borders of Christianity.' In Hansen, Mesøy and Tuncay (eds): *Borders of Islam: exploring Huntington's faultlines.* London: Hurst, 2009; *Islamism in the Horn of Africa: Assessing Ideology,* Report no. 2. Oslo: International Law and Policy Institute, 2010.

REGNUM EDINBURGH 2010 SERIES
Series Listing

David A. Kerr, Kenneth R. Ross (eds.)
Edinburgh 2010
Mission Then and Now
2009 / 978-1-870345-73-6 / xiv + 343pp (paperback)
2009 / 978-1-870345-76-7 / xiv + 343pp (hardback)

No one can hope to fully understand the modern Christian missionary movement without engaging substantially with the World Missionary Conference, held at Edinburgh in 1910. As the centenary of the Conference approaches, the time is ripe to examine its meaning in light of the past century and the questions facing Christian witness today. This book is the first to systematically examine the eight Commissions which reported to Edinburgh 1910 and gave the conference much of its substance and enduring value. It will deepen and extend the reflection being stimulated by the upcoming centenary and will kindle the missionary imagination for 2010 and beyond.

Daryl M. Balia, Kirsteen Kim (eds.)
Edinburgh 2010
Witnessing to Christ Today
2010 / 978-1-870345-77-4 / xiv +301pp

This volume, the second in the Edinburgh 2010 series, includes reports of the nine main study groups working on different themes for the celebration of the centenary of the World Missionary Conference, Edinburgh 1910. Their collaborative work brings together perspectives that are as inclusive as possible of contemporary world Christianity and helps readers to grasp what it means in different contexts to be 'witnessing to Christ today'.

Claudia Währisch-Oblau, Fidon Mwombeki (eds.)
Mission Continues
Global Impulses for the 21st Century
2010 / 978-1-870345-82-8 / 271pp

In May 2009, 35 theologians from Asia, Africa and Europe met in Wuppertal, Germany, for a consultation on mission theology organized by the United Evangelical Mission: Communion of 35 Churches in Three Continents. The aim was to participate in the 100th anniversary of the Edinburgh conference through a study process and reflect on the challenges for mission in the 21st century. This book brings together these papers written by experienced practitioners from around the world.

Brian Woolnough and Wonsuk Ma (Eds)

Holistic Mission

God's plan for God's people

2010 / 978-1-870345-85-9

Holistic mission, or integral mission, implies God is concerned with the whole person, the whole community, body, mind and spirit. This book discusses the meaning of the holistic gospel, how it has developed, and implications for the the church. . It takes a global, eclectic approach, with 19 writers, all of whom have much experience in, and commitment to, holistic mission. It addresses critically and honestly one of the most exciting, and challenging, issues facing the church today. To be part of God's plan for God's people, the church must take holistic mission to the world.

REGNUM STUDIES IN GLOBAL CHRISTIANITY

(Previously GLOBAL THEOLOGICAL VOICES series)

Series Listing

David Emmanuuel Singh (ed.)

Jesus and the Cross

Reflections of Christians from Islamic Contexts

2008 / 978-1-870345-65-1 / x + 226pp

The Cross reminds us that the sins of the world are not borne through the exercise of power but through Jesus Christ's submission to the will of the Father. The papers in this volume are organised in three parts: scriptural, contextual and theological. The central question being addressed is: how do Christians living in contexts, where Islam is a majority or minority religion, experience, express or think of the Cross? This is, therefore, an exercise in listening. As the contexts from where these engagements arise are varied, the papers in drawing scriptural, contextual and theological reflections offer a cross-section of Christian thinking about Jesus and the Cross.

Sung-wook Hong

Naming God in Korea

The Case of Protestant Christianity

2008 / 978-1-870345-66-8 / xiv + 170pp

Since Christianity was introduced to Korea more than a century ago, one of the most controversial issue has been the Korean term for the Christian 'God'. This issue is not merely about naming the Christian God in Korean language, but it relates to the question of theological contextualization—the relationship between the gospel and culture—and the question of Korean Christian identity. This book examines the theological contextualization of the concept of 'God' in the contemporary Korean context and applies the translatability of Christianity to that context. It also demonstrates the nature of the gospel in relation to cultures, i.e., the universality of the gospel expressed in all human cultures.

Hubert van Beek (ed.)

Revisioning Christian Unity

The Global Christian Forum

2009 / 978-1-870345-74-3 / xx + 288pp

This book contains the records of the Global Christian Forum gathering held in Limuru near Nairobi, Kenya, on 6 – 9 November 2007 as well as the papers presented at that historic event. Also included are a summary of the Global Christian Forum process from its inception until the 2007 gathering and the reports of the evaluation of the process that was carried out in 2008.

Paul Hang-Sik Cho

Eschatology and Ecology

Experiences of the Korean Church

2010 / 978-1-870345-75-0/ 260pp (approx)

This book raises the question of why Korean people, and Korean Protestant Christians in particular, pay so little attention (in theory or practice) to ecological issues. The author argues that there is an important connection (or elective affinity) between this lack of attention and the other-worldly eschatology that is so dominant within Korean Protestant Christianity. Dispensational premillennialism, originally imported by American missionaries, resonated with traditional religious beliefs in Korea and soon came to dominate much of Korean Protestantism. This book argues that this, of all forms of millennialism, is the most damaging to ecological concerns.

Dietrich Werner, David Esterline, Namsoon Kang, Joshva Raja (eds.)

The Handbook of Theological Education in World Christianity

Theological Perspectives, Ecumenical Trends, Regional Surveys

2010 / 978-1-870345-80-4/ 759pp

This major reference work is the first ever comprehensive study of Theological Education in Christianity of its kind. With contributions from over 90 international scholars and church leaders, it aims to be easily accessible across denominational, cultural, educational, and geographic boundaries. The Handbook will aid international dialogue and networking among theological educators, institutions, and agencies. The major objectives of the text are (1) to provide introductory surveys on selected issues and themes in global theological education; (2) to provide regional surveys on key developments, achievements, and challenges in theological education; (3) to provide an overview of theological education for each of the major denominational / confessional traditions; and (4) to provide a reference section with an up-to-date list of the regional associations of theological institutions and other resources.

David Emmanuel Singh & Bernard C Farr (eds.)

Christianity and Education

Shaping of Christian Context in Thinking

2010 / 978-1-870345-81-1/ 244pp (approx)

Christianity and Education is a collection of papers published in *Transformation: An International Journal of Holistic Mission Studies* over a period of 15 years. It brings to life some of the papers that lay buried in shelves and in disparate volumes of *Transformation,* under a single volume for theological libraries, students and teachers. The articles here represent a spectrum of Christian thinking addressing issues of institutional development for theological education, theological studies in the context of global mission, contextually aware/informed education, and academies which deliver such education, methodologies and personal reflections.

REGNUM STUDIES IN MISSION

Series Listing

Kwame Bediako

Theology and Identity

The Impact of Culture upon Christian Thought in the Second Century and in Modern Africa

1992 / 1-870345-10-X / xviii + 508pp

The author examines the question of Christian identity in the context of the Graeco–Roman culture of the early Roman Empire. He then addresses the modern African predicament of quests for identity and integration.

Christopher Sugden

Seeking the Asian Face of Jesus

The Practice and Theology of Christian Social Witness in Indonesia and India 1974–1996

1997 / 1-870345-26-6 / xx + 496pp

This study focuses on contemporary holistic mission with the poor in India and Indonesia combined with the call to transformation of all life in Christ with micro-credit enterprise schemes. 'The literature on contextual theology now has a new standard to rise to' – Lamin Sanneh (Yale University, USA).

Hwa Yung

Mangoes or Bananas?

The Quest for an Authentic Asian Christian Theology

1997 / 1-870345-25-8 / xii + 274pp

Asian Christian thought remains largely captive to Greek dualism and Enlightenment rationalism because of the overwhelming dominance of Western culture. Authentic contextual Christian theologies will emerge within Asian Christianity with a dual recovery of confidence in culture and the gospel.

Keith E. Eitel

Paradigm Wars

The Southern Baptist International Mission Board Faces the Third Millennium

1999 / 1-870345-12-6 / x + 140pp

The International Mission Board of the Southern Baptist Convention is the largest denominational mission agency in North America. This volume chronicles the historic and contemporary forces that led to the IMB's recent extensive reorganization, providing the most comprehensive case study to date of a historic mission agency restructuring to continue its mission purpose into the twenty-first century more effectively.

Samuel Jayakumar

Dalit Consciousness and Christian Conversion

Historical Resources for a Contemporary Debate

1999 / 81-7214-497-0 / xxiv + 434pp

(Published jointly with ISPCK)

The main focus of this historical study is social change and transformation among the Dalit Christian communities in India. Historiography tests the evidence in the light of the conclusions of the modern Dalit liberation theologians.

Vinay Samuel and Christopher Sugden (eds.)

Mission as Transformation

A Theology of the Whole Gospel

1999 / 0870345133/ 522pp

This book brings together in one volume twenty five years of biblical reflection on mission practice with the poor from around the world. The approach of holistic mission, which integrates proclamation, evangelism, church planting and social transformation seamlessly as a whole, has been adopted since 1983 by most evangelical development agencies, most indigenous mission agencies and many Pentecostal churches. This volume helps anyone understand how evangelicals, struggling to unite evangelism and social action, found their way in the last twenty five years to the biblical view of mission in which God calls all human beings to love God and their neighbour; never creating a separation between the two.

Christopher Sugden

Gospel, Culture and Transformation

2000 / 1-870345-32-0 / viii + 152pp

A Reprint, with a New Introduction, of Part Two of Seeking the Asian Face of Jesus
Gospel, Culture and Transformation explores the practice of mission especially in relation to transforming cultures and communities. - 'Transformation is to enable God's vision of society to be actualised in all relationships: social, economic and spiritual, so that God's will may be reflected in human society and his love experienced by all communities, especially the poor.'

Bernhard Ott

Beyond Fragmentation: Integrating Mission and Theological Education

A Critical Assessment of some Recent Developments in Evangelical Theological Education

2001 / 1-870345-14-2 / xxviii + 382pp

Beyond Fragmentation is an enquiry into the development of Mission Studies in evangelical theological education in Germany and German-speaking Switzerland between 1960 and 1995. The author undertakes a detailed examination of the paradigm shifts which have taken place in recent years in both the theology of mission and the understanding of theological education.

Gideon Githiga

The Church as the Bulwark against Authoritarianism

Development of Church and State Relations in Kenya, with Particular Reference to the Years after Political Independence 1963-1992

2002 / 1-870345-38-x / xviii + 218pp

'All who care for love, peace and unity in Kenyan society will want to read this careful history by Bishop Githiga of how Kenyan Christians, drawing on the Bible, have sought to share the love of God, bring his peace and build up the unity of the nation, often in the face of great difficulties and opposition.' Canon Dr Chris Sugden, Oxford Centre for Mission Studies.

Myung Sung-Hoon, Hong Young-Gi (eds.)

Charis and Charisma

David Yonggi Cho and the Growth of Yoido Full Gospel Church

2003 / 1-870345-45-2 / xxii + 218pp

This book discusses the factors responsible for the growth of the world's largest church. It expounds the role of the Holy Spirit, the leadership, prayer, preaching, cell groups and creativity in promoting church growth. It focuses on God's grace (charis) and inspiring leadership (charisma) as the two essential factors and the book's purpose is to present a model for church growth worldwide.

Samuel Jayakumar

Mission Reader

Historical Models for Wholistic Mission in the Indian Context

2003 / 1-870345-42-8 / x + 250pp

(Published jointly with ISPCK)

This book is written from an evangelical point of view revalidating and reaffirming the Christian commitment to wholistic mission. The roots of the 'wholistic mission' combining 'evangelism and social concerns' are to be located in the history and tradition of Christian evangelism in the past; and the civilizing purpose of evangelism is compatible with modernity as an instrument in nation building.

Bob Robinson

Christians Meeting Hindus

An Analysis and Theological Critique of the Hindu-Christian Encounter in India

2004 / 1-870345-39-8 / xviii + 392pp

This book focuses on the Hindu-Christian encounter, especially the intentional meeting called dialogue, mainly during the last four decades of the twentieth century, and specifically in India itself.

Gene Early
Leadership Expectations
How Executive Expectations are Created and Used in a Non-Profit Setting
2005 / 1-870345-30-4 / xxiv + 276pp

The author creates an Expectation Enactment Analysis to study the role of the Chancellor of the University of the Nations-Kona, Hawaii. This study is grounded in the field of managerial work, jobs, and behaviour and draws on symbolic interactionism, role theory, role identity theory and enactment theory. The result is a conceptual framework for developing an understanding of managerial roles.

Tharcisse Gatwa
The Churches and Ethnic Ideology in the Rwandan Crises 1900-1994
2005 / 1-870345-24-X / approx 300pp

Since the early years of the twentieth century Christianity has become a new factor in Rwandan society. This book investigates the role Christian churches played in the formulation and development of the racial ideology that culminated in the 1994 genocide.

Julie Ma
Mission Possible
Biblical Strategies for Reaching the Lost
2005 / 1-870345-37-1 / xvi + 142pp

This is a missiology book for the church which liberates missiology from the specialists for the benefit of every believer. It also serves as a textbook that is simple and friendly, and yet solid in biblical interpretation. This book links the biblical teaching to the actual and contemporary missiological settings with examples, making the Bible come alive to the reader.

Allan Anderson, Edmond Tang (eds.)
Asian and Pentecostal
The Charismatic Face of Christianity in Asia
2005 / 1-870345-43-6 / xiv + 596pp
(Published jointly with APTS Press)

This book provides a thematic discussion and pioneering case studies on the history and development of Pentecostal and Charismatic churches in the countries of South Asia, South East Asia and East Asia.

I. Mark Beaumont

Christology in Dialogue with Muslims

A Critical Analysis of Christian Presentations of Christ for Muslims from the Ninth and Twentieth Centuries

2005 / 1-870345-46-0 / xxvi + 228pp

This book analyses Christian presentations of Christ for Muslims in the most creative periods of Christian-Muslim dialogue, the first half of the ninth century and the second half of the twentieth century. In these two periods, Christians made serious attempts to present their faith in Christ in terms that take into account Muslim perceptions of him, with a view to bridging the gap between Muslim and Christian convictions.

Thomas Czövek,

Three Seasons of Charismatic Leadership

A Literary-Critical and Theological Interpretation of the Narrative of Saul, David and Solomon

2006 / 978-1-870345484 / 272pp

This book investigates the charismatic leadership of Saul, David and Solomon. It suggests that charismatic leaders emerge in crisis situations in order to resolve the crisis by the charisma granted by God. Czovek argues that Saul proved himself as a charismatic leader as long as he acted resolutely and independently from his mentor Samuel. In the author's eyes, Saul's failure to establish himself as a charismatic leader is caused by his inability to step out from Samuel's shadow.

Jemima Atieno Oluoch

The Christian Political Theology of Dr. John Henry Okullu

2006 / 1-870345-51-7 / xx + 137pp

This book reconstructs the Christian political theology of Bishop John Henry Okullu, DD, through establishing what motivated him and the biblical basis for his socio-political activities. It also attempts to reconstruct the socio-political environment that nurtured Dr Okullu's prophetic ministry.

Richard Burgess

Nigeria's Christian Revolution

The Civil War Revival and Its Pentecostal Progeny (1967-2006)

2008 / 978-1-870345-63-7 / xxii + 347pp

This book describes the revival that occurred among the Igbo people of Eastern Nigeria and the new Pentecostal churches it generated, and documents the changes that have occurred as the movement has responded to global flows and local demands. As such, it explores the nature of revivalist and Pentecostal experience, but does so against the backdrop of local socio-political and economic developments, such as decolonisation and civil war, as well as broader processes, such as modernisation and globalisation.

David Emmanuel Singh & Bernard C Farr (eds.)

Christianity and Cultures

Shaping Christian Thinking in Context

2008 / 978-1-870345-69-9 / x + 260pp

This volume marks an important milestone, the 25th anniversary of the Oxford Centre for Mission Studies (OCMS). The papers here have been exclusively sourced from Transformation, a quarterly journal of OCMS, and seek to provide a tripartite view of Christianity's engagement with cultures by focusing on the question: how is Christian thinking being formed or reformed through its interaction with the varied contexts it encounters? The subject matters include different strands of theological-missiological thinking, socio-political engagements and forms of family relationships in interaction with the host cultures.

Tormod Engelsviken, Ernst Harbakk, Rolv Olsen, Thor Strandenæs (eds.)

Mission to the World

Communicating the Gospel in the 21st Century: Essays in Honour of Knud Jørgensen

2008 / 978-1-870345-64-4 / 472pp

Knud Jørgensen is Director of Areopagos and Associate Professor of Missiology at MF Norwegian School of Theology. This book reflects on the main areas of Jørgensen's commitment to mission. At the same time it focuses on the main frontier of mission, the world, the content of mission, the Gospel, the fact that the Gospel has to be communicated, and the context of contemporary mission in the 21st century.

Al Tizon

Transformation after Lausanne

Radical Evangelical Mission in Global-Local Perspective

2008 / 978-1-870345-68-2 / xx + 281pp

After Lausanne '74, a worldwide network of radical evangelical mission theologians and practitioners use the notion of "Mission as Transformation" to integrate evangelism and social concern together, thus lifting theological voices from the Two Thirds World to places of prominence. This book documents the definitive gatherings, theological tensions, and social forces within and without evangelicalism that led up to Mission as Transformation. And it does so through a global-local grid that points the way toward greater holistic mission in the 21st century.

Bambang Budijanto

Values and Participation

Development in Rural Indonesia

2009 / 978-1-870345-70-5 / x + 237pp

Socio-religious values and socio-economic development are inter-dependant, inter-related and are constantly changing in the context of macro political structures, economic policy, religious organizations and globalization; and micro influences such as local affinities, identity, politics, leadership and beliefs. The three Lopait communities in Central Java, Indonesia provide an excellent model of the rich and complex negotiations and interactions among all the above factors. The book argues that the comprehensive approach in understanding the socio-religious values of each local community is essential to accurately describing their respective identity which will help institutions and agencies, both governmental and non-governmental, to relate to these communities with dignity and respect.

Young-hoon Lee

The Holy Spirit Movement in Korea

Its Historical and Theological Development

2009 / 978-1-870345-67-5 / x + 174pp

This book traces the historical and theological development of the Holy Spirit Movement in Korea through six successive periods (from 1900 to the present time). These periods are characterized by repentance and revival (1900-20), persecution and suffering under Japanese occupation (1920-40), confusion and division (1940-60), explosive revival in which the Pentecostal movement played a major role in the rapid growth of Korean churches (1960-80), the movement reaching out to all denominations (1980-2000), and the new context demanding the Holy Spirit movement to open new horizons in its mission engagement (2000-). The volume also discusses the relationship between this movement and other religions such as shamanism, and looks forward to further engagement with issues of concern in wider society.

Alan R. Johnson

Leadership in a Slum

A Bangkok Case Study

2009 / 978-1-870345-71-2 xx + 238pp

This book looks at leadership in the social context of a slum in Bangkok from an angle different from traditional studies which measure well educated Thais on leadership scales derived in the West. Using both systematic data collection and participant observation, it develops a culturally preferred model as well as a set of models based in Thai concepts that reflect on-the-ground realities. This work challenges the dominance of the patron-client rubric for understanding all forms of Thai leadership and offers a view for understanding leadership rooted in local social systems, contrary to approaches that assume the universal applicability of leadership research findings across all cultural settings. It concludes by looking at the implications of the anthropological approach for those who are involved in leadership training in Thai settings and beyond.

Titre Ande

Leadership and Authority

Bula Matari and Life - Community Ecclesiology in Congo

2010 / 978-1-870345-72-9 xvii + 189pp

This book proposes that Christian theology in Africa can make significant developments if a critical understanding of the socio-political context in contemporary Africa is taken seriously. The Christian leadership in post-colonial Africa has cloned its understanding and use of authority on the Bula Matari model, which was issued from the brutality of colonialism and political absolutism in post-colonial Africa. This model has caused many problems in churches, including dysfunction, conflicts, divisions and a lack of prophetic ministry. Titre proposes a Life-Community ecclesiology for liberating authority, where leadership is a function, not a status, and 'apostolic succession' belongs to all the people of God.

Frank Kwesi Adams

Odwira and the Gospel

A Study of the Asante Odwira Festival and its Significance for Christianity in Ghana

2010 /978-1-870345-59-0

The study of the Odwira festival is the key to the understanding of Asante religious and political life in Ghana. The book explores the nature of the Odwira festival longitudinally - in pre-colonial, colonial and post-independence Ghana - and examines the Odwira ideology and its implications for understanding the Asante self-identity. The book also discusses how some elements of faith portrayed in the Odwira festival could provide a framework for Christianity to engage with Asante culture at a greater depth. Theological themes in Asante belief that have emerged from this study include the theology of sacrament, ecclesiology, eschatology, Christology and a complex concept of time. The author argues that Asante cultural identity lies at the heart of the process by which the Asante Christian faith is carried forward.

Bruce Carlton

Strategy Coordinator

Changing the Course of Southern Baptist Missions

2010 / 978-1-870345-78-1 xvii + 268pp

In 1976, the Southern Baptist Convention adopted its Bold New Thrusts in Foreign Missions with the overarching goal of sharing the gospel with every person in the world by the year 2000. The formation of Cooperative Services International (CSI) in 1985 and the assigning of the first non-residential missionary (NRM) in 1987 demonstrated the Foreign Mission Board's (now International Mission Board) commitment to take the gospel message to countries that restricted traditional missionary presence and to people groups identified as having little or no access to the gospel. Carlton traces the historical development along with an analysis of the key components of the paradigm and its significant impact on Southern Baptists' missiology.

Julie Ma & Wonsuk Ma
Mission in the Spirit:
Towards a Pentecostal/Charismatic Missiology
2010 / 978-1-870345-84-2 xx + 312pp

The book explores the unique contribution of Pentecostal/Charismatic mission from the beginning of the twentieth century. The first part considers the theological basis of Pentecostal/Charismatic mission thinking and practice. Special attention is paid to the Old Testament, which has been regularly overlooked by the modern Pentecostal/Charismatic movements. The second part discusses major mission topics with contributions and challenges unique to Pentecostal/Charismatic mission. The book concludes with a reflection on the future of this powerful missionary movement. As the authors served as Korean missionaries in Asia, often their missionary experiences in Asia are reflected in their discussions.

GENERAL REGNUM TITLES

Vinay Samuel, Chris Sugden (eds.)
The Church in Response to Human Need
1987 / 1870345045 / xii+268pp

Philip Sampson, Vinay Samuel, Chris Sugden (eds.)
Faith and Modernity
Essays in modernity and post-modernity
1994 / 1870345177 / 352pp

Klaus Fiedler
The Story of Faith Missions
1994 / 0745926878 / 428pp

Douglas Peterson
Not by Might nor by Power
A Pentecostal Theology of Social Concern in Latin America
1996 / 1870345207 / xvi+260pp

David Gitari
In Season and Out of Season
Sermons to a Nation
1996 / 1870345118 / 155pp

David. W. Virtue
A Vision of Hope
The Story of Samuel Habib
1996 / 1870345169 / xiv+137pp

Everett A Wilson
Strategy of the Spirit
J.Philip Hogan and the Growth of the Assemblies of God Worldwide, 1960 - 1990
1997 /1870345231/214

Murray Dempster, Byron Klaus, Douglas Petersen (eds.)
The Globalization of Pentecostalism
A Religion Made to Travel
1999 / 1870345290 / xvii+406pp

Peter Johnson, Chris Sugden (eds.)
Markets, Fair Trade and the Kingdom of God
Essays to Celebrate Traidcraft's 21st Birthday
2001 / 1870345193 / xii+155pp

Robert Hillman, Coral Chamberlain, Linda Harding
Healing & Wholeness
Reflections on the Healing Ministry
2002 / 978-1- 870345-35- 4 / xvii+283pp

David Bussau, Russell Mask
Christian Microenterprise Development
An Introduction
2003 / 1870345282 / xiii+142pp

David Singh
Sainthood and Revelatory Discourse
An Examination of the Basis for the Authority of Bayan in Mahdawi Islam
2003 / 8172147285 / xxiv+485pp

For the up-to-date listing of the Regnum books see www.ocms.ac.uk/regnum

regnum

Regnum Books International

Regnum is an Imprint of The Oxford Centre for Mission Studies
St. Philip and St. James Church
Woodstock Road
Oxford, OX2 6HR
Web: www.ocms.ac.uk/regnum